GOING
PUBLIC

GOING PUBLIC

(
MY ADVENTURES
INSIDE THE SEC
AND HOW TO PREVENT THE
NEXT DEVASTATING CRISIS
)

NORM CHAMP

New York   Chicago   San Francisco
Athens   London   Madrid   Mexico City
Milan   New Delhi   Singapore   Sydney   Toronto

ISBN   978-1-259-86120-8
MHID   1-259-86120-1

e-ISBN   978-1-259-86121-5
e-MHID   1-259-86121-X

McGraw-Hill Education books are available at special quantity discounts to use as premiums and sales promotions or for use in corporate training programs. To contact a representative, please visit the Contact Us pages at www.mhprofessional.com.

Where the author uses quotation marks at times in reconstructing conversations, he is being as accurate as possible to the exact wording as based on his research and recollection.

*To those quiet patriots on the staff
of the U.S. Securities and Exchange Commission
who pursue the mission despite the obstacles.*

CONTENTS

ACKNOWLEDGMENTS

You often read an acknowledgments section of a book in which the author writes that a book takes a team effort. After seeing the number of people involved in *Going Public*, I will never scoff at those acknowledgments again! There are so many people I want to thank, that I know I will miss some. Apologies and please do accept my sincerest gratitude nonetheless.

I will start with the members of my family, as they are the most important people in my life. My wonderful wife, Sally, supported the five years of public service described in this book. I just don't have an adequate way to thank her for everything. I would also like to thank my four amazing children.

As Chapter 2 makes clear, I owe so much to my late uncle Joseph C. Champ, it is hard to express. Man, do I miss you even after 25 years.

The idea of a book about my experiences at the SEC began with a comment from the dean of Harvard Law School, Martha Minow, in January 2014. The law school has been unfailingly supportive of me since then dean (now associate justice of the U.S. Supreme Court) Elena Kagan asked me to teach a class at the school in 2008. Dean Minow has continued to invite me back to teach my investment management law class. One day in January 2014, I was in Dean Minow's office telling her about the good and the bad at the SEC when she said, "You have to write this down." Thank you, Martha, so much for starting me on this journey. Early guidance came from several people associated with Harvard including Elizabeth Knoll and Catherine Claypoole and her husband, Toby Lester.

The man who turned the idea of a book into a practical reality was my publicist, Adam Friedman, who tirelessly searched for an agent to market the book at the same time he was building my website. Adam's unfailing efforts, steady resolve, and sage guidance have been invaluable in making *Going Public* a reality.

Thank you to my agent, Cathy Hemming, who saw in my half-baked book proposal the kernel of what would become the book. Cathy introduced me to my editor, Herb Schaffner, who has been my invaluable companion on this journey.

A number of students at Harvard Law School helped with research on various parts of the book. They are of course only responsible for the good parts; I'll take the blame for any mistakes. Amanda Liverzani, Jacqueline Trudeau, and Cam Nunery were invaluable in all their help. Stephen Adams and Phil Chang graciously helped out with some early research projects.

Thanks to McGraw-Hill for its support of the book and in particular to editor Donya Dickerson for seeing what the book could be. The marketing team at McGraw-Hill has been so helpful in positioning the book.

Professionally I have been privileged to get to know some of the most talented people in the investment management field including Yukako Kawata, Richard L. Chilton, Jr., Patty Mallon, Bill McNabb, my fellow board members at MFA including Mike Neus, Steve Kessler, Adam Cooper, and many others. My partners and colleagues at Kirkland & Ellis LLP, including John O'Neil, Andrew Wright, Aaron Schlaphoff, Jamie Walter, and Daniel Lavon-Krein, have been tremendously supportive in my return to private practice.

My heartfelt thanks to so many of the staff of the U.S. Securities and Exchange Commission who work tirelessly for investors with no public fanfare. The list is so long I know I will omit some names, but I hope all of you know who you are. Thanks to George Canellos, Jim Capezzuto, Joe DiMaria, Dawn Blankenship, Carlo di Florio, Joan Forrester, Robert Fishman, Julius Leiman-Carbia, John Polise, Carolyn Grillo, Judy Lee, Jon Hertzke, Kevin Goodman, Jane Jarcho, David Woodcock, Marshall Gandy, John Walsh, Dave Grim, Brian Murphy, Diane Blizzard, Susan Nash, Liz Osterman, Doug Scheidt, Barry Miller, Bob Plaze, Marian Fowler, Aidan O'Connor, Richard

Rodgers, Jennifer McHugh, Brian Johnson, Sarah ten Siethoff, Ammani Nagesh, Ken O'Connor, Lou Casais, Dan Townley, Dan Kahl, Jennifer Duggins, and countless others across the agency who give their all for American investors. And of course to the Tuesday lunch gang Andrew Ceresney, Keith Higgins, Steve Luparello, John Ramsay, Drew Bowden, Marc Wyatt, Craig Lewis, and Mark Flannery.

Finally, thank you to the chairs and commissioners of the U.S. Securities and Exchange Commission. I had the privilege of reporting to the first three women to chair the agency, Mary Schapiro, Elisse Walter, and Mary Jo White. Over my five years I worked closely with Commissioners Kathy Casey, Troy Paredes, Dan Gallagher, Luis Aguilar, Mike Piwowar, and Kara Stein plus had the guidance of former Commissioner Paul Atkins. I appreciate all their support and their commitment to the agency's mission to protect investors, ensure fair and orderly markets, and facilitate capital formation. The three pillars of that mission have made the United States the greatest engine of wealth creation in world history. As I hope *Going Public* explains, we face some serious challenges in keeping that record going. I hope we can keep the country on that path for the benefit of all Americans.

FISH OUT OF WATER

He's got more guts than sense.
> —*To Hell and Back* (1955)

FIRST DAY

On January 25, 2010, I dropped two of my sons at their school in Manhattan. It was a typical cold winter day in New York City with the added twist of severe winter storm warnings bearing down on the city. After saying goodbye to the boys, I jumped on the express subway train and headed downtown to report for my first day at the New York regional office of the U.S. Securities and Exchange Commission (SEC) at the World Financial Center. The SEC is located in the American Express Tower building, which has tight security procedures, so I had to wait near the building's main security desk for an administrator to come get me. Upstairs she handed me two thick black binders of the statutes governing federal employment and explanations of federal employee benefits. This was my first day as an employee of a U.S. government agency, and no one gave me an orientation. No one discussed "onboarding" for my duties. No one gave me a job description of my responsibilities in my new role as head of examinations of investment firms in New York and New Jersey—or advised me of the problems at the SEC and other regulatory agencies supposedly leading our nation out of the 2008 financial crisis.

Eventually, as there was no clear label for my position, I made up my job title for my business card: Associate Director of Investment Management Exams for the New York Region. The formal name of the nationwide SEC Exam office is the Office of Compliance Inspections and Examinations, a label that reminded me of some shadowy bureaucracy out of Dickens where people will be doing things to you with cold steel. SEC staff and we in the industry simply called it Exam or OCIE. The office conducts examinations by visiting broker-dealers, investment adviser and investment companies, securities exchanges, clearing agencies, transfer agents, and credit rating agencies to assess their compliance with the federal securities laws. Exam leaders decide which firms to visit and then send a team of examiners, typically from one of the SEC regional offices, to go to the firm and review trading records, e-mails, and the like to look for any wrongdoing. For investment management firms, Exam employs about 450 investigators covering more than 12,000 firms, so it relies on the data that firms present to decide on which companies to review. As part of this new adventure I was embarking on, I would now supervise about 100 of those 450 examiners, and we were responsible for policing investment managers in New York and New Jersey, where the bulk of the investment assets managed in the United States are located.

After having an ID picture taken, I sat in my office and thought about what to do first. My mind drifted back to a lunch I had a few months before with a high-ranking SEC official while interviewing for the job. He and I met at a Cosi restaurant in what was then the dingy food court of the World Financial Center. We grabbed salads, and I offered to buy lunch since I was in the private sector and not on a government salary. He said that as a government employee he couldn't accept lunch from someone in the hedge fund business.

We squeezed into a booth. After eating quietly for a few moments, he looked over at me.

"Listen," he said. "If you leave your job in the hedge fund business and come to the SEC hoping to change how exams of investment firms are done, certain employees in the New York office are capable of anything in trying to stop change."

I told him that I thought my expertise in the investment management business could be helpful to the examiners after the SEC's spectacular failure to discover the massive frauds committed by Bernie Madoff and Allen Stanford. He responded that some of the supervisors and employees in the New York office would resent any help from the outside, particularly from someone like me who had not conducted exams before.

When I asked what these people might do, he said that they could try to ruin my career. I was taken aback by these words, but I could not believe that examiners at an agency that had failed to detect fraud would not want assistance from someone with a background in the investment fund world.

I would soon be proved very wrong.

Later that day, back in my office at my hedge fund firm in Midtown Manhattan, I thought over what this official had said but was undeterred in my desire to join the SEC. I wanted to serve my country at this difficult time and believed I had the experience and legal expertise to handle myself in this new world. Looking back, I can see I was also a little naive in thinking that an organization that had suffered a massive failure would be open to outside help. During 20 years in the private sector practicing law and serving as general counsel of a hedge fund, I interacted with the SEC both as a lawyer seeking approval of transactions for clients and as an industry representative trying to educate the SEC staff about hedge funds. It was clear to me that many SEC employees did the best they could on hedge fund issues, but the agency had few people with expertise in the field. I had registered our firm with the SEC in the early 2000s and helped expand the business to offices in London, Hong Kong, and mainland China, working with regulators in all those places. I respected the regulators I worked with in the United States and abroad for their dedication to public service and for their efforts to police the industry. But the boom real estate market of the mid-2000s was too frothy to last, and I knew that a slowdown was inevitable, although in my wildest nightmares I did not foresee the massive crash of September 2008. After the crisis hit, I found it difficult to fathom what happened at the SEC, which was so embarrassed by its failures and savaged by critics in politics and the media that I had to avert my eyes.

I believe in the power of the U.S. securities markets and the prosperity they have brought the country for more than 200 years by providing capital for innovative businesses. Such healthy markets periodically produce manias like the one leading up to the 2008 crisis, but they also finance businesses too numerous to list. The usual sign of impending disaster is the inevitable article saying that "this time is different." Many such pieces ran in 2006 and 2007 predicting that real estate would keep rising in value. I worried that the reaction to the crisis would harm the position of the United States as the financial center of the world. I believed my expertise in private funds and securities laws, which I had spent 20 years building, would be helpful to the SEC as it tried to recover from its debacle. So despite the prescient warning, I continued with my application to join the SEC's New York office.

Once I'd made the decision, I felt excited to be entering public service for this great country—but also hesitant about what was to come. I gave up a partnership in a prestigious, established hedge fund manager at a time when my wife and I were raising four kids. I was not only taking a massive pay reduction but also stepping out of the industry where I'd made a good career. Happily, despite the challenges, it turned out to be the best experience of my working life.

I had been hired by New York office head George Canellos, with the approval of SEC chair Mary Schapiro, to overhaul the SEC's processes in order to unearth the next Madoff or Stanford—*before* that person fleeced unwitting investors. When I started, the fallout from these failures was still reverberating. The SEC inspector general (IG)—a position created by Congress to investigate legal and compliance deficiencies and failures within the commission—had issued reports on the Exam division's blunders. Congressional committee members demanded answers. The press was doggedly examining the negligence of the SEC.

I liked my new office more than I expected to. I had envisioned a cubbyhole with worn metal furniture that belonged in a government surplus warehouse. Instead I had a decent wooden desk and a small conference table. In addition I had access to a conference room across the hall that was big enough to meet with my direct reports and two counsels. The office exposed a wonderful view to the south of Ellis Island and New York Harbor. After 15 years in Midtown Manhattan, where you usually looked into another building, I took the splendid view to be a good sign.

However, I detected one oddity about the desk. Tradition holds that each U.S. president writes his successor a letter and leaves it in the desk in the Oval Office. The legacy left by my predecessors was more practical in nature: they had stuffed my desk with office supplies. Every drawer was chock-full of staplers, notepads, writing paper, paper clips, you name it. I even found a couple of metal mechanical items so archaic I wasn't sure exactly what they were meant to do. I soon learned the reason for this stash: office supplies were chronically in short supply, so employees often hoarded them. (I packed up cardboard boxes of the supplies and asked my assistant to return them to the supply room so they would be available for everyone.)

The supply room itself in the New York office was always worth a laugh (or tears). You found very few if any pens, staples, or other useful items people needed. However, someone had shoved a large wooden pallet against the wall and stacked it nearly to the ceiling with packs of 8½- × 14-inch legal-size copier paper. Since almost nothing is printed or copied on legal-size paper anymore (except a few court filings), the stack stayed about the same size for years.

Most days, the regular 8½- × 11-inch copy paper, always in great demand, was not to be found. To print a document, I sometimes scavenged from copy room recycling bins for paper that I could load in my printer. It certainly wasn't the sort of problem I encountered at my private sector jobs.

The SEC's New York offices stood directly across the West Side Highway from the site of the new Freedom Tower—now called One World Trade—that was rising where the World Trade Center buildings collapsed on September 11, 2001. During law school I worked one summer in One World Trade Center. New Yorkers used the Trade Center's Twin Towers to orient themselves since you could see them from almost anywhere; their absence felt strange to me. I was unnerved that something so familiar was no longer there. As it happened, on the awful day of the attacks, the SEC's New York office, located in the World Trade Center complex, was destroyed. SEC staff moved first to a temporary location and then to these new offices. Thankfully, no SEC personnel were lost on 9/11.

Our offices were on the fifteenth floor of the American Express Tower, where the SEC had three other floors: one for examiners who inspected broker-dealer firms and two for enforcement lawyers and investigators. We had conference rooms on the fourth floor with armed guards posted at a security desk. When I was in the hedge fund business, brokers, lawyers, accountants, tech vendors, and others visited our offices all the time to pitch us products or work with us. At the SEC, however, outsiders were limited mostly to the fourth floor and not allowed upstairs without warnings e-mailed from security to the staff.

The SEC had good reasons to control visitors: the agency ran legally sensitive examinations and enforcement investigations that were high stakes for the targets of those activities. But no one had made the effort to consider the public image the SEC presented by failing to make the office space comfortable or welcoming for those who did visit us, including our customers, the American taxpayers. The conference rooms had ominous-sounding names like Hearing Room and Testimony Room, which made the investment professionals who visited us voluntarily to discuss policy or exam issues seem uneasy. The people in those rooms who'd come involuntarily because they were testifying or being investigated looked haggard and nervous. It was not a place that radiated trust or seemed open to input from the outside world. Later I will touch on the impact this isolation had on the agency's ability to do its job.

But perhaps the most disheartening aspect of the layout is how poorly lit all four floors were. Even on a gorgeous sunny day the light remained dim inside most of the offices. Light fixtures were sparse and powered with extremely low-wattage bulbs. (Whether this was a budget issue or simply poor design I still cannot say for sure.) It also didn't help that the office color scheme was a drab brown that absorbed what little light there was. I was literally—and figuratively—stumbling in the dark.

Early on I befriended Ken O'Connor, a supervisor in the Exam division who had been there for more than 10 years and who had a great sense of the absurdity of the government. Ken worked hard to rise above the impediments the SEC tossed at him but heard all the stories of the futility of it all. Ken also had a good working knowledge of construction, from his house renovations. So I asked him once why the office was so dark.

Adding to the absurdity, Ken said that when the space was being prepared for the move from the temporary post-9/11 location, the government hit its budget limit; since the lighting had yet to be installed, the agency had no choice but to skimp on the number of fixtures! It didn't take me long to realize that almost everything at the SEC was passed down by word of mouth like a child's game of telephone. Ken's renovation budget story may have been true, but like all the other SEC lore passed along over the years, you never really knew. Regardless, the effect the lighting created was of an office environment with the appeal of the furniture pickup warehouse at IKEA.

A NOT SO SUBTLE WARNING

It was one of those old-fashioned interoffice envelopes, the brown manila kind that most of us haven't seen in years. As I untied it, I noticed it had been coiled shut many times, and I wondered what could be in the thick package that couldn't have been e-mailed to me as a PDF. It was my second week at the SEC, and I'd entered a time capsule of pre–digital era conventions where fax confirmation sheets were still a part of daily office life and people still waited in line at the copying machine.

I pulled out an anonymous letter, and my stomach sank with dread.

The letter amounted to a 10-page tally of allegations against my friend and predecessor, Tom Biolsi, dated about six months before he walked out the door from the SEC in 2009. According to this document, he'd engaged in serious wrongdoings: holding staff parties with alcohol in the office, using ethnic slurs I can't imagine him making, showing favoritism to certain staff. The letter described everyday events with toxic innuendo and seemed to distort well-meaning actions into politically incorrect blunders. For instance, it suggested an office gathering, which I suspect was intended to promote team unity, was exclusionary because of its St. Patrick's Day theme.

Tom Biolsi did not remotely resemble the person described in the letter. Because Tom died a few years later in 2013 at age 57, he can no longer defend himself, but I knew it was all a lie. I attended his funeral along with hundreds of others from our industry who admired, trusted, and respected him. Tom served in the U.S. Air Force from 1974 to 1978 before working two stints at the SEC, where he was highly regarded. Early in his career he had spent nine years in the New York office as an examiner and then branch chief, supervising other examiners. In 2006 he left a lucrative compliance consulting practice at Price Waterhouse to be the associate director for examinations in New York until he returned to consulting in 2009. Before he left, Tom encouraged me to apply to take his place, and that was one of the main reasons I wound up at the SEC in early 2010. Anyone who knew Tom would find the memo preposterous—unless it was written with other motives.

I reached inside the envelope and found a stack of fax confirmation sheets showing that while Tom was still working at the SEC, this anonymous screed had been sent to every senior official at the SEC as well as members of Congress—essentially all around Washington. It was a missile sent to destroy someone's life, the work of a coward. There was only one reason why a copy would have been sent to me in my second week at the SEC. Clearly this was a warning to me not to step out of line. Someone wanted to intimidate me right away before I even got acclimated to the job.

Was this what I could face if I instituted the changes I had come there to make: an anonymous note faxed all over Washington? Had I been incredibly naive to come to the SEC? I left the office at 7 p.m., scared and wondering if the author of the libel was watching. (I learned I didn't need to worry. The flexible work schedules and work-from-home programs enjoyed by some SEC employees meant there was almost never anyone else in the office at that hour.)

Later I shared the document with Carlo di Florio, the head of Exam, who also knew Tom well. I told Carlo that I thought the letter, which at this point was more than a year old, had been an attempt to force Tom out because he was trying to revamp the New York Exam office, including trying to fire the deadwood. I saw the delivery of a copy of the letter to me as a warning of what would happen if I followed a similar path. Carlo nodded in agreement as he marveled at the petty tone of the letter, especially given that there was so much else to do at the agency.

Even before the copy of the letter arrived, I concluded that trying to fire anyone, no matter how derelict, was a losing proposition. My counsel Jim Capezzuto and other colleagues had explained to me how civil service protections and union grievance procedures made it nearly impossible.

Grasping for a silver lining, I naively thought that perhaps retaining staff would help me avoid the poison pens of unidentified witchhunters—but I was wrong.

ANONYMOUS COMPLAINTS ARE FREE WEAPONS

I soon learned that the anonymous complaint is a common tool in the SEC and throughout the federal government. I gave a copy of the note to Mary Schapiro's chief of staff, Didem Nisanci, who told me that she received anonymous notes all the time! Carlo and I later spoke to the SEC inspector general, David Kotz, who had of course received the note directly at the time it was first sent. Kotz did not have to investigate the note since Tom had left the agency. However, he indicated he would be required to investigate the allegations, no matter how ludicrous, if Tom ever wanted to return to the SEC. Kotz routinely received anonymous notes and had to determine if they were worth investigating.

During my time as a senior manager at the SEC, I received many complaints against other managers and employees. This had never happened before in my entire professional career, not in my law practice or at the hedge fund. In the private sector, it wouldn't take long for people to figure out who was making anonymous complaints, and they would not trust that person going forward.

While I am sure there are exceptions, in the worlds of finance and law we try to establish clear lines of authority and accountability to make sure everyone is moving in the same direction. For the most part, we put issues about performance on the table and discuss them openly to reach solutions.

Anonymous notes undermine what is generally a fairly transparent system where supervisors give their direct reports meaningful feedback. Talented, ambitious people aren't going to tolerate a toxic environment where unsigned notes are allowed to float around the company. They'll take their talent and ambition elsewhere.

As with staff in other bureaucracies, SEC employees cannot be disciplined, fired, or sanctioned except for the most extreme behavior such as committing fraud or sexual harassment. Congress has passed job protection measures practically guaranteeing federal employees lifetime employment, thereby giving some SEC staffers license to send the IG and others these types of anonymous grievances without fear of consequences. Those opposed to change use anonymous notes to protect the status quo. As a result, it became part of SEC culture for some staff members from around the country to use such weaponized notes to advance their personal agendas and for vendettas against supervisors, colleagues—whomever they chose. During the five years that I was involved in efforts to transform the SEC into a businesslike, more rational organization, these nameless complaints appeared constantly.

INVESTIGATING COMPLAINTS

While some of the SEC's functions are handled centrally in Washington, DC, the Exam and Enforcement divisions primarily are administered regionally in cities across the country.

When I later became the deputy director of Exam, I teamed up with one of the senior officials in Enforcement, Margaret McGuire, to investigate anonymous complaints in several of these regional offices. We spent a great deal of time traveling the country together visiting regional offices and interviewing employees to see what we could learn about the charges.

You might ask yourself, why didn't we just ignore these complaints when they seemed to come from certain employees with their own agendas? My answer is that we knew that the complaints also could have been made to the agency's internal watchdog (the inspector general) or to Congress. Then *we* might be questioned about how we responded.

When complaints did go to the inspector general, he sometimes sent them to us for action. As much as I would have liked to announce that we refused to act on many of these "nastygrams," as we began calling them, that was a nonstarter because the IG would be breathing down our necks. In fact, if we did nothing, we could have been investigated. Our efforts rarely turned up any facts to substantiate the misconduct alleged in the anonymous notes.

I found it hard to follow up on these complaints because they inevitably left out critical details such as the office where the note originated or specific examples of wrongdoing. Most importantly, I couldn't interview the person who made the complaint. (The SEC copes with the same phenomenon regarding the many anonymous complaints made by the public alleging misconduct by investment managers.) The time we spent on chasing down the illegitimate complaints could have been spent on improving exams or enforcing the securities laws, our one true mission. Keep in mind, at Exam our 450 investment management investigators only completed on average a little more than two exams per person per year!

The SEC didn't have a single formal procedure for dealing with the myriad means that nameless complaint writers could use to attack managers or coworkers. Yes, you read that correctly. For the most part, the SEC lacked formal procedures for anything—which some of us changed in the years ahead. When I was there, we did the best we could with the complaints we received. At least I could investigate complaints that came to me; some complaints were made to other forums where the damage could be even worse.

A BUNCH OF COMPLAINTS

I'm sure some of my colleagues saw the anonymous notes as one of the annoying, unavoidable quirks of having a safe, secure job in the federal government. Something to put up with—and stay clear of. But what if your career is put in the crosshairs for petty or personal reasons? What's more, many of us saw the hitman culture as another symptom of a fundamental loss of direction at the agency. I quickly realized that an agency in which its employees are guaranteed life-time employment, have complete flexibility in setting their hours (including in one group up to five days a week at home), and enjoy myriad other taxpayer-funded benefits, cannot be laser-focused on its mission of protecting investors and the country's entire financial system.

I told Mary Schapiro that I found it unbelievable that some staff had time to fire scud missiles at colleagues without any concern about blowback. While unemployment and home foreclosures were near record highs and banks and other financial institutions were fighting to survive with bailouts, I was squandering my precious hours and energy on anonymous political hit jobs. Mary had been at the commission before, in the late 1980s and early 1990s, but did not remember character assassins during that period, let alone tolerating such behavior. She was of the same mind—that the crisis facing the United States was so dire that we each needed to be working as if the economy were a runaway prairie fire we could only extinguish by working together. Mary brought that sense of urgency to all of us who were empowered to rebuild the agency and the economy.

When an organization is in crisis, everyone who has a stake in it must charge directly into the emergency at hand. Internecine scores can be settled later. At least that's how most organizations act. But at the SEC, where a staffer's sworn duty is to protect U.S. investors, we had a lot of work to do yanking some heads on straight and making improvements to help all employees succeed. Without Mary's support and leadership in the wake of the 2008 financial crisis, we could not have done it.

The Madoff and Stanford disasters put Exam on its heels. In addition, the major broker-dealers (such as Goldman Sachs and Morgan Stanley) needed to become banks during the crisis to survive and were now subject to Federal Reserve supervision. The Fed likes to keep its oversight behind its thick closed doors, so the SEC was on the outside looking in at the fate of these major firms. Congress had a field day firing questions at Mary and Carlo about the SEC's humiliating breakdowns in Madoff and Stanford. If our senators, House members, and the media swept open the curtain on other aspects of the SEC—the anonymous notes, the lax schedules, the telecommuting—the embarrassment would have been far worse, as this conduct persisted even after the crisis.

So what could have been the motivation for certain employees to ambush their superiors or colleagues, guns a-blazing, especially in the throes of a world economic meltdown? One of my fellow senior officers was convinced that some members of the staff simply did not want any supervision over what they were doing. They couldn't be fired, but we on the leadership team could be! I came to believe that the bomb hurlers could not abide change, just like the difficult employees in any institution. But Congress had inadvertently empowered them to resist any urgency to fix the kinds of problems that led to the Madoff and Stanford failures.

Mary, Carlo, and I were charged with making the kinds of changes that would ensure that the agency would catch the next Ponzi scheme before it did violence to innocent investors' savings. We'd have to use all our leadership prowess to inculcate our mission into the bloodstream of the staff so problem and passively resistant employees would redirect their weapons toward the bad guys, not fellow staffers. More importantly, we needed to streamline processes and remove bureaucratic obstacles so the hardworking, dedicated staffers could do their jobs. I realized early on that we had a big challenge ahead of us. While daunting, we made positive change to support the efforts of motivated staffers and it was incredibly rewarding.

THE MANY, MANY INSPECTORS GENERAL

If the nameless authors of accusations characterize a manager's actions as a violation of federal rules or equal protection, they can anonymously send them to the SEC inspector general or the Equal Employment Opportunity (EEO) office, both of which, by statute, are obligated to evaluate such complaints. The deadliest weapon in the federal employee arsenal is the IG. Most federal agencies have an office of the inspector general to root out wrongdoing at U.S. government agencies and departments, particularly in places like the Department of Defense, where procurement programs are at risk of being defrauded by corrupt government employees. But as with so many well-intentioned plans out of Washington, the inmates have taken over the asylum. The mission of the inspectors general across the government has been undermined by the bureaucracy and twisted into a tool for subverting accountability.

David Kotz, the IG when I arrived at the SEC, took a wide view of what he should investigate, which led to a great deal of confusion about whether he was investigating wrongdoing or simple incompetence. During an inspector general investigation, an SEC employee is not entitled to representation by SEC lawyers. Those employees who can afford outside counsel are much better off in these investigations. But those who cannot are at a tremendous disadvantage facing investigators without the assistance of counsel. Supervisors are on their own, but the union can send shop stewards with staff. As a lawyer I found this abhorrent: all people subject to investigation should have a right to counsel. I spoke with an official in New York, who recounted the ordeal of being questioned by the IG without counsel. He was called to a meeting to discuss Madoff failures but not advised that he would be questioned by IG investigators. He ended up fine although a little shell-shocked by the experience.

The EEO offices pursue discrimination complaints. This is another mechanism for employees to file grievances anonymously, which in turn saddles the supervisors who are targeted with costly expenses to defend themselves. In one instance, our human resources department announced a new policy about how pay would be calculated that applied to everyone in the agency. An employee who was a member of a minority group told me about a plan to talk to EEO because the policy discriminated against the employee as a member of a minority group, a novel argument given that it affected all employees similarly situated. These kinds of complaints put the director of the EEO office of the SEC, Alta Rodriguez, in a tough spot. Alta had to investigate complaints and report on those investigations to Congress, but she tried her best to mediate some of the more fantastic ones to see if a resolution could be worked out. Alta was one of the most professional and helpful executives at the agency, constantly making efforts to broaden the SEC's hiring across all groups of Americans.

JOB SECURITY NOT ENOUGH

The sheer volume and variety of these complaints mystified me, because staff members had no fear of losing their jobs whether they were making the complaint or were the object of one. What was the point then of the whole process? I was coming from a world where the primary mission was to make sure that the funds my firm managed performed well for investors. If they did, you got to keep a job that was stimulating and paid well. In general in the hedge fund business, two years of bad performance leads to investors fleeing and traders and other employees shown the door marked exit. At the SEC, on the other hand, in my five years on the job I was involved in a grand total of two people getting canned, one after she was arrested for a fraud and the second after he failed to show up for work for at least five years!

Joe DiMaria was an assistant director on my Exam staff who always helped put things in perspective. He pulled together a talented team who got exams done quickly and frequently uncovered wrongdoing such as an investment manager charging client accounts fees that he was not entitled to collect. I asked Joe why it was so hard to fire people at the SEC. He described how even when human resources staff would help a manager compile the detailed record needed to substantiate action against an employee, HR would ultimately not terminate the employee who would be retained. I wondered whether HR managers also feared complaints against them that would suck up all their time and energy defending. I loved talking to Joe. He was superb at hiring excellent supervisors, and he motivated them by trusting them and turning them loose to find infractions at investment firms.

He and I would talk about the different ways to encourage people, first by finding out what motivates them. Some of our staff who
performed exams wanted more public recognition, so we asked the
PR folks at the Enforcement division to include examiners' names in
press releases when their efforts resulted in violations and enforcement actions. Other staff members desperately wanted to avoid the
spotlight but relished knowing they'd helped in making wronged
investors whole by having the investment firms that overcharged
them make payments to clients called recoveries. These recoveries
provided immediate gratification to examiners because they did not
have to slog through a long enforcement action to win a penalty.

An article in *USA Today* in 2011 captured the problem of lifetime
employment in the federal government when it reported that federal
employees had a far better chance of dying before they retired than
being fired. That same article showed that for the fiscal year ending September 30, 2011, five SEC employees were ousted out of a
workforce of almost four thousand. That is about one-eighth of one
percent of the workforce. By contrast, the article stated that the private sector fires around 3 percent of its employees each year for poor
performance. The data in the article showed that the majority of the
firings in the federal workforce occurred during the initial two-year
probation period in use at many agencies, including the SEC. After
that, job security was almost total.[1]

For those in the private sector, the job security enjoyed by federal
workers sounds like an artifact from the 1950s. In many ways, it is. Civil
service employment protections were originally intended to prevent
each new presidential administration from coming in and canning all
the workers and replacing them with their supporters. The process
that is required to fire someone, including the appeal that often results
in reinstatement, has had the unintended consequence of making
federal civilian employment equivalent to a Supreme Court appointment. When the SEC staff voted in 2000 to be represented by a public
employee union, they added another buffer between managers and
the employees on their team. In a 1937 letter to Luther C. Steward, the
president of the National Federation of Federal Employees, President

Franklin Roosevelt (notoriously for many labor groups) wrote, "All Government employees should realize that the process of collective bargaining, as usually understood, cannot be transplanted into the public service. It has its distinct and insurmountable limitations when applied to public personnel management. The very nature and purposes of Government make it impossible for administrative officials to represent fully or to bind the employer in mutual discussions with Government employee organizations."

The SEC collective bargaining agreement allows unionized employees to file grievances on many issues, including termination, and, together with civil service rules, provides one obstacle after another for managers seeking to get rid of poor performers.[2] In one case, when an employee using civil service procedures made an appeal outside the SEC to the Office of Special Counsel—which I had never even heard of—its ruling returned this problematic employee to his job because of some perceived procedural violation by his supervisor. The aftermath of all this futility: managers rarely even bother to weed out the worst performers in their midst.

One day I was in Ken's office down the hall from mine when he mentioned the difficulty he was having even getting an employee to accept some constructive feedback on his performance. I worried that the SEC staffer could feel free marching up and down the halls, if not working from home, shouting gripes at the top of his lungs without any consequences. A supervisor might appeal to him to be a little quieter, but that was about it. And because the SEC and the union representing SEC employees had never agreed on a "pay for performance" system, compensation rose automatically every year for all employees regardless of the quality of any individual's work, the state of the economy, and the taxpayers who shoulder the burden. Union-won benefits were generally extended to supervisors as well. This is fair, but it also erodes motivation in managers. I saw over and over again where hard chargers came into the agency but gradually were worn down by a system that provided little reward for working hard.

I have to give credit to one of the SEC's most famous whistle-blowers for not remaining anonymous when she believed supervisors were also engaged in unaccountable behavior. Julie Preuitt, an assistant director in the Fort Worth office, had lobbied others at the SEC to further investigate the Stanford Financial Group for running a massive, $7 billion Ponzi scheme. Preuitt had been the examiner for the Stanford Group in 1997 and immediately called out the company's financial returns as ludicrously unsound. As reported in the *Washington Post* after the 2011 hearings held by the House Committee on Financial Services, "The SEC then flagged Stanford Group as a 'possible Ponzi scheme.' . . . In the years that followed, SEC examiners repeatedly pressed the agency to investigate, but the SEC enforcement staff made little if any meaningful effort to do so, Kotz said." The article contended that leaders in the SEC's Fort Worth office believed that headquarters wanted more cases, which meant that complicated cases (Stanford supposedly invested in Antigua) did not warrant investigation as they would not produce quick results.[3]

Julie didn't hide behind anonymity in warning the SEC that she believed the Texas regional bosses were marginalizing her for having warned about the Stanford mess. She sent "rocket" e-mails to Chair Schapiro complaining about her treatment. Not only did she sign her name, but she had the courtesy to copy me so that I could be ready when a member of Mary's staff, usually Chief of Staff Didem Nisanci, would inevitably call me soon after the e-mail.

When Preuitt testified at the 2011 hearings, she said she interpreted a job transfer as an effort to drive her out of the agency, and she argued that the move was "part of a cultural problem" that continues to undermine the SEC's effectiveness.[4]

I accompanied Julie and her mother to the House hearing for her testimony. Julie's mother worried that Julie could encounter further repercussions from SEC management. I told her that she didn't have to worry, that going public shielded her, but also promised to alert the SEC chair and protect her if any incidents came to pass.

I HAD MY SHARE

During my five years at the agency, at least two bellyachers sent anonymous notes about me to my boss, the chair of the SEC, and the inspector general. One complained about my office being located in the New York Regional Office, which had been the case from my first day, and the other lodged various complaints about one of the reorganizations I implemented at the SEC even though no staffers were ever let go. Both the inspector general and the Equal Employment Opportunity office were forced to investigate me based on these screeds. Once again, it was an entire waste of the chair's, the IG's, and the EEO's time, and in each instance, it was found that I'd done nothing wrong. But that only tells the end of the story.

I was not going to lose sight of a key part of my mandate: to reform the dysfunctional aspects of the agency that were crippling our mission and preventing dedicated staffers from doing their jobs. That's not to say that they weren't a distraction and time suck. The chair's office and the EEO showed me the nastygrams. No matter how many times I read notes about others, to see fictitious, ghastly allegations against me in writing took my breath away. All for trying to do the right thing for the agency and U.S. investors. I was met with gratitude from the chair's office for taking the time to refute each nonsensical charge in the nastygrams against me. I was gladdened by the support but didn't need it, because I was determined to defend my good name against these attacks.

One reward when I decided to serve the federal government was having to dole out thousands of dollars on a lawyer to help me navigate these investigations; and thousands more on an accountant to prepare my required annual financial disclosure form to make sure it was accurate. I was one of the lucky ones who could bear such unforeseen expenses. It was awful to witness the devastating personal cost to managers and staff who weren't so fortunate when they were targets of bogus accusations of misconduct made against them, need I say it again, anonymously. It was an epidemic of falsehoods, but that did not mitigate the pain, emotional and financial, that they inflicted. And the repercussion: a culture of fear and paranoia. And this is the agency meant to protect our country's citizens. As you will discover in later pages, the time and energy wasted on these internecine battles could have been better used on examinations and enforcement to catch fraudsters such as Bernie Madoff.

The failure to document policies and procedures, as any well-run business would, left the motivated examiners without the tools to do better.

That said, I was mightily inspired by those of the staff and managers at the SEC who tirelessly persevered to make the agency better despite all the obstacles and deceptions. They were the best of the best, so I jumped in the foxhole with them to do battle with inertia and soulless bureaucracy, to rebuild a broken system, and to make a real difference for U.S. investors and the U.S. financial markets.

MY EXPERIENCE AT THE SEC

Despite my frustrations with the decayed and debilitated culture of parts of the SEC when I arrived that I have described in this chapter, the surprising truth is, for all the challenges, my time there will always be the epitome of my professional career. I was given the gift of making real change in an agency that, arguably more than any other government entity, suffered the most damage to its reputation in the financial crisis. I served with many dedicated individuals who devoted their lives to public service and the preservation of the U.S. capital markets, the financial center of the world. It was an honor that I will cherish for the rest of my life. More than once I would pinch myself and ask, "Did you really come to the SEC and get to do these jobs?" The opportunity was humbling, and I never took for granted the opportunity the role afforded me. I endured the deceptions, the character assassinations, and the bureaucratic fatuousness as the cost of admission: to make policy at the highest levels of American government in a time of crisis.

MANAGING CHANGE AT THE SEC

When I started in Exam, the second largest group at the agency with about 950 of the agency's nearly 4,000 employees, my team in New York helped me adjust to the different and difficult realities of government service. My counsel, Jim Capezzuto, was a talented lawyer who helped me grapple with the fact that hundreds of investment management firms in our region had never been examined by the SEC. He patiently answered all my questions and was brutally honest about the challenges we faced. I was thrilled that after I left the New York job to be national deputy director, Jim took my place.

Carlo di Florio became another trusted colleague, mentor, and ally. Carlo took his oath of office as the national director of Exam in Washington, DC, on the same day I started at the SEC in New York. Carlo and I had met shortly before we both started at the agency (through Tom Biolsi), and we worked together almost nonstop for the next 2½ years, developing a deep friendship. Within six months Carlo asked me to be his deputy. Carlo had been a consultant at Price Waterhouse and had a great understanding of governance and how to assess the changes that an organization needed. We teased Carlo a little about some of the consultant lingo he used, such as "operationalizing" a change that we were discussing, but he was a strong leader who patiently gathered information about the problems and led the effort to craft solutions to address them. Carlo and I had the backing of our boss, Mary Schapiro, who was committed to improving the expertise of Exam and making it better equipped to find fraud and inform policy choices at the SEC. We did this by following the money—that is, by taking the hard facts the examiners discovered about how financial firms were running their businesses and ferreting out any issues that needed to be addressed.

For example, I was surprised to learn that Exam operated with no cohesive set of written policies and procedures on how to conduct examinations and carry out other critical functions. It wasn't an oversight on my first day that I wasn't given a manual for the operation of New York exams: it didn't exist! Carlo and I, working with a team of Exam lawyers, started reorganizing the office to address the issues uncovered by the crisis. We wrote a much-needed policy manual so everyone would play by the same rules, hired more experts who knew how the securities business operated, automated exam reports so all examiners could see them in a national database, and put more supervisors in the field to do the actual exams.

During the reorganization of Exam, I got to know SEC Chair Mary Schapiro much better. Ultimately, Mary entrusted me with an assignment to avert the imminent collapse of a massive broker-dealer, which would have been the largest failure ever of such a firm (it had about a million customers and 3 million accounts). On the basis of this experience and other projects where we worked together, Mary ultimately asked me to be the director of the Division of Investment Management.

I was thrilled with the offer. Imagine that you are asked to become the chief policymaker for the federal government in your field of expertise. But it was also a culture shock, as the division had the same problems that plagued Exam, as well as some of its own. Having acclimated to Exam, I was once again the proverbial fish out of water at Investment Management (or IM, as it is known at the SEC and around the industry). However, soon after the appointment, I was asked to wade into national policy issues such as implementing the Volcker Rule and reforming the troubled money market fund industry. If I was going to make other changes within IM, I'd have to find the time. Thank goodness I'd already learned something about changing the tires on a moving car.

As the director of one of the SEC's principal policy divisions, I started working closely with staffers at the U.S. Treasury, the Federal Reserve, the FDIC, and other federal regulators within the newly created Financial Stability Oversight Council. Having joined the SEC six months before the postcrisis bill called Dodd-Frank passed and was signed into law by President Obama, and having stayed until 2015, I had a front-row seat at numerous financial regulation mixed martial arts battles.

The story that follows is my five-year journey through the SEC as I and other leaders tried to make the agency work for investors again. Whether it was in Exam where I started or in the Division of Investment Management where I ended up, we reorganized the programs to tear down the walls encasing the fiefdoms and replaced them with a culture of cooperation. We savored the successes and bemoaned the failures; we rode out moments of high drama and weathered periods of hopelessness. At some points when we beheld progress being made, dispiriting times would follow, and I feared nothing would change. All the while it was a human endeavor: people showing strength and courage to make the agency function better but sometimes suffering setbacks at the hands of powerfully determined bureaucratic and institutional forces opposed to change. This is an intensely personal story of leaders making sacrifices to try to repair an agency that had become terribly insular and ill-equipped in significant ways to perform its functions in the fields it regulated. The U.S. capital markets are still the deepest and best in the world, one of the shining strengths of the U.S. economy, and the SEC plays a critical role in preserving and expanding those markets for the prosperity of future generations of Americans. In spite of all the black eyes, bloody noses, and sleepless nights, I would do it all over again in a heartbeat because it was the most rewarding experience of my professional life.

TAKING MYSELF PUBLIC

I'm gonna walk before they make
me run.

—Rolling Stones

I recall the moment I heard about Bernie Madoff's arrest. It was December 2008, and I was at a holiday party standing with several acquaintances when a friend walked up to us and said that Madoff had been arrested.

I knew then that everything was about to change. Madoff—an investment manager who was a former vice chair of Nasdaq—running a multibillion-dollar Ponzi scheme. Lives would be destroyed. The news couldn't have been more stunning.

The financial world had already absorbed many shocks in 2008. But Madoff's arrest would put the SEC in the crosshairs of Congress, the media, and the world. That fall I'd been seriously thinking about leaving the private sector and about whether I could get a job at the SEC. This news pushed me over the edge.

Was I ready to go public?

I had the financial industry and compliance experience. I had the love of policy and knowledge of deal making. But making the leap from my great gig at a hedge fund manager to the beleaguered SEC was about something more.

Part of that was an interest in public service. You see, I had loved clerking for Judge Charles S. Haight, Jr., of the New York federal district court during my second and third years out of law school. I was willing to endure the bureaucratic bungling of government in order to experience the intense rewards of serving the United States. Somewhere inside I knew that after 10 great years at Chilton Investment Company I wasn't sure if I wanted to make working at a hedge fund manager my entire career. I was also drawn to the challenge of making a difference in what I figured to be a chaotic and messy situation. My ability to stay focused and steer through anarchic dysfunction is a mindset that helped me succeed against the odds at the SEC. I view this ability to focus as a residual gift—and curse—of navigating a chaotic childhood with alcoholic parents and, truth be told, a lot of isolation.

I grew up in Ladue, Missouri, one of the wealthiest towns in the United States, with its brick mansions and expansive grounds, custom pools, country clubs, and open spaces, all linked by winding roads shaded by overhanging oak and maple branches. I was lucky to have many financial advantages growing up. But I spent years largely alone in a big house with a swimming pool and tennis court while my mother (divorced from my dad early on) suffered through severe mental illness and my father and stepmother drank themselves into oblivion on a nightly basis. It took a lot of serious skills in reading people and staying compartmentalized, not to mention a loving uncle, to escape with my confidence intact and start life on my own at Princeton University.

POLITICS EARLY ON

I grew up around politics and public service, but politics was always served with an open bar. My father, Norman Champ, Jr., worked for years in local Democratic politics in Ladue and made himself a local personage largely through his high school friendship with U.S. senator Tom Eagleton. Some of my earliest memories are of fund-raisers that my father hosted for various candidates in Missouri races.[1] He served as a Democratic committeeman, which is at the lowest level of local politics and meant he could get people to run for state legislature jobs. But it mostly meant he could attend as many political fund-raisers, cocktail parties, and dinners for the arts as he wanted to. That was a big part of the real motivation behind his life in politics.

I remember my father hosted fund-raisers in 1975 for several Democratic presidential candidates, including one for then Georgia governor Jimmy Carter.[2] When candidate Carter visited our house, he came complete with a Secret Service detail that guarded the candidate and set up a perimeter around my father's house. For a 12-year-old boy who already liked to hunt birds at our farm about an hour outside of St. Louis, having an armed group of Secret Service agents in the house was fascinating. The agents showed great patience as I quizzed them about the weapons they carried. Carter struggled as a president, but he was magnetic when I met him in person. It didn't hurt that he looked me in the eye and said, "Norm, you look like a fine young man."

My father's side of the family has long roots in St. Louis dating back to at least the 1880s when one of my ancestors moved to St.

Louis from Ohio and began a business making heavy leaf springs for wagons and buggies. We manufactured stacked steel springs of about 10 or so 3-inch-wide bars that sit between the axle and body of a vehicle. When the United States moved from horse-drawn conveyances to motor vehicles, leaf springs survived and are now used in heavy trucks. This led to the family saying that we were happy our ancestor chose to make buggy springs and not buggy whips! The Champ Spring Company lasted from 1882 until 2007 when we shut the company down after my dad's death in 2005 because it was no longer making a profit. The Champs also diversified into the farm outside St. Louis and other real estate which my family still owns. The experiences I had salvaging these companies helped me understand the nonstop nature of keeping a business profitable and in compliance with government regulation.

Through my dad's connections, I spent a couple of summers in high school working as a page on the Senate floor in DC and an intern in Senator Eagleton's office. Pages occupied the lowest rung on the congressional staff ladder; U.S. Senate officials made us run errands all day long. I remember one time I was told to go to the Senate floor and retrieve Senator John Stennis's favorite dress shoes that he'd stashed under his desk in the chamber. Stennis wanted the shoes because he was heading out to an event. I walked onto the mostly empty Senate floor casual as you please, scrabbled around under his desk, found his shoes, and stuffed them into a large manila envelope.

I liked working inside the Capitol—and I took advantage of my freedom. Most Friday afternoons, the other interns and I would sneak out and buy beer (no one carded us) and take it right through security to bring back into the senator's office. We'd also hit the bars after work most nights and then return to our apartment on what was then a rough block on East Capitol Street. These days, we all smile at the term "helicopter parents" in our era—those of us who like to hover in place to make sure their kids are safe—but my dad was more like a Huey pilot who dropped me off on a remote mission and then flew away until I called in for pickup.

ROCKY TIMES

Jimmy Carter came to my father's house for that fund-raiser (at that time my parents had been divorced for three years, and I lived with my mother, Anne Champ, in another suburb of St. Louis). My parents separated when I was seven years old and divorced in 1972 when I was nine. Divorce in St. Louis in the 1970s was pretty rare. In an unusual twist even by twenty-first-century standards, my mother and I moved out of the house in Ladue where we had lived with my father and lived in an apartment. After the divorce was final, my mother bought a house in Clayton, another suburb, and I moved to a new school there in the middle of fourth grade. After finishing primary school, I applied to and was accepted at a private seventh-to-twelfth grade school called John Burroughs.

All of this bouncing around did not stop, as I had to move back in with my father during eighth grade when my mother suffered what was then termed a "nervous breakdown." Mom struggled with manic depression, or bipolar disorder, for my whole life. Medication controlled her illness for certain periods, but then she relapsed. In the classic pattern she took turns being extremely manic and high and then plunging into depressive episodes. The mania usually evidenced itself by her buying lots of clothes, and so she had racks of clothes in her basement with the price tags still on them. My mother developed additional health problems, including diabetes and Parkinson's, and went to a nursing home at the relatively young age of 64. Part of my sadness for her: did all the tranquilizers and antidepression drugs she took for decades trigger or hasten the onset of Parkinson's? It seemed so terribly unfair after her many struggles.

The night I moved back in with my father was in late December 1975, just before Christmas. My mother always did worse as the holidays approached. On that particular night, I was at home with my mother and was in my room reading. I knew she was spiraling down—as a kid you soon become like an amateur doctor studying and identifying your ill parent's warning signs. I heard her call my father.

"Come pick him up," she said. "You have to get over here. And get the guns too. I'm afraid I'll hurt him or myself."

I heard her hang up and strained to listen for her movements from her bedroom next door, but she must have been sitting quietly after she hung up the phone. My dad stopped by in about an hour. I came downstairs and watched him collect the guns we kept in the basement, including the Browning shotgun that my Uncle Joe gave to me on my birthday that I used for bird shooting.

I'll never forget my father as he turned to me and said, "OK, Norm, I've got the guns, so you'll be safe," and he walked out through the door. Just left. I sat there staring gap-jawed at the door. Dad, I thought, don't you think you should be getting me out of here? Fortunately, after another call from my mother, he figured out the right thing and came back for me later that night.

Living with my father didn't provide much more stability. As I mentioned, he drank in great quantity, and I'm sure one of the reasons he divorced my mom was that she couldn't or wouldn't keep up with him. Dad remedied that issue when he got married to my stepmother who was every bit his equal as an alcoholic. It was a bit like *Days of Wine and Roses* with Jack Lemmon and Lee Remick, except they didn't want to go straight. The two of them drank themselves into a stupor every night of the year, with no exceptions. He preferred gin on the rocks in a brandy snifter; she went with vodka and white wine. They drank at parties or dinners they went to most nights and then returned to keep drinking at home. They always finished the night with a fresh bottle of champagne. Up in my room, I'd hear them come in the door and then about 15 minutes later the sound of the cork popping.

My stepsister, stepbrother, and I pretty much lived on our own while these two were out partying. I never got along with my stepmother, so the dynamic in the house felt uncomfortable. I often spent weekends at my mother's house. While my dad was a difficult person, ultimately he did leave me a legacy—the devastating truth about what addiction does to families.

I threw myself into my studies as an antidote to the craziness around me. I made some great friends at the John Burroughs School, like my lifelong pal Rod Krause, another guy in my class with divorced parents, who helped me through the rough times. I escaped as well to music, in particular becoming a Rolling Stones fan as their songs resonated with me.

Somewhere in early childhood I decided I wanted to be a lawyer. I'm not sure where I got the idea, but no one was going to stop me. One family story I like to tell goes back to when I was 9 or 10 and visiting the Champ Spring Company long before I worked there as a teenager. I told my father that I was going to grow up to be a lawyer and shut down factories like his. I was inspired by the grassroots crusades for clean air and clean water that were in the news during the 1970s and probably on a subconscious level wanted to show my dad my independence. Even at that age, I felt the tug of public service.

LOTS OF TIME IN SCHOOL

My mother and father rarely agreed on much, but both supported me when I wanted to attend a private school. I started at the John Burroughs School in seventh grade and graduated in 1981. When I got to Burroughs, I found a history teacher named James Alverson who turned me on to history and gave me the confidence to dive into the topic with a lot of scholarly passion.

I had always been, and still am, devoted to studying history. As a kid I read most of the hundred or so Ballantine $1 Illustrated History of World War II books. That war fascinated me because it was only a few decades before and my parents remembered so much about it. I also liked to visit several military surplus stores around St. Louis because they had medals and other gear from the Second World War. Even to this day I read a variety of history books with a particular focus on military history. Mr. Alverson was a brilliant teacher who made history come alive for me, particularly as he taught his course on European history.

Armed with some good grades from Burroughs and high test scores, I was able to compete for a highly selective college in the East. My mother was from New York and graduated from Wellesley College, and my father had gone to MIT and Harvard Business School in Cambridge, Massachusetts, so I had a sense that I wanted to go to the East Coast for college. At the same time, I wanted to get away from St. Louis, as I had no desire to return there after college and law school. In the spring of my junior year of high school, a friend named Barry Parness and I struck out from St. Louis in a station wagon to visit Princeton, Yale, and Columbia, among other colleges in the Northeast. My mind still boggles that two 17-year-olds from Missouri drove into Manhattan in 1980 and visited Columbia University.

The Upper West Side of Manhattan was a tougher, grittier place at the end of the 1970s that looked a lot more like the streets of Martin Scorsese's *Taxi Driver* than the Manhattan of my time. I remember the guy we stayed with had at least three deadbolt locks and a metal pole braced against the door. After our tours at Columbia we emerged unscathed and traveled on to several other colleges up the coast. My wife, Sally, and I would never send one of our four kids at age 17 on a 2,000-mile drive with a buddy, but expectations were definitely different in 1980. I didn't find it particularly remarkable, as I'd been making most of my own decisions for years already.

I emerged from our tour of colleges intent on attending Princeton. I found the academic rigor attractive, coupled with a sense that people worked hard but also stayed well rounded. I loved the stately open plazas and imposing campus buildings from the Gothic-style Nassau Hall (once the capitol building of the United States) to the massive Firestone Library. It helped that it was near Revolutionary War sites at Princeton and Trenton.

I felt extremely fortunate to go to Princeton. The academic buffet on display was so large I could have stayed for 10 years instead of 4. I had enough AP credits to graduate in 3½ years instead of 4 but soon realized what a mistake that would be.

My father and stepmother had continued to drink and spend down our finances, so my dad refused to pay my tuition for college. Fortunately my uncle Joe Champ, who had no children of his own, stepped in and paid for college and eventually law school. Uncle Joe would keep an eye on me through the years and helped fill the dark void my dad's drinking had left in our family. My uncle never finished college, but he had tremendous wisdom about life and used it to guide me along the way.

I majored in history and graduated with highest honors after writing my senior thesis on American pacification programs in one province in the northern part of South Vietnam. I loved having access to the most amazing historians in the world. I got to study with James McPherson, the foremost historian of the Civil War, and John Keegan, author of a book called *The Face of Battle* that revolutionized military history with its focus on the experience of the frontline soldier in several eras. Professor McPherson took a group of us to tour Civil War battlefields from Gettysburg to the Battle of Bull Run at Manassas. I wish every schoolkid could walk the grounds of these consecrated sites with Professor McPherson. Not only did I make many friends through those experiences, but I was so smitten with the academic life that I nearly gave up the law for a PhD in history.

I decided to test the academic waters and applied to some scholarship programs to pursue military history further after graduating. I won a Fulbright Scholarship to travel to London and pursue a master's degree in war studies at King's College London. Going to London was a thrill and exposed me to a year of living in another country while I earned my master's degree. I had by this time decided that academia didn't offer the marketable skills that I wanted for a career, and I had returned to my desire to be a lawyer.

I got accepted to Harvard Law School in December 1985 and started there in the fall of 1986. I enjoyed the rigor involved in studying law and learning how our legal system brought about a level of logic and fairness to human affairs in the United States. I found corporate law fascinating and wanted to practice in New York at one of the large law firms with major practices in finance and mergers and acquisitions transactions.

After Harvard, I started at the Wall Street law firm of Davis Polk & Wardwell. Practicing as a young lawyer meant endless days, nights, and weekends assisting senior lawyers negotiate and document financing and merger transactions. Davis Polk had two major areas of practice—litigation and corporate transactions like mergers and acquisitions. I vastly preferred the latter. For me litigation is after the fact, a dispute over failures. It was backward looking. I wanted to learn how big companies made deals happen, found financing, and created value through growth and restructuring. I also interacted with SEC staffers as they reviewed securities filings for transactions I worked on. I liked helping businesses change and pursue opportunities. I did work on securities litigation at times, including one case that pretty much required living in a storage room full of hundreds of boxes of documents that needed to be reviewed.

MY FIRST EXPERIENCE OF PUBLIC SERVICE

In my first year of practice, a Davis Polk partner named Dennis Glazer approached me and asked if I would be interested in clerking for a federal trial judge in Manhattan. I had applied for a few appellate court clerkships in my last year of law school, but my heart was not really in it, as I wanted to be a corporate lawyer. My first year of practice had included some interesting litigation assignments, and a clerkship in federal court would enhance my understanding of how litigation worked. I soon interviewed with Judge Charles S. Haight, Jr., and started as his law clerk in the fall of 1990. Judge Haight was a throwback to a courtlier and kinder time in the New York bar. Both the judge and his father had been partners in the admiralty law firm of Haight Gardner that dealt with legal matters arising out of New York's shipping industry. Judge Haight was committed to public service and spoke eloquently about serving this great country and the better work-life balance that public service usually involved. As an ambitious young lawyer, I wasn't completely receptive to the judge's message at the time, but it gradually sank in over the years and influenced my thinking about what was important.

Clerking for a federal trial judge is one of the best jobs in the law. Other clerks and I lamented that only in the law do they give you such a great job so early in your career. It was a heady combination. We dug into all kinds of federal cases from complex securities laws cases to large drug arrests. We had a close-knit "chambers family" consisting of courtroom deputy Corinne Szalay, assistant Cecilia Rudden, and my co-clerks David Finn and Beth Grossman that functioned like a small law firm dealing with the more than 1,000 cases on the judge's docket.

It was great.

Near the end of my clerkship in June 1992, I suffered an awful personal loss when my uncle Joe Champ, who had given me so much guidance and support throughout my life, died of smoke inhalation in a house fire. His wife, who had been disabled by a stroke, fell asleep with a lit cigarette and started a large fire. I still miss Uncle Joe's great humor and the well-grounded guidance he gave me—as well as the newspaper clippings about the football and baseball Cardinals he'd send to me every few weeks while I was in school and at Davis Polk.

After two years of clerking, I returned to Davis Polk, and excited after spending time in federal court, I spent a couple of years as a litigator working on securities cases in federal and state court in Manhattan. The United States had been in a recession from 1990 to 1992, and as the economy heated up, corporate work on mergers and financings began to pick up again. In 1994 the managing partner at Davis Polk asked if I would return to corporate work since I had experience with it in my first year of practice. I readily agreed and joined the mergers and acquisitions practice at Davis Polk working on private and public company deals.

At about the same time as I moved back to corporate law, I began dating a beautiful, smart, and funny lawyer named Sally Shreeves, who became my wife in 1996. When Sally and I had our first child, our daughter, in 1998, I knew the mergers and acquisitions lifestyle would force me to miss most of my kids' lives.

Given my background, I was particularly concerned about being the kind of dad who wouldn't give my kids nightmares or lifelong neuroses. A recruiter named Judy Kross introduced me to Richard L. Chilton, Jr., who ran a successful hedge fund firm and hired me as his general counsel. Over the next decade I had a challenging and professionally rewarding experience as a partner and general counsel of Chilton Investment Company. Because I ran the small legal office at Chilton, used outside counsel in a pinch, and acted as my own boss for most day-to-day business, I had more flexibility to set my schedule and be available to my family. The hours were still long, but I had more control. I was a hedge fund lawyer.

I had one more lesson to learn about being my father's son. I was a drinker since high school and continued to drink most every day for a long time even after we started a family. While I took pride in never losing control, I'm sure my drinking brought out the worst in me while I was juggling a demanding job and helping Sally raise our four children. I finally got smart after I discovered that I had atrial fibrillation in 2004, which necessitated not drinking for a while. After that, I realized my drinking behaviors had been handed down to me by my dad, and I didn't want to follow in his path any longer.

I never picked up another drink.

HEDGE FUND WORLD

I found my life as the general counsel and partner of a hedge fund demanding but also interesting. I often compared it to being a country lawyer, because one day I might be analyzing a new security and the next day I would be looking at the office space lease because the roof leaked. I handled many business development tasks, and I opened the firm's offices in London, Hong Kong, and two cities in mainland China. When the funds expanded overseas, I was responsible for all the logistics in those locations, clearing registration and compliance with foreign governments and setting up our offices. As in the judge's chambers, my coworkers and I formed a close-knit family and became great friends. While I was in the hedge fund business, my three sons were born. Most of the partners were around my age and having their own families, so we were all going through similar life experiences.

When our number of funds grew, we were required to register our business with the SEC. I headed up the team responsible for assembling the documentation and reporting the information the SEC required. In preparation for registering with the SEC, I also brought people from the firm together to complete an operations and compliance manual for handling allocations and clients. By this time in my career, I had built a reputation around Wall Street as someone who knows how to get things done—the right way.

In 2007 I was elected to the board of directors of the trade group for the hedge fund industry called the Managed Funds Association (MFA), a member organization composed of most of the largest and most prominent hedge funds in the United States.[3] Smaller hedge funds are also members, but the large funds pay higher dues and generally control the direction of the organization, primarily by placing senior people from their firms on the board of directors. Some of my fellow directors were senior executives at well-known hedge funds such as D.E. Shaw, Renaissance Technologies, and Citadel Capital Management. For years, no one paid much attention to the tiny MFA, which held a few industry events that were sparsely attended.

That changed as investors, media, and Congress grew more interested about the power and profits of hedge and private equity funds. MFA raised its profile with Congress and regulators as the bull market, coupled with the high-profile exploits of hedging and derivatives, began attracting more and more interest—and concern. Before this, Congress generally ignored what was seen as an uncontroversial niche of funds except for the occasional kerfuffle over whether to tax long-term investment earnings allocated to successful managers as ordinary income instead of capital gains.

From 2007 to 2009 I took part in regular MFA meetings with Fed chair Ben Bernanke, Treasury secretary Hank Paulson, and other top financial policy makers. With Bernanke we always convened in the Fed's "map room," one of the largest rooms in the federal government. Huge maps of the Federal Reserve districts covered the walls. The Fed had a photographer so that every visit ended with a group photo. Bernanke was always interesting though he said little. He certainly fulfilled the image of the Fed chair as an oracle who maintains a mysterious silence. Later, as I'll discuss in Chapter 8, when I worked with Bernanke and the Fed on the Volcker Rule, it was much the same.

During 2007 and 2008 I also briefed members and staff on the Hill about what hedge funds were and how they worked. We wanted to educate regulators and Congress about what hedge funds actually did so they could make more informed voting decisions and benefit from knowing us and having people they could reach out to with questions. During the initial controversy over hedge fund taxation in the mid-2000s, one of the House committees hosted a briefing for all staff in an elaborate room in the Capitol building. Staffers varied in their level of knowledge. Some understood the impacts of what Congress might do, and others did not. One staffer in the latter category told us, "Even if we raise taxes on you, you will continue on as before with your business and employ people." At this panel I was joined by a professor from Emory Law School who replied, "If you tax something, you have less of it." It was disheartening to see the Obama administration impose major tax hikes after the Great Recession and then seem puzzled that we had the slowest recovery since the Second World War.

I got to know legislators including Barney Frank, who was one of the smartest guys in DC I met when he was in office. Although I disagreed with his politics, I was impressed by how much he knew about how the Street worked. As events unfolded before the fall of Lehman, Congress and the media kept the klieg lights focused on hedge funds. I begin to feel like the sick patient in the hospital—you know you are in trouble when all the medical specialists arrive. In our case it seemed that every political professional I met wanted to work for the MFA. The MFA full-time staff expanded from two to maybe a dozen in no time.

WHAT ARE HEDGE FUNDS?

I loved working in the hedge fund business in large part because participating in a well-run hedge fund manager showed me the genius of the American capital markets. Many hedge funds created wealth for a lot of people by investing in stocks while avoiding mortgage securities such as collateralized debt obligations (CDOs). In some corners of the media and on the Hill, hedge funds became caricatured as irresponsible. I took every opportunity to educate influencers about the long history and sound practices of well-managed mutual and hedge funds.

Investors have been pooling their money in common investment vehicles for much of modern financial history in Europe and the United States of America. By investing in a stock or bond directly, stockholders place their money on the fortunes of a particular business. Pooling money in investment funds is one level removed. Investors put their money in a fund and ask the manager of the fund to invest the money in stocks and bonds on their behalf.

European merchants and capitalists established precursors to the mutual fund as far back as 1774, a business dominated until the late nineteenth century by the Dutch.[4] Early U.S. mutual funds operated as what came to called "closed-end" funds. These funds issued a fixed number of shares that then traded on the market. The funds did not issue more shares to meet investor demand. If an investor owned shares, he or she had to sell them to a buyer to cash out. The first American "open-end" mutual fund—which accepted a limitless number of investors by adding more shares to meet demand and that are redeemable daily—opened in Boston in 1924 and was called the Massachusetts Investor Trust.[5]

A riskier variation of the mutual fund was wildly popular in the years leading up to the stock market crash in 1929. These investment "trusts" pooled investors' money while fund managers bought and sold stocks and other instruments with no regulatory oversight. The funds became highly leveraged and collapsed in 1929 as securities in them plunged in value and those securities had to be sold to pay for debt that been taken on by the trusts. As a result, Congress stepped in to pass a series of tough new laws regulating mutual funds. These included the 1933 Securities Act, the 1934 Securities and Exchange Act, the 1936 Revenue Act, and the Investment Company Act of 1940.[6] These laws established the U.S. Securities and Exchange Commission and required that mutual funds register with the SEC. They set up tax rules for funds and mandated fund structures. They also imposed strict limits on leverage and required that the funds be redeemable on a daily basis at the net asset value of the fund.

These funds helped fuel post–World War II growth with U.S. securities markets that provided ample capital for expanding businesses. However, the U.S. economy hit a pothole in the late 1960s and 1970s, as spending on the war in Vietnam, oil shocks from the Middle East, and inflation resulted in the slow growth and high inflation that was termed "stagflation." During these years private pools of capital, now known as hedge funds and private equity funds, began to rise to prominence. They were organized under a provision of the mutual fund law that exempts such funds from most regulation if they are offered privately to certain sophisticated investors.

The best-known manager of a private pool of capital that we now refer to as a hedge fund is someone that no one would associate with hedge funds today, Berkshire Hathaway CEO, founder, and principal investor Warren Buffet.[7] Buffett, a math genius, had gone to work at a brokerage firm in the 1960s where he helped trade securities for clients and did research on public companies. Buffett soon went out on his own and formed a private hedge fund where he could trade stocks in the markets based on his view of a stock's value. Buffett raised capital for his fund from friends, family, and acquaintances in the Omaha, Nebraska area. Investors who started with Buffett and stayed with him throughout his subsequent changes in investing vehicles became fabulously wealthy. A pair of college professors at the University of Nebraska who invested early with Buffett owned over $100 million worth of Berkshire Hathaway stock by the time they passed away.[8]

Buffett's hedge fund ultimately purchased all the shares of an obscure Rhode Island textile firm called Berkshire Hathaway, and Buffett offered his fund investors the opportunity to take Berkshire

Hathaway shares in return for their fund interests or be cashed out of the fund. The lucky ones took Berkshire Hathaway stock, and the return on their share of Berkshire Hathaway stock from the time Buffett distributed to his fund investors in the 1970s until 2016 has been phenomenal. Buffett runs his public company in a similar manner except now he buys businesses and adds them to his conglomerate.

Hedge funds buy and sell securities for the fund and "hedge" their exposure to the market by selling stocks short—that is, by borrowing these securities from a broker and selling them. If the price of the security goes down, the fund can later purchase shares at a cheaper price to replace the borrowed shares and make money based on the amount the price of the security has declined. Shorting is not for the faint of heart, because if the price of the security goes up instead, the potential loss is infinity! Shorting will always have its critics because investors are betting on and profiting from failure, but this activity is healthy for markets as it provides liquidity. Mutual funds cannot short stocks to the same degree as hedge funds because of their regulated role as less-leveraged funds for ordinary retail investors.

Some of the most famous hedge fund managers of the last decades, such as George Soros, have been investors who trade around the globe on so-called macro considerations.[9] Such investors seek to profit from price mismatches in global markets, for example by buying futures on cheap grain in the United States because they know there is a weak crop in Russia. Other investors such as Julian Robertson founded Tiger Management that ran so-called long-short equity strategies to buy the best companies long and sell the worst companies short.[10]

While hedge funds invest in publicly traded securities, private equity funds largely invest in private firms, and then implement strategies to increase the company's value. Often, they then sell the company later in an IPO or other arrangement. Managers of private equity funds provide capital and management know-how to businesses in exchange for ownership of all or part of the business. These businesses are sometimes publicly traded companies "taken private" or privately held businesses. Private equity pioneers including Kohlberg Kravis

Roberts (now known as KKR) used investor capital to take public companies private in leveraged buyouts and then make them public again later with added value. Private equity funds typically have a much more limited ability for investors to obtain their money once it is invested in the fund. For a standard hedge fund, investors typically can ask for their money back once each year. But private equity funds usually last 8 to 12 years, and investors only receive their capital back when an investment in the fund has been sold or taken public.

Private equity firms often specialize in providing funding to businesses at a certain stage of their growth. Venture capital firms typically offer early seed capital to businesses at the beginning stages. Private equity funds like to step in and make their play at later stages of a business during its growth phase when it is only a few years away from an initial public offering.

CRISIS

After the Madoff arrest, the financial crisis continued as the biggest story in the world. The headlines screamed about banks needing bailout money, tsunamis of home foreclosures, and metastasizing job losses. Even when the immediate panic of 2008 had passed, Americans knew the U.S. economy had plummeted to a historic low, that the recession would last, banks were in trouble, and their futures were incredibly shaky.

By the spring of 2009 I was hearing about drafts of legislation to reform the entire U.S. financial system that were in circulation, including provisions that would require all hedge fund managers to register with the SEC.* Other legislative measures were rumored to require the SEC to craft rules in response to broad requirements that would be set by Congress. The SEC would ultimately need to translate whatever law Congress passed into rules and regulations that the securities industry would have to follow.

---

*Under the law at that time, private fund managers could remain outside SEC scrutiny if they ran fewer than 15 funds.

I knew I could help give the SEC's examiners the tools to do a better job of identifying fraud and malfeasance before they exploded into front-page news. My experience both as a senior executive in the hedge fund industry and as a securities lawyer wouldn't hurt much either. Investors lost huge amounts of money when Bernard Madoff and Allen Stanford were revealed to be running massive Ponzi schemes that cost investors billions of dollars. Serious regulators and lawmakers needed to know everything they could about how the Street operated from people who had worked there.

In April I had a fateful lunch with Tom Biolsi. Tom held the position of associate director for investment management examinations in the New York SEC office, but we knew each other from the speaking circuit around the New York legal world. We both attended a conference at the Practicing Law Institute, which was then on Seventh Avenue on Manhattan's West Side and agreed to have lunch afterward. As we ate, I told Tom that the crisis and its impact on the SEC were starting to make me think about the possibility of public service at the SEC. Tom replied that I should apply for his job, as he was going to leave the SEC in the summer. I had no idea Tom was thinking of leaving, but I was also excited, as this seemed to be the perfect way to reenter public service. In the summer I completed the voluminous online application for Tom's job and waited to see what would happen.

ENTERING PUBLIC SERVICE

After I applied for the Exam position in New York, I got a call scheduling an interview with George Canellos, the SEC's regional director of the office. I called Tom before the interview to ask for his advice. Tom told me that George was a great guy, and per usual he was spot on. I met George in the New York office and took an instant liking to one of the best people in the securities law business. George came to the SEC only about eight months before I got there. Before joining the SEC George had been a partner at the historic and prestigious Wall Street law firm of Milbank Tweed. George is an affable, funny guy who cares deeply about ferreting out wrongdoing in the securities

industry. When George decided to hire me as the head of investment management exams in New York, SEC chair Mary Schapiro
endorsed the hire, and she requested that I agree to stay three years.

George called me at my office in October 2009 and offered me
the job to head up investment management exams in New York. I was
eager to join the SEC, but I told George I would think about it and
call him back. I went home and talked to Sally about the offer. I struggled with giving up a great job at Chilton to join the SEC. However,
I only planned to stay at the SEC for three years, and I thought the
experience would strengthen my skills for my career after the SEC.
The allure of returning to government service made it worth taking a
pay cut. Sally supported the move all along; she knew this was a challenge I'd thought about tackling for years.

George and I agreed I would start at the end of January 2010 after
I taught my private funds class at Harvard Law School in January, a
class I started teaching in 2008 before the crisis.

The reality of my decision hit hard when the SEC wanted to do a
press release on my hire in November 2009.[11] Mary Schapiro wanted
to show Congress and the public that the SEC could hire people with
industry and management experience to turn the agency around.
After the release I knew my world had changed when I dialed in for
the next meeting of the MFA Executive Committee. When the chair
of the committee took roll call, I gave my usual "Norm Champ." The
line went silent for a bit, and the chair politely told me to get off the
phone. Even though I didn't start at the SEC until January, I was no
longer in the hedge fund industry.

SWEARING AN OATH
TO SERVE MY COUNTRY

On my first day, I joined George Canellos's weekly meeting with
the heads of the SEC groups located in New York. Around the table
were Bob Sollazzo, the head of broker-dealer examinations; Andy
Calamari, the chief of enforcement; Bruce Karpati, who ran asset

management enforcement; and a handful of other senior enforcement officials. George opened the meeting by asking me to raise my right hand and repeat the oath of office after him (the oath of office is set by statute)[12]:

> I, Norm Champ, do solemnly swear that I will support and defend the Constitution of the United States against all enemies, foreign and domestic; that I will bear true faith and allegiance to the same; that I take this obligation freely, without any mental reservation or purpose of evasion; and that I will well and faithfully discharge the duties of the office on which I am about to enter. So help me God.

As I sat down at George's conference table, my eyes were welling up with tears. I really didn't want to cry in front of my new colleagues, and I managed not to. Nevertheless, it was exhilarating and emotional to think that I could do some small part to help the United States recover its position as the world's leading financial center.

I started to contribute in that meeting as we discussed various management issues in the New York office. I remember thinking that all my experience in the private practice of law, the clerkship for a federal judge, the hedge fund business, and teaching would come in handy as we all tried to make the SEC better than it had been before and more able to police the markets so that investor confidence in the United States would be restored. We'll see how I fared in the chapters ahead.

PUNCHING
THE CUSHION

The administration of government,
like a guardianship, ought to be
directed to the good of those who
confer, not of those who receive the
trust.

—Cicero

It's my nature to solve problems. I tend to take a proactive approach based on the input I can get. I talk to the people involved, get the facts, and make my charge. That's how I've operated as a lawyer, executive, and entrepreneur. I assumed that this kind of background would make me a great fit for the SEC. After all, the agency had a lot of problems, and coming up with solutions was one of my major strengths. And while this was indeed true, it didn't unfold as I expected. Not in the least.

I assumed going in that the SEC was mired in excessive rules and regulations, with bureaucrats hiding behind reams of policies that had grown year by year like coral on a sunken chest. No problem. I was prepared to do my homework and grapple with dense pages of procedure manuals that I planned to be reading at home over the weekends. I'm a lawyer; I read the documents. If I could grind through thousands of pages of securities litigation documents as a first-year law firm associate, I could handle all the three-ring binders they could throw at me.

Nothing was what I expected. I soon learned that the SEC wasn't a typically dysfunctional bureaucracy that needed to fix what had been broken. Rather, there were parts of it that had never been built.

Government bureaucrats tend to thrive under the layers of red tape that they devise and master in order to protect themselves from the vicissitudes of politics, their superiors, and the media. In the case of government agencies, these rules begin with laws. The SEC was formed by a law passed by Congress and President Franklin Roosevelt in 1934.[1] In fact, Dodd-Frank set a deadline for all SEC examinations to be completed 180 days after the last documents are requested from a regulated business because Congress was concerned about examinations taking too long.[2]

Soon after I started in 2010, I scheduled a regular weekly meeting with my three assistant directors. Our purpose would be to review and solve problems that needed attention.

It was the second or third time we'd met. We gathered in a sizable conference room with black leather rolling chairs and a light wood table. Each of the assistant directors supervised a team of inspectors who conducted exams in the New York and New Jersey area, where the bulk of U.S. asset managers are located.

My direct reports took their chairs. Counsel Jim Capezzuto sat on my left. Joe DiMaria usually parked himself on my right about halfway down the table. Joe turned out to be a quiet, steady performer who got exams done. An experienced professional who had started his career with the New York regional office as a securities examiner in 1986 and worked his way up, Joe looked to be in his midfifties, balding up top, with steel wire-rimmed glasses.

Dawn Blankenship tended toward the left side of the conference table and liked some space around her. She was somewhere around Joe's age with dark hair and prominent eyes. I soon learned she had an incredible commitment to her work. She was known to be a tireless auditor in performing exams, sometimes camping out at a firm for months or even years, digging for evidence of bad conduct, self-dealing, or conflicts of interest. She had a reputation for not always knowing when to pull up stakes and close an exam, which could be inefficient. But she took her mission to protect investors very seriously, and I thought that was great, particularly because some examiners seemed to be just going through the motions.

Another assistant director, William Delmage, was a little younger than the rest but had been around the SEC for a long time. He usually sat next to Joe.

At one of the first weekly meetings, Dawn started reviewing a concern she had about an investment manager allocating securities trades among client accounts in a way that might favor one client over another when Bill Delmage interrupted and began talking to me directly.

He asked me how I wanted to deal with these kinds of issues on exams. Bill related that when Tom Biolsi was in charge, he specified how he wanted to do different types of procedures.

"What's the SEC's internal guidance on how to do these exams?" I asked. "Where can I read up on it?" I looked up at their neutral expressions.

"Well, there isn't any," Dawn murmured. "There's no set way we do it. Each new New York associate director tells us how they want it done."

So I asked them about nationwide standards for conducting exams. That's when I learned that among the 12 offices from California to New York, we lacked any published guidance on how the SEC went about its investment management exams.

No framework. No policies about who talked to whom. No required approvals or guidance for communications. In short, nothing had been put in writing. Employees were more or less left to use their best judgment.

"We all pretty much know how to do this stuff," one of the assistant directors explained.

Shocked, I gathered my thoughts.

John Adams said that constitutional democracy was to be a government of laws and not of men. It didn't seem that anyone here had gotten the memo. The next week at our meeting, the assistant directors were discussing how examiners should check if investment managers had a conflict of interest between trading for their own accounts and trading for clients. Dawn began digging through a stack of papers that she had brought to the meeting and found the rumpled piece of paper she was looking for. "Oh yes, Norm," she said. "We have a procedure for that. A supervisor e-mailed it out about five years ago."

So this was how our assistant directors were finding their guidance? Dug up from five-year-old e-mails? Later I learned that the staff members had to print out their e-mails in order to store them in safety. Evidently, the New York office server was scrubbed periodically to free up storage space. Dawn couldn't save e-mails on her computer for long.

I didn't know whether to laugh or cry. A five-year-old crumpled paper copy of an e-mail in one employee's files held crucial documentation for a federal agency? If SEC inspectors ever arrived at a financial firm for an examination and discovered that the firm had no manual on how to comply with federal securities laws, that firm would immediately be cited for deficiencies and most likely subject to enforcement action.

Looking around the table, I could see the assistant directors didn't notice the irony that they themselves had no formal manual capturing how they would go about their job. The SEC requires that investment advisors have a "code of ethics" to specify how advisors manage conflicts of interests with their clients. SEC leaders frequently gave speeches about the sanctity of the compliance manual.

"Thanks, Dawn," I told her. "Could you see what else you can find in your files?"

Was it like cracking the Watergate scandal? No. Did this lack of written rules really matter? Absolutely. With benchmarks and guidelines, the SEC might have detected the wrongdoings of Madoff, Stanford, and other significant frauds *before* the 2008 financial crisis.

Indeed many of the SEC's breakdowns prior to the financial crisis stemmed from this very issue. The commission desperately needed national procedures that ensured a consistent standard of work to govern its examination, monitoring, and enforcement activities. With no documented, agreed-upon system for how to conduct its responsibilities, each SEC division or office made up its own rules for how to do its job—but rarely wrote them down. The SEC had evolved to rely on managers in every office to act as village elders passing down the knowledge to new members of the tribe. The longer I stayed, the more I felt like I had stumbled into some ancient society where all knowledge was handed down by oral tradition from generation to generation.

The problem was that the system had turned into the game of "telephone." With each transmission, the original message got a bit more garbled. As my conversations with key staff who remembered the original discussions revealed, many procedures bore little resemblance to their intent. Not surprisingly, some of those changes along the way were slanted toward what was best for government workers—not enforcement of the federal securities laws. The inspector general's report recounted that examiners at Madoff's firm actually drafted a letter asking the options exchange self-regulatory organization for records of his trading, but the examiners appear to have decided not to send the letter because it would pull in too many records that would have taken a long time to review.[3] If those examiners had had procedures requiring them to verify at least some trading, they would have sent the letter and Madoff might have been unmasked because he did not trade at all—on the exchange or anywhere else.

Most SEC employees were and are committed to the mission of the agency. They wanted to do the right thing. But without proper management and process, they barely stood a chance of being successful.

Why did policies and procedures matter? In the case of the Stanford disaster, examiners had no consistent way of escalating issues such as written examiner concerns over Stanford that identified him as carrying on a "possible Ponzi scheme" years, and billions, before he was caught.[4] In these circumstances, everything comes down to the judgment and on-the-job training of examiners. That is a pleasant place to be when you are doing your work, as it allows you to decide what you want to do. For a leader of the agency, it was an unpleasant place to be when Congress kept calling and asking why no one was being held accountable for the Madoff and Stanford disasters. It is hard to hold people accountable when there are no standards.

Over the next few years, I would lead a number of battles to force this aspect of the SEC into the sunlight of the twenty-first century. Some I lost, some I won—but we ultimately got manuals in place in Exam and IM that gave staff a consistent set of polices to follow.

PHONING IT IN

The worst blowback I witnessed during my time at the SEC started with a widespread trend in federal government agencies that is unknown to most of the public (every person outside the government I have told this to didn't know about it). Public employee unions along with their allies in Congress have pushed through various measures encouraging federal employees in most agencies to work from home, sanctifying the practice in legislation. The most recent statute put on the books allowing employees to "telework" as much as possible: the Telework Enhancement Act of 2010.[5]

You can't find much media coverage or compelling research to show telework's benefits or explain why it has become so dominant. The SEC to my knowledge lacked any internal plan to measure the impact of telework. It was allowed to move into the house like a crazy old uncle in the family and stay as long as it wanted. One report I found from the Office of Personnel Management ("2013 Status of Telework in the Federal Government") mustered scant evidence for the benefits of telework, beyond highly subjective employee surveys.[6] The report oohed and aahed over the expansion of telework as if that trend in itself made our nation better. In 2012, over a quarter million federal employees had telework agreements in place, up from 144,000 the previous year, the report said. One-third of the 1.02 million of Uncle Sam's employees who were allowed to telework in 2012 did so. The report gushed that a greater share of employees were able to telework *three or more times a week* in 2012 than the year before.

Are we all sure this is a good thing? I'm not. One is hardly blown over by the evidence put forward to justify telework in this report written to cheerlead the policy with as much favorable data and framing as possible. The survey from employees—whom I don't blame in the least for liking telework—reported they were "more satisfied with their jobs," "experienced greater support for performance on the job" (whatever that means), and had "a greater sense of empowerment." The objective, more rigorous criteria set out to evaluate telework were less convincing: "Goals of reduced commuter miles, energy use, and real estate costs continue to be less common" (i.e., of so little significance, they won't even be included here). And you know what; it was all too darn complicated anyway: "Unlike data for human resources related metrics [that is, employee surveys], data for energy and environmental goals is often difficult to access, and requires complex analysis to identify the impact of telework." (By all means, then, let's skip it.)

Further, the report buried the hidden force behind telework expansion: bargaining demands by public employee unions. The public employee union representing SEC employees, the National Treasury Employees Union, has used the leverage provided by the telework statutes to bargain to give SEC employees more latitude to work from home. The 2013 collective bargaining agreement governing working conditions for SEC nonsupervisory employees goes as far as to provide that a certain number of employees can work from home five days a week.

I'm not a telework grump. But I've seen its limitations in the private sector, and I experienced how it went down at the SEC. Can professionals really collaborate, share critical information, and communicate with their supervisors when they are 20 miles from the office two, three, or even five days a week? The concept of occasional telework for federal employees is not a bad one. I took advantage of it sometimes so that I could avoid commuting downtown to the New York office of the SEC on a day when I had an event in one of my children's schools and on some Fridays in the summer.

But without procedures and oversight, telework can make a mockery of work-life balance. At the SEC, I saw too many examples of telework eroding common sense and really, even common decency. While I was at the agency, an employee asked SEC chair Mary Schapiro in a town hall meeting, if he was called into the office for a meeting while he was on telework, would the SEC pay for his commuting costs?

Here's the killer. Soon after I arrived in my job, supervisors approached me with a dilemma. They were concerned that certain employees were not being productive while working at home, but the supervisors felt constrained because there was a "labor arbitration ruling" that said they were not allowed to check on what teleworking employees were doing.

"No way," I said, shaking my head. "Could you get me a copy of this ruling? I need to understand what the parameters are." We went on to chat about the issues with the particular employees, such as how telework made it difficult to schedule exams and team meetings and coordinate efforts.

In the following weeks I asked numerous times to see a copy of the "arbitration ruling" prohibiting supervisors from monitoring employees on telework. In the end, the supervisors never provided me with a copy because no such ruling existed. My colleagues found e-mails about various disputes over telework but no evidence that they were forbidden by law from asking their reports what they were doing each day. I asked Greg Gilman, the head of the SEC's union local, about this later on. Greg said of course supervisors could check on employees when they were home teleworking.

In the culture of the SEC where policies and procedures are rarely documented, nonsensical rules about whether supervisors can check on employees working at home were passed down by oral tradition. This of course worked out quite well for employees who were spared pesky supervisors asking them what they were doing at home. It also gave the less motivated supervisors an easy excuse for not managing the people who reported to them. The SEC's culture made such accommodations commonplace. It was easier for everyone to cite a fictional arbitration ruling rather than challenge the status quo. Plus, challenging the status quo might get you an anonymous complaint to the inspector general or Congress, so the cost could be quite high. Not surprisingly, the supervisor who raised this issue was someone who did his best to carry out as many exams as possible despite the impediments of the way the SEC does business.

The issue of making it up as you go along is prevalent across the parts of the federal government I came to know. As I worked with other regulators on rule-making required by the Dodd-Frank financial reform legislation, I saw repeatedly where an individual's personal opinions about an industry practice became a rule. Later I'll describe how this tradition of "knowing it when you see it" contributed to arbitrary rules and regulations that reflected the personal and political beliefs of bureaucrats, often with immediate adverse consequences.

NOTHING TO SEE HERE.
JUST KEEP MOVING

Over my first few months, I talked to a number of employees about the agency's well-publicized failures. Most believed individual instances had nothing to do with broader issues of how the agency went about its duties. Rather, staffers believed that the failures were the result of a few isolated mistakes by broker-dealer examiners in the SEC's New York office (Madoff) or enforcement staff in the Fort Worth, Texas, regional office (Stanford). The thinking was that these failures occurred in some far-off place and had nothing to do with how well most people did their jobs.

Many in the SEC saw no personal responsibility for anything that had happened. Even though their prevailing thinking was that Madoff and Stanford were isolated mistakes in regional offices, the same staffers thought those mistakes could not be charged to anyone individually. The possibility that individuals in the agency might be held accountable for the Madoff and Stanford disasters was inconceivable to most agency employees. I often heard from employees that the problem might be the system or lack of resources but that individuals had never been and could never be held accountable for their actions on an exam.

If an organization is almost entirely free from consistency in policy and procedures, fiefdoms (or to use a modern term, "silos") will rise up, and each one will guard its own territory and power, often in competition. This creates an environment where staffers refuse to share information with their coworkers. Therefore, many SEC employees never reached out or collaborated beyond their immediate work team, but stayed in their silos repeating the same informal practices. The two largest groups at the agency, Examination and Enforcement, operated independently such that examiners had no access to the detailed tips that the lawyers in Enforcement had received on Madoff.

Since no one was conducting exams on any kind of consistent basis, each fiefdom was convinced that it was doing things the "right" way and others were doing things the "wrong" way. In reality, almost no one was doing anything in a consistent or agreed-upon manner, and so their chances of finding frauds like Madoff and Stanford were severely hampered.

This vulnerability revealed itself in small decisions. I remember early on someone in the LA regional office of the SEC sent me a FedEx envelope with materials about suspicious activities regarding an investment firm in New York. Again, this could have been the next Madoff. But no one called me or sent an e-mail to give me a heads-up that evidence of serious issues at an investment manager in my area was being sent my way. What if it had been misdelivered? What if it sat in my inbox for a few weeks because I didn't know to look for it? We ended up sending examiners to investigate, and the issues were not that serious—but the lack of coordination scared me.

The great Supreme Court justice Felix Frankfurter wrote in his 1947 opinion for the *United States v. United Mine Workers*: "If one man can be allowed to determine for himself what is law, every man can. That means first chaos, then tyranny. Legal process is an essential part of the democratic process."[7] Many people had lost sight of what FDR and Congress had designed the SEC to do, but I had no intention of using my time at the SEC just to throw darts at well-meaning employees who had been given no leadership or bad leadership. I wanted to help the staff by giving them better processes for doing their jobs, so I had no intention of sitting back and complaining. I was right about my new job after all: a guy who likes legal process and wants to charge at problems should love the SEC.

I met a number of colleagues, some of whom I've already introduced, who believed in what we were there to do and wanted to make the agency work better for investors and taxpayers. When you find people who believe in your mission, they become your allies. People like Carlo di Florio, director of the Exam division, and Mary Schapiro supported me when I talked about reorganizing Exam, establishing written rules of the road, and strengthening the SEC's workforce through better training and recruitment. A number of people in my division liked these ideas when they found out what they were and signaled they would not actively oppose them.

But I would be frequently reminded that the status quo at the SEC would not easily give way.

RED FLAGS

Later on during my first year, I met John Polise, a senior manager in Exam, who supervised exams of securities exchanges like the New York Stock Exchange and Nasdaq. John is a smart guy with a quick, open smile and warm demeanor. He ran an excellent program, steering a middle course to try to get exams done without too much fanfare. I used to kid John that he was the "Mayor of the SEC" because he knew everyone and was always generous in introducing a new guy like me. I often stopped by John's office when I was in the SEC's Washington headquarters because he always had good information about what was happening, and I enjoyed talking to him.

I was chatting with John one day in his eighth-floor office that had a comfortable couch. As always, he had papers stacked everywhere, and he had the TV on with a business news channel showing the stock crawl along the bottom. Every trade room I've ever been in has the TV going all the time, and John did the same, as he was the chief examiner for the U.S. securities markets. As we talked, I asked John why there seemed to be no urgency for change in the exam program after the Madoff and Stanford disasters. John told me that he had been around the SEC almost 20 years and had seen new managers come and go. He explained to me that the SEC is like the cushion he had on his office couch. You can punch it and make a dent, but the cushion always bounces back to its original shape. He said that in his time at the SEC he had seen leaders put changes in place, but when those leaders left, some people at the SEC bounced back to keep doing things the way they had always been done.

As I had discovered already, bureaucracies tend to cultivate a palace guard of permanent civil service employees who see it as their job to protect institutional prerogatives against the tides of political and policy change. Some SEC employees I met spoke freely of waiting out new managers who will eventually leave the agency and allow supervisors and employees to return to the way they have done things in the past. This was echoed by the standard line around the agency about any change that "this too shall pass." But if a new manager is too dedicated and makes too many attempts to change practices that have been followed for decades, then SEC supervisors and employees can be more active in opposing those who push too hard for change.

One day in Washington we threw a party in the hallway outside Carlo di Florio's office on the seventh floor of SEC headquarters. Carlo had a nicely furnished, large corner office that looked out at a school that was behind the building. The hallway outside the office had an open space that we used for the comings and goings events that happened occasionally. This time we were toasting someone who was leaving the agency. Carlo's wonderful assistant, Joan Forrester, had arranged a nice food spread along one wall. (The money for this kind of function always came out of the pockets of managers, as there was no budget for it.) It was crowded as I watched Julius Leiman-Carbia make a few remarks at the party. Julius had recently come over to the SEC as a new national associate director who was trying to improve the examinations of broker-dealers to better detect issues that harm investors. It was members of the broker-dealer exam group in the SEC's Fort Worth Office that had spotted Stanford's Ponzi scheme but not been able to get the Enforcement division to take the case, so change was needed. Julius brought a high level of energy and intelligence in trying to improve both the quality of exams and their frequency, but I worried about him because at times he handled the career folks with a bit of a "bull in a china shop" attitude. Once in a meeting of headquarters broker-dealer exam group personnel, he seemed to imply that if anyone decided to leave the group, that would be fine with him. This did not go over well!

At the party I was standing next to a supervisor in the broker-dealer exam program who had been at the SEC for many years and didn't like the changes Julius was implementing. Nonetheless, even though I knew this, my blood ran cold when she said to me casually of Julius, "He doesn't realize we can destroy his career." Here was a brillant lawyer who had passed up lucrative opportunities in the private sector to join the SEC to try to improve its ability to detect fraud. His reward from some longtime staff at the SEC would be career destruction during his tenure. Julius only stayed at the SEC for about two years and, escaping career harm, went on at first to JP Morgan.

CHANGING SEATS ON THE BUS

I knew from the start we needed to develop our staff through training and by hiring new people. To paraphrase Jim Collins, you at the least want the right people driving the bus, even if some of the passengers aren't paying for their ticket. During my years at the SEC, I was consistently looking to hire, promote, or find the right job for folks who exemplified certain qualities. When I found motivated people who believed in the SEC's mission, I did everything I could to get them in the right spot in the organization where they could do some good. Carlo felt the same way, and with Mary Schapiro's backing, we brought in many experts to help improve knowledge in the agency. But I had to be patient—investing in our workforce was like the proverbial elephant pushing a peanut across the room with his trunk.

Early on, some folks approached me suggesting people I should hire. Other managers didn't even bother to consult with me about filling a position. I quickly found that some people would do their own thing unless I interfered, while those who were more interested in positive, proactive change came to me with suggestions.

That was the case with Dawn Blankenship, who lobbied me to hire financial data wizard Erozan Kurtas, because the examiners so desperately needed more analytic tools. We were in a staff meeting, and Dawn asked, "Norm, do you know who Erozan Kurtas is?"

"No, I don't, Dawn."

"He's this brilliant computer and math PhD who's been at S&P and some other places. He would be amazing and help us do something with all our data."

"All right," I said. "Let me think about it. I'll look him up."

Dawn never lets go that easily. She kept pushing Kurtas every time she saw me. I brought Kurtas in for an interview, and Dawn was proved right. Hiring the friendly, curly-haired Turkish scientist succeeded beyond my wildest expectations. Erozan turned out to be a huge asset and became one of the SEC's first "quants" who could deploy advanced analytics. Erozan led the development of a software system called the National Exam Analytics Tool, which allowed SEC examiners to analyze large amounts of trading data to detect insider trading, improper allocations of investment opportunities, and other types of misconduct. (In Chapter 9, I'll talk more about how the SEC stepped up to use analytics and other data-crunching tools to keep tabs on the vast investment management sector.) Erozan later went to work for the Financial Industry Regulatory Authority (FINRA) as its head of advanced data analytics and senior vice president.

Erozan is of Turkish descent and has a dark complexion, a rarity at the SEC. This highlighted another odd fact about the workforce at the New York regional office: the lack of diversity among employees. Coming from the private sector into government, I expected to see a diverse workforce from management on down. When I started at the SEC, imagine my surprise when I realized that of the 100 staff members in the investment management examination group in New York, only one or two were African American. Most of the New York managers were white males from Long Island and New Jersey who had tended to "hire themselves." They went to Long Island University, Fordham, or Rutgers, so that's where they recruited. George Canellos and I established hiring committees to try to broaden the candidate pool and consider candidates more objectively. I did the same thing in IM to try to open up the hiring process to consider all candidates, which I'll talk about more later on.

I also focused on training as another early priority for change in developing our workforce. Most people were starved for it, and employees consistently (and fairly) complained about the lack of quality training opportunities. During the seemingly nonstop budget fights while I was at the commission, the administrative folks would inform me that we had something like $50 per person for training. Not only did the SEC make it difficult to hire new people and not only did some groups suffer from an insular culture, but it skimped on training. While there is a great deal of training material available for purchase online, the constrained budget made it hard to purchase quality training offerings. Union leaders also complained to me about the lack of training because they saw a risk for their examiner members who might miss the next Ponzi scheme.

In 2010, I went down to headquarters in Washington to meet with Deborah Smith Cook, who was the head of training for SEC University, a central training resource for the whole agency. One of the branch chiefs in DC, Marita Bartolini, accompanied me to this meeting as she was a liaison assigned to help me with issues in DC. Deborah is a lovely woman who always tried to be helpful in providing training content that would help the examiners do their jobs better. We met in the HR office of headquarters and sat across from Deborah at a large conference table to discuss what to do about training.

The three of us talked about how to be creative with our budget dollars by training large groups of examiners at one time, because we did not have the money to send them out to external conferences that often cost a thousand dollars a person or more to attend. Deborah said she would do her best to bring in outside providers so that we could stretch the training dollars we had available, as paltry as they were.

Since we were in the meeting with the training chief, I took the opportunity to raise another issue that was incredibly frustrating to me. I had noticed e-mails circulated to all SEC employees inviting them to attend the SEC book club to hear talks from authors who were promoting their books. Inconveniently for the running of any serious organization, the book clubs sometimes took place for two hours in the middle of the workday afternoon. A two-hour book talk while we're in the crosshairs of Congress didn't seem like the best use of employee time. I told Deborah about how Exam management was trying to increase the productivity of SEC Exam staff. I went on, pointing out that we were urging examiners get out in the field and be more proactive and we needed to reduce distractions. Using the book club to discuss essential finance and management topics could help build a learning culture, but not at the cost of half the workday.

Nonetheless we did succeed in more training for examiners, often by drawing on experts we had on hand to share what they knew. In February 2012 I started teaching the syllabus from my law school course to about 120 SEC staff members. Bob Sollazzo from the New York office did a broker-dealer class for a wide audience where I learned a tremendous amount. We also brought in outside experts who were happy to do free training for the staff until Ethics decided that this was a problem. At the SEC, there's usually a tarnished side to every good coin. Rules against outsiders giving "gifts"—e.g., free training—to the government killed the use of outside speakers.

I am proud that throughout my time at the SEC, we strengthened the workforce by bringing in great people, finding better roles for others, securing new resources for training, and giving my colleagues a larger voice in reorganizing the agency. We'll learn more about this in the chapters ahead.

GOVERNMENT BY PASS-FAIL

As I settled in over a few months, I wasn't feeling so much like a fish out of water. I had found great allies who shared my enthusiasm for improving the SEC. As upsetting and strange as my indoctrination was to the bureaucratic machine, like many financial and business folks I still admired and respected the SEC's role as it was founded in 1934. I saw its potential to truly function as the investor's watchdog, and it had the statutory authority to do so and a generally strong team of commissioners.

What could I do to make things better as long as I was at the SEC? I concluded that during my time I would make progress on three of these entrenched concerns: One was the disturbing number of decisions that came down to one person's judgment because there was no written guidance to follow. The second was the degree to which improvement at the SEC depended on the efforts of a small group of people willing to endure the anonymous notes and all the other chaos in order to make the agency better. The third was the outsized clout of the employee union and the "me-first" culture all the benefits created; we had to deal with the union constructively.

As with other government agencies, the combination of civil service protection and public employee union contracts over the decades had wired the wrong incentives into the management of the agency. People followed their own self-interests because they were encouraged to, and that changed their priorities and ultimately the SEC's culture.

The telework example illustrates my point. The union pushed relentlessly for expanded telework benefits, as I talked about earlier in this chapter. Because public employee unions only survive if they deliver new improvements for their workers with each contract, I wasn't surprised that union leadership wasn't going to back down on telework. I understood the union's position and would have done much the same in the union's place. The union leaders occupy elected positions and must deliver for their constituents. After all, SEC employees already enjoy a gold-plated employment compact in many respects. There wasn't much else the public union could deliver on top of lifetime employment, competitive salaries, great hours, and tremendous benefits. They were putting fresh new icing on top of icing and cake.

The SEC already matched employee 401(k) contributions at generous rates and provided an additional pension benefit based on years worked. Private-sector workers would love to have either one of those. The contributions of federal employees to healthcare insurance are smaller than in the private sector. Most federal workers are covered by a guaranteed pension program that is a result of Reagan-era reforms needed to make federal pensions sustainable. That gives them a retirement pension equal to 1 percent of their average top salary for each year they work, with some adjustments. While the current federal pension plan pales in comparison with some state and local government pensions, federal employees enjoy a pension where most private-sector workers do not. In particular, at the SEC the move to "pay parity" in the 1980s, which was meant to increase SEC wages to provide some competition with the private sector, has made wages at the SEC some of the most generous in the federal government. Still, going to the SEC required a pay cut for many qualified midcareer professionals in the financial and consulting industries.

While Congress apparently meant for pay parity to help the SEC attract talent from the financial services industry, the decision, as with many government actions, had an unintended consequence. Workers who were at the commission when pay parity went into effect received massive raises from where they had been paid. The typical lawyer at the SEC makes $150,000 or more as of 2015.[8] These wages provide a comfortable living with almost no threat of ever being fired from the job and an enviable work-life balance. Consequently, many people who were at the SEC when pay parity came have simply stayed for decades. Similarly, new recruits often stay for extended periods of time. I'm all for people getting paid well, but I'm not for people getting paid well and then not being held to any performance standard.

The long-time SEC staff generally were well meaning, but it would be hard for anyone to stay fresh after decades in the same job, particularly when their supposed expertise lies in the complex and fast-moving world of financial services. Until Mary Schapiro started hiring outside experts, many supervisors at the SEC did not have experience in the financial service industry. These officials knew every aspect of SEC regulations. They knew the letter of the law as to how the SEC rules for the industry worked. But the SEC as structured made it very difficult for them to keep up with the products and services continually on offer from the industry that they regulated.

THE CARROT-FREE MANAGER

The combination of higher levels of pay, a far better work-life balance than the private sector offers, and statutes that make it almost impossible to fire poor performers makes for a federal workforce that stays in its job and is resistant to change. Supervisors like me in the federal government must cope with the lack of either "carrots" or "sticks." Budgetary restrictions mean that supervisors can pay relatively small bonuses to their best employees. In my last year at the SEC, Chair White gave me the highest rating possible and a bonus of about 3 percent of my salary. While I was grateful for the bonus, it was emblematic of the difficulty in rewarding performance. For nonsupervisory employees, the SEC and the union for the staff have been unable to agree on a meaningful evaluation system that would allow "pay for performance" for SEC staff members. Performance ratings are done essentially on a "pass-fail" system where almost all employees pass. I kid you not.

When SEC managers and outside groups conduct surveys to get feedback from employees, a consistent refrain is that those who work harder are not rewarded for their additional effort. In both the Exam and Investment Management divisions, we created programs to recognize employees through division directors' awards to try to address this issue. However, without the ability to distinguish among employees with actual pay differences, managers are extremely limited in their ability to make change.

Without an internal system of incentives and limit setting, you get a culture where employees demand more and more. At one of our weekly staff meetings in the spring of 2010, Bill Delmage let me know there was a problem on one of our exams.

After I asked what it was, Bill explained that one of the examiners on the exam worked a 4–10 alternative work schedule where he worked 10 hours each day Monday through Thursday to get Friday off. In this situation, the investment firm being examined was only open 9:00 a.m. to 5:30 p.m., so the examiner could not work his 10 hours in each day.

One of the other assistant directors told me that under the collective bargaining agreement, the examiner is supposed to go off his 4–10 schedule in these circumstances.

Bill mentioned that the exam team asked the investment firm to extend their opening hours to be 10 hours, but they refused.

"Bill, tell the examiner to go off his work schedule as per the collective bargaining agreement," I said, barely concealing my astonishment. They asked the firm to stay open longer! So that the examiner could get Fridays off? Unbelievable.

When there is no risk to one's job from demanding behavior, the demanding behavior gets worse and everyone's expectations get lower. With all the telework and alternative work schedules, every Friday the New York office was so emptied out you could have used it as a roller skating rink. One Friday SEC Commissioner Troy Paredes was in town and wanted to stop by and visit our offices. George Canellos and I were mortified about how empty the place would be, but fortunately Troy's plans changed. Perhaps it would have been a good thing for him to see what was happening.

FORGET THE STICKS

Trying to fire someone takes so much energy and time that most managers decide as I did that if anything is going to get done, you find people with whom you can work and identify those whom you have to work around or keep away from your important projects. For example, in the New York office I was faced with an employee who rarely did any work. Early on I decided that it was just a cost of doing business to have him in the office and that I would not spend the effort to try to get rid of him. Tom Biolsi, my predecessor, had made some efforts to fire a few of the absolute worst performers. Wise voices on my team informed me of the length of time such moves could take. You will pour a ton of energy into moving a bad employee, and with low probabilities of making a change.

Anyway, not content with his cushy and nearly no-show job, one day the employee asked if we could meet, and I said yes. As we spoke, this employee told me that he wanted more responsibility or perhaps more visibility in the office to take advantage of the talents he thought he possessed. However, he was careful to state that he didn't actually want to do any work to get such responsibility. He made it clear to me that more work would not fit in with his schedule of activities outside the SEC. I heard him out and simply never got back to him on his request. I felt guilty about simply tolerating this person being on the federal payroll, but I knew it would be nearly impossible to have him fired.

Occasionally employee misbehavior would get so bad that an employee actually was fired. As I mentioned in Chapter 1, in one case an SEC supervisor had not shown up at the office in about five years. Undeterred, each year the human resources department gave him the standard annual raise given to all employees. When a new manager discovered that he had an employee who was a no-show for five years, he succeeded in having the person terminated.

I had colleagues in management who couldn't believe that the union would ask for so much, particularly when the SEC was under such fierce scrutiny. But I never saw it that way. The system was so rigged in the union's favor, it didn't surprise me at all that the union kept asking for more and more. As I noted earlier, the union leaders only get reelected if they obtain ever-increasing benefits for the members. I made a decision early on that I set aside my frustration and political views and see if I could work with the SEC's union leader Greg Gilman to tackle the SEC's challenges. As I'll show later in this book, this worked out surprisingly well.

As I was wrestling with work rules and the dysfunction in the New York regional office, I also encountered a lack of rules from our national headquarters in Washington, DC. In many areas, headquarters didn't set national priorities or govern how the exam program was run. I thought the headquarters teams for investment management exams and broker-dealer exams seemed the logical choice to coordinate a national exam strategy. But the people from the examination headquarters simply did exams around the country where they were interested in doing so. Instead of managing the national exam effort, they did exams of their own.

I remember my discussion with a capable manager in headquarters who ran exams using two branches of examiners. As we began to think about how to manage the national exam program from headquarters, the obvious question was whether the headquarters personnel should simply continue plugging away at exams or rather assume a role supervising the rest of the country and trying to standardize their operations. The manager was a tremendously talented exam supervisor and very smart about finding wrongdoing at investment advisors. But when I asked why the staff did exams at headquarters as opposed to managing the national program, the manager responded, "We do exams in headquarters because we've always done exams in headquarters." It was said without irony and without an appreciation that in the twenty-first-century management world, no one ever uses the excuse that "we've always done it this way." But for folks in the Exam division, it seemed a perfectly natural way to do things because that's the way it was always done.

A friend of mine once said that the obligation of anyone in a leadership position, be it in a private company, a nonprofit, or even the government, was to leave the organization better than you found it. There could be no better legacy than to make the organization better and make sure you have the leadership in place to take over after you are gone. I count as one of my deepest successes as a manager the fact that I had three jobs at the SEC. When I left each of those jobs, an internal candidate whom I had helped position for success ended up taking my place after the normal competitive search procedures required by the government. That perfect record meant that I had found three people who were ready to step in and take my place and continue the great work that we had started.

Each of those three individuals—Jim Capezzuto, Drew Bowden, and Dave Grim—are talented and committed lawyers who have forgotten more about the securities laws than I will ever know. My goal as a manager had been to get out of the way and give them the exposure and experience that would let me let them shine and be noticed by the senior officials of the commission. I saw it as part of my mission to get the best people we could get, give them the opportunities to make things better, and develop their skills so they could carry on after I eventually left the agency.

Mary Schapiro hired a number of us from the financial sector to help save the commission as it faced an existential moment with

Congress because of the Exam division's failures in the Madoff and Stanford cases and the rising power of the Fed and Treasury, which could absorb the SEC's role. I could have quietly put in my time working within the existing ad-hocracy at the SEC, but Schapiro had charged us with the urgent task to change the exam program and gave us the backing to make it happen.

Schapiro also equipped the exam program with consultants to help us think about how to instill long-lasting changes in the SEC's culture and byways that would endure beyond the next set of political appointees. These consultants were instrumental in helping Carlo, the leadership team, and me determine how to go about change in a way that would not only implement good ideas but excite and engage the senior leaders and staff in the Exam division. Change mandated from the top without getting thorough input and buy-in from the rest of the exam program would have been meaningless. What did Jeremiah say? Laws must be written not only on stone but in our hearts. Without in-depth communication and dialogue, managers and employees would simply go into a four-corners defense, go slow, and sabotage any change that was mandated without their buy-in. One highly placed official was quite honest with me about it. I was trying to explain to him that once we had received everyone's input and crafted solutions, the senior leadership team had to lock arms and support change together—no matter what our personal views had been. I asked him what he would do if there was a management decision that all of management agreed on but that he disagreed with. He informed me that he would resist the change for as long as he could, undermine the change, and hope to have the decision reversed ultimately either by existing leadership or eventually by new leadership. All I could think was at least he was being honest.

He'd soon discover that I and others were determined to change the SEC's culture and way of doing business and that many of his colleagues wanted to be included in that change. If this official and a few others like him wanted to form a wall against reform, the rest of us would find a way over or around that wall.

POSTCRASH TRIAGE IN THE SEC EMERGENCY ROOM

Triage: the assignment of degrees of
urgency to wounds in order to decide
the order of treatment of a large
number of patients or casualties.
—Jeff Solheim, *Emergency Nursing*

Some days during my first years at the SEC (I ended up staying for five years), I felt like a trauma surgeon in the ER of the financial sector. In the wake of the financial train wreck of 2008 and the early casualties from the Madoff and Stanford scandals, patients kept getting wheeled through the doors of the SEC, and I was racing from table to table operating on the toughest cases. And while we juggled many priorities, we simply had to save as many investors as we could. The truth was, after decades of the SEC's more or less enjoying widespread respect from the financial community, Congress, and independent experts, its spectacular failures revealed how much had gone wrong and how much the agency needed a major transformation to address the underlying weaknesses in its processes and culture.

In working with Carlo di Florio, who was a former management consultant with years of "doing change" at big companies, we frequently talked about what was happening at Exam and other SEC departments from the perspective of "change management"—that is, changing culture and getting people to buy into new roles and responsibilities as a result of a major failure of management.

Bestselling business author John Kotter and other experts cite key steps in making change work that include communicating a sense of urgency, building a coalition of leaders who support the change strategy, communicating principles and goals with a clear vision, reducing obstacles throughout the organization, and building ownership for this new way among employees at all levels.[1] Carlo and I saw Exam as needing this kind of major change package. But we didn't have an agencywide coalition or clear goals to talk about. It reminded me of a McKinsey case study. A Canadian hospital undertook a major change effort to reduce waiting times in the emergency room. A handful of managers piloted in-patient initiatives within the neurosurgery unit that cut waiting times and improved patient morale, but they failed when the time came to scale up those changes to other clinical units. Too few leaders across the entire hospital had bought into the initiative, and the rank and file showed widespread resistance to change. The consultant team had to start the entire program over from scratch.[2]

In New York, we were trying to make our ER work better, but the rest of the hospital required attention as well. As mentioned in Chapter 3, if Exam and the SEC were going to rediscover the value of their mission, we needed more converts at the national level.

A MEETING WITH ALL THE FACTIONS

Carlo decided early in 2010 to forge a national change plan for how Exam's people would do their work for America's taxpayers. It wasn't enough for us just to improve the New York office. If we were going to shake up the culture of the SEC, Carlo knew, we needed a strategy for reform that included Exam leaders in every region. We called in associate and regional directors from every region for meetings in Washington, DC. (Each region has at least one associate director for exams, and New York and LA have two—one for investment management firms and another for broker-dealers.)

We not only wanted to make our case for modernizing how the SEC did its business; we needed to see who the regional players were. We had to find out who was strong and who was not. We needed to know who had innovative ideas for change, who would go along, and who would work against us behind the scenes. We had to try.

Soon divides appeared. Sometimes newer directors expressed far more support for change than the "lifers," but some lifers advocated a great deal of change. (And I really mean lifers—some had been at the SEC for decades.) I didn't hesitate to drive a lot of ideas and push the group to embrace reform. It wasn't long before Carlo spoke to me one day in my office in New York.

"Norm," he said, "I want you to become my deputy director. You should start coming down to Washington."

"Carlo, I'd love to," I told him. "But I can't do it now. I just left 10 years of constant travel in the hedge fund business, and I am here in New York on a regular basis, and my family likes it."

"All right, take your time," he said. "I'll catch up with you in a few months."

We continued pushing for a national leadership *idea*, a set of operating principles that everybody in the Exam office followed. To do that, we needed cooperation from leaders in each department. That wasn't a familiar role for them. Like New York, each of the other regions in Exam was doing its own thing. Nothing written down. No manual. Every region was convinced it was doing the right thing and the others were doing the wrong thing.

We introduced the classic five-part approach to strategic change: strategy, structure, people (including training), process, and technology.[3] Then we formed teams around each aspect and charged them to come up with recommendations. I continued to take an active role in all the working groups, putting in monumental hours on top of trying to run the exam program in New York. Carlo came back to me late in the spring and said, "Look you're the change agent in this crowd. You are leading all these different things. You have to be the deputy director."

In June I finally agreed. "OK, Carlo, I'll do it." I enjoyed what I was doing in New York, dropping the kids at school, taking the subway to work, and not having to travel across too many time zones. But I'd come to relish the management challenges at the SEC and the opportunity to improve the agency for the staff. I knew if another major fraud scandal slipped through our process, it could be the SEC's death blow.

So by July 2010 Carlo promoted me to deputy director of Exam. I now had responsibility for examinations and personnel problems all around the country. Soon after that I became caught up in new legislation aimed at reforming Wall Street and preventing another financial crisis. The Democratic-controlled Congress and the Obama administration passed a law, now known as Dodd-Frank, named after its sponsors Senator Chris Dodd and Congressman Barney Frank, that was the most sweeping financial services law our nation had seen since the original Glass-Steagall Act. It was our government's answer to all that had happened, and it was also loaded up with many policy ideas that had little or nothing to do with the 2008 crisis, including requiring public companies to disclose whether they made payments for "extractive resources" like oil! Little did any laypeople (or even me to some extent) know at the time that it would be the SEC's job to make a large part of this law work.

After all, until the SEC writes and implements revamped rules, financial legislation is only words in the United States Code. I found a talented SEC lawyer, Judy Lee, whom we asked to coordinate the effort to track the almost 50 Dodd-Frank rules in which Exam had data and experience to offer. Judy is at the SEC instead of a corporate law firm so she doesn't spend long hours away from her two children, and yet she worked nonstop on this project.

Dodd-Frank became law in July 2010 just weeks after my promotion. One provision required the SEC to examine and report on the 10 credit rating agencies, such as Standard & Poor's (S&P) and Moody's, and assigned the task to the national exam group. It was time to get to work.

TIGHTENING THE LEASH ON THE CREDIT RATING AGENCIES

What exactly are credit rating agencies? (And I'm not talking about the consumer outfits that give you your credit score, though they too are quite important.) When people in and around the financial industry talk about credit rating agencies, they're usually referring to Standard & Poor's, known as S&P Global, Inc. at the time of this writing,* and Moody's. These two agencies each control about 40 percent of the ratings business.[4] Henry Poor began what became S&P in 1860 when he wrote a history of the finance of railroads and canals in the United States as a guide for investors. The Standard Statistics Bureau was founded in 1906 to examine the finances of nonrailroad companies. The two merged in the 1940s. John Moody started the company bearing his name in 1909 to publish his analyses of railway finances,

---

*At the time of the crisis, the McGraw-Hill Companies was the parent company of this book's publisher and Standard & Poor's. However, the educational and publishing divisions were spun off as a separate company long before my book was published. The publishing group and S&P have nothing to do with each other.

grading the value of railroad stocks and bonds. Fitch is another ratings agency, established in 1913, with a much smaller share of the market.[5]

The agencies grade the issuers of bonds (loans that pay back the purchaser based on a fixed period of time), whether they are corporations or governments, from AAA down to CCC or lower, based on their analysis of the debt issuer's ability to pay back its loan. The higher the risk of default, the higher the interest rate paid by the issuer. Michael Milken allegedly coined the notorious term "junk bonds" to describe the highest-risk paper offered by financially fragile or highly leveraged companies (or governments with very high debts and weak economies) and therefore that paid the fattest interest rates.[6]

The SEC's relationship with rating agencies began in 1975 when it set up an endorsement system for rating agencies called Nationally Recognized Statistical Ratings Organizations, or NRSROs.[7] The endorsement told investors and investment funds (some of which the SEC requires to carry only highly rated bonds) the agencies that could be viewed with the highest degree of trust and objectivity. The first three NRSROs were S&P, Moody's, and Fitch. By 2008, however, the SEC had ten NRSROs on its approved list, including a Canadian and two Japanese agencies. Because of these endorsements, the SEC essentially placed the stamp of approval of the U.S. government on these agencies as objective referees of creditworthiness in the bond market.[8]

The 10 NRSROs at the time were A.M. Best Company, DBRS, Inc., Egan-Jones Ratings Co., Fitch, Kroll, Japan Credit Rating Agency, Moody's Investors Service, Morningstar Credit Ratings, Rating and Investment Information, Inc., and Standard & Poor's.[9]

This context makes it easier to understand the reaction of Congress and the regulatory agencies about the rating agencies' role in the crash. In the aftermath of 2008, Congress grew enraged with the credit rating agencies for rating collateralized mortgage obligations—bundles of mortgage debt—and other complex housing debt instruments as AAA when such instruments were far riskier. The bundles' value depended upon an overheated housing sector fueled by skyrocketing house prices and resulting increases in home values for mortgage holders.

Mortgage companies and to some extent banks were giving home loans to most anyone who breathed and who wanted one, often without documentation ("no doc" mortgages). "Lawmakers, regulators and investors have trained their cross hairs on S&P and its peers for assigning rosy ratings to thousands of complex securities that were later downgraded within the span of a few months, deepening the crisis," one trenchant *Wall Street Journal* article by Jeannette Neuman and Jean Englesham reported in September 2011.[10]

Dodd-Frank called for two solutions. One created an office of credit rating agencies at the SEC to promulgate further rules for the agencies and require annual exams of the agencies and a public report on the findings of those exams. The second significantly increased the agencies' liability for issuing inaccurate ratings and made it easier for the SEC to impose sanctions and bring claims against them for material misstatements and fraud.[11]

By the fall of 2010, the SEC's new office hadn't been created yet, but the statute did require the SEC to examine the credit rating agencies each year. Dodd-Frank directed no other requirements for our division other than the credit rating agencies' exams. In a good example of how things go wrong between writing and regulating a law, Dodd-Frank required the SEC to examine and report on the agencies annually, but it didn't say whether the report should be completed in the next fiscal year or the next calendar year. Since the statute passed in July, did that mean a report was due for 2010 or 2011? Calendar or government fiscal year? In the end, we decided to go with the government fiscal year; the statute passed in July 2010 so we made our deadline for the first set of exams to be completed by September 30, 2011.

Dodd-Frank charged the SEC with policing the raters to make sure they abided by their own procedures, but we were prohibited from meddling in the ratings process itself. Instead, we reviewed whether or not agencies complied with their own written procedures and policies and avoided conflicts of interest. This could include ensuring that agencies protected market-sensitive information and that their rating committees properly met to discuss any rating decision. The SEC was empowered to refer cases to enforcement authorities if it found problems.[12]

Now Exam had to get it done. When I met Jon Hertzke in August in my office in Washington, I felt great relief about our prospects. Jon brought a nice presence. He was big, was taller than I am, and had a thick beard and a ready open smile. He grew up in Utah, but as a gay man, he didn't find Mormon culture was a great fit. After getting his law degree, Jon left Utah for the East Coast. At the SEC, Jon had starred in a number of staff roles including working as an examiner for the broker-dealer and securities markets exam groups.

Because a 2006 law that was passed when President Bush was in office gave the SEC some oversight tasks for the rating agencies, the SEC was ahead of the curve. Jon's securities markets team at the SEC was among the first to see signs amid the smoking wreckage of the crash that the agencies had issued some questionable ratings. Had the big agencies become empires unto themselves? Was more oversight needed? To get the exams done in a year, I needed a team of examiners to start digging into the methods and potential conflicts at the ratings agencies. Jon volunteered to lead the examinations, a big leap for him at the time because he wasn't known as a credit ratings expert and could have been second-guessed if he made any wrong moves.

As I got to know Jon, I understood his decision. Jon likes to take on new projects and grow into them because he is tremendously devoted to the mission. He's fearless that way. Jon likes to be where the action is, and he didn't give a lot of thought to how it would "sell" around the SEC.

"Look, we have to examine all of these credit rating agencies," I told Jon at our August meeting. "This is the only thing that the exam program has been assigned out of Dodd-Frank. It is our responsibility. We are monitoring 50 of the rules, and Judy Lee is working on that whole thing. But this one is on us."

The exam program was at the nadir of its existence, having missed Madoff and Stanford. We had 10 high-profile exams to complete, and our report would be read very carefully by many denizens of Capitol Hill and the media.

"Jon," I went on, "we are not going to screw this up! If this has to be done within the year, we are going to do it within the year."

"Sure," he said, "I'm in. Got to be done."

Oh, that was refreshing. This guy isn't getting away from me, I thought.

Then our conversation yielded another example of the bizarro* decisions produced by the SEC bureaucracy. Jon told me that, in the wake of the 2008 crisis, the SEC actually hired several qualified analysts from the credit rating agencies. But the SEC required these examiners to move to Washington, DC, and operate from national headquarters. How absurd! These folks were overseeing three major credit rating agencies located within blocks of the SEC's New York office. In fact, I used to walk past the Moody's offices every day on my way to work. Shortly after the meeting I authorized the credit rating agency examiners to move back to the city if they wanted and work in the part of the New York regional office reserved for personnel who reported to groups actually located at the SEC's Washington headquarters. In fact some of them did so, although one or two opted to stay in Washington.

As bizarro decisions tend to do, assigning the examiners to Washington eventually served up bad karma. The Republicans had recaptured the House of Representatives in the fall elections of 2010, riding the success of Tea Party candidates who ran on a limited-government platform. As a result, the House joined with the Senate in giving the SEC a "flat" budget—that is, the same dollar figure as

---

*Bizarro was a character created by DC Comics as a villain in the Superman/Superboy/Supergirl universes. As his creator, Alvin Schwartz, explains, "I was striving, you might say, for that mirror-image, that opposite. And out of a machine which would reveal the negative Superman, came the mirror image—always remembering that in a mirror everything is reversed . . ." "Bizarro," *DC Comics Encyclopedia*, p. 631 (2008).

the year before.[13] This actually curtailed our spending, because items like the union's collective bargaining agreement mandated steadily rising pay no matter what the budget situation was. As is common in many agencies, the SEC responded by redlining travel spending because it could control that cost. As the guy who had to carry out the credit rating agency exams with the few examiners we had located in Washington, a sudden ban on travel was a real issue. We were able to free up limited funds to send some of the examiners to New York for the exams. Nonetheless the decision to locate the examiners in Washington made our lives extremely difficult.

Given all of Exam's failures relating to Madoff and Stanford, which we had to explain on nearly a daily basis to Congress or the press, I was determined we'd get these exams done and the public report issued in a timely manner. However, our team faced an unusually tough deadline conducting 10 exams and issuing a public report on them in a little over 12 months. Exam teams would need to visit all agencies, including the two in Japan, draft the report, and have the commission approve it. For high-profile assignments of this nature, Mary Shapiro's office made sure we had the funding we needed to travel.

We borrowed examiners from the investment management and broker-dealer programs despite their other duties. As deputy director I had the authority to do this, but it wasn't fun. Borrowing another group's staff amounts to an act of bureaucratic warfare. My assistant directors were not happy that we took their people, which resulted in more work for them and everyone else. I would have felt similarly frustrated in their place. But there wasn't a choice. Congress and the media were watching. If we screwed up, the entire country would be watching, in truth. It was our mission, and we were going to complete it.

Dodd-Frank charged the SEC with reviewing the raters on the following grounds:

- Did the raters ensure they follow policies and procedures regarding each rating?

- Are they managing conflicts of interest by making sure there is a separation between sales and people doing the ratings?
- Do they follow their ethics policies?
- Is their governance aboveboard?
- Are they allowing their designated compliance officer to perform his or her duties appropriately?
- Do they follow guidelines in managing conflicts and implications of postemployment activities for former staff?[14]

By the spring of 2011, our team did complete all 10 ratings agency exams. It took an all-out effort. We finished the report on time as well, and the SEC released it in September. You can find a link to the report on my website at http://www.normchamp.com.

THE CREDIT RATING AGENCIES STRIKE BACK

By early August 2011 my team was finishing the report on the raters. The exams were done, and we were getting the latest patient into recovery and ready for discharge. I remember it was a wet, windy August with many thunderstorms (which culminated when Hurricane Irene hit the New York and New England region late in the month with significant flooding). I was hoping things would slow down so I could get out to Martha's Vineyard to join my family for our vacation. And that's when the ambulance pulled up, and the next crisis came through the double doors. I was in the office early on Thursday, August 4, answering e-mails. My phone rang, and caller ID showed "Hertzke, Jon," who by now had become one of my most trusted allies.

"S&P is going to downgrade the credit rating of the United States," he told me. "The story's going to be page one in all the papers."

Oh, great. I didn't think it would really happen. The roots of this went back to April 2011 when S&P announced a ratings review of the U.S. government, which is like saying we're going to audit your taxes aggressively.[15] As with most preliminary announcements of this kind, it barely drew a look from anyone except Treasury, the SEC, and some members of Congress. But during the summer of 2011, the Tea Party Caucus with the new Republican majority in the House of Representatives tried to get a handle on massive deficit spending by the Obama administration and Democrats by refusing to raise the debt ceiling. This is the legislative limit placed on the entire debt of the U.S. government in the form of bonds and securities. The administration and Congressional Democrats racked up massive annual budget deficits that necessitated the issuance of more government debt. The budget is in surplus or deficit each year depending upon the annual difference between the federal government's revenue (taxes and fees) and its allocated expenditures for that year. The federal government's debt is all of Uncle Sam's obligations added together.

The debt ceiling controversy continued into the summer, and the Tea Party Caucus vowed as a protest to block any votes raising the debt ceiling limit. Raising the ceiling was necessary, many argued on the other side. Without a debt ceiling hike, not only could the United States be in default with its creditors, but the federal government wouldn't be authorized to pay its bills, and all nonessential government operations would be closed. This is what led to the familiar "government shutdown" rhetoric of that time. S&P identified these events as significant enough to pose a threat of instability to the good credit of the United States—that is, S&P saw an increased risk to repayment of U.S. bonds, i.e., "Treasuries."

Jon was right about the coverage the next day. There's the *New York Times* headline: "S.&P. Downgrades Debt Rating of U.S. for the First Time."[16] The lead sentence in the *Washington Post's* story read: "Standard & Poor's announced Friday night that it has downgraded the U.S. credit rating for the first time, dealing a symbolic blow to the world's economic superpower in what was a sharply worded critique of the American political system."[17] And the *Wall Street Journal* carried parts of S&P's press release: "We lowered our long-term rating on the U.S. because we believe that the prolonged controversy over raising the statutory debt ceiling and the related fiscal policy debate indicate that further near-term progress containing the growth in public spending, especially on entitlements, or on reaching an agreement on raising revenues is less likely than we previously assumed and will remain a contentious and fitful process."[18]

Behind the scenes (as we later learn) President Obama, his team, and Treasury secretary Tim Geithner were angry about the downgrade and had already told the folks at S&P that they'd made a mistake in their model that added $2 trillion to S&P's claims about the U.S. deficit.[19] (S&P disagrees it had made this error.) S&P and the U.S. government litigated for years afterward over whether a phone call Geithner made to S&P after the downgrade led to a lawsuit by the government against S&P for its failures in the crisis.[20] But we didn't know anything about this kind of acrimony. We were in the throes of finishing our new report on the exams of the rating agencies, and here S&P had taken a huge whack at the hornet's nest of the Beltway budget fight, generating tons of controversy and news.

My thought was that we needed to go and talk to S&P. That's what I told Jon, and he concurred. So I called Schapiro's chief of staff in the afternoon.

"Look," I told Didem, "we want to let you know that we are planning to visit S&P on Monday and talk to them. We want to ask about their policies and procedures in downgrading the rating. What's behind this mistake in their model? Have you analyzed it?" The chair's office agreed with what we were planning, and I called over to S&P to set up the meeting. Jon flew up Sunday, and we arranged to meet outside S&P's offices at nine o'clock Monday morning.

Before I headed over, I got a call from a reporter asking about our plan to visit S&P about the downgrade. I nearly spit out my coffee. This was meant to be a no-drama sit-down just to understand what procedures S&P followed on the downgrade. You have to be kidding me! I told the reporter we had no comment. How the hell did this get to a reporter? Only a half-dozen people knew, and I doubted anyone at the SEC would have leaked this. It wasn't our way.

We showed up at S&P at 55 Water Street. Jon and I walked in and went through security, got our badges, checked in, and headed upstairs.

We got off the elevator and walked into the hall that always seemed unusually long and quiet. I'd had a few meetings on this floor before with management, and the conference room was at the end of the hallway perhaps 50 yards away. Jon and I were a few strides from the door when a senior executive of S&P came out of the room, turned toward us, and started screaming: "How the hell can a reporter know that you are coming here this morning?! How was this meeting leaked?"

Jon and I stopped. "Listen," I said, raising my hand in the universal palm-facing-out, chill-out-for-a-second gesture, "We didn't leak this. Jon and I and Schapiro and a few other people knew about it, and we'd have no interest and no benefit in leaking this. We haven't leaked anything about the agencies during the whole examination. So I don't know what is going on. Let's just go inside, and let's just calm down."

We crossed into the conference room. The upset executive had taken a seat, refusing to look our way. I saw S&P's new CEO Doug Peterson getting up as we came in. The heads of S&P's government ratings group were there as well as the head of European ratings and some of that group's senior ratings people. Peterson came from Citibank as a steady, seasoned global financial manager, and I had grown to like him so far. He shook our hands and turned to say, "This is Floyd Abrams down here at the end of the table."

There he is, indeed, the famous constitutional scholar on the First Amendment. I'd know him anywhere. S&P had hired one of the world's name-brand lawyers to advise it on this meeting.

Peterson conveyed his concern that we were there to muzzle the credit rating agency based on S&P's downgrade of the United States government's credit rating.

Floyd Abrams looked up as we sat down. Abrams said, "We're here to preserve their [S&P's] First Amendment rights to say what they please."

Once again, I gave the universal palm-out, calming gesture. "Look, can we just take a time-out here?" Keeping my voice calm though I'm getting aggravated, I went on: "As you know, we were charged by Dodd-Frank to regulate you and to conduct regular exams of you. We just finished the first exam. We saw your rating downgrade of the U.S., and we saw that there might have been a problem with the model. We are civil servants. We work for the government. We are following our statutory responsibility to dialogue with you about these issues.

"What are we going to do? Stay home? No. We are going to come, and we are going to talk to you. And we are going to ask you about whether you followed your policies and procedures. I don't care if you downgrade or not. I don't care what ratings you issue, but we do care about your process. We are not here to muzzle your First Amendment rights. But we are here to understand if you acted the way a regulated entity is supposed to act in these circumstances. That's it."

I saw heads nodding in agreement all around as the room calmed down. And then Peterson said, "How was this leaked to a reporter?"

I replied, "I had the same reaction. The only people at the SEC who know this is happening are me, Jon, Mary Schapiro, the chief of staff and a few others. We didn't even tell the commissioners we were coming. There are maybe half a dozen people at the SEC. I doubt any of them are leaking it. So I don't know where it is coming from." Later I thought that S&P might have leaked it because it was under fire from Treasury, and it wanted to create the impression that it was being harassed. Or who knows? Perhaps someone in the SEC chair's office leaked it to show the administration and Congress that the SEC was on the case. We never found out who it was.

But if Jon and I were caught leaking this kind of information, we'd lose our jobs. That's it. I said to Floyd Abrams and his band of merry men, "You guys leaked this—or someone on our side did, someone way above our pay grade. I can promise you that Jon and I didn't."

Abrams shook his head slightly and half smiled, Peterson murmured something to him, and the meeting went smoothly after that. With his usual professionalism, Jon grilled the S&P leadership about its process, and we went back to the office satisfied with the answers.

I must say that I am proud that S&P later countersued Treasury for harassment over the downgrade but not the SEC.[21] We did our jobs under the law and did not overstep our responsibilities.

TRIAGE

The SEC chair's office is headquartered in a sleek, white granite and curved glass building connected to Washington's Union Station not far from the Capitol. It provides a spectacular view of the skyline of Washington and the Capitol dome. For SEC chair Mary Schapiro, the sight of the congressional building served as a daily reminder of the cost of further failures in the financial sector. "I like to tell the staff we are going to act like our hair is on fire," Schapiro told reporters in the first weeks after she was appointed.[22]

Schapiro promised Congress during her confirmation hearing that she would take the handcuffs off the SEC's Enforcement division and use them to apprehend fraudsters like Madoff before they could do further damage to the economy. The case of Allen Stanford particularly haunted Schapiro as an avoidable tragedy—and one that she would not allow to be repeated.[23]

The SEC's examiners in Texas had suspected fraud at Stanford's operation from as early as 1997, when examiners went to his firm for the first time. Stanford should have been an obvious outlier in that he purported to be able to make money for U.S. investors by investing in certificates of deposit issued by a bank in the Caribbean island nation of Antigua. Stanford himself was a prominent figure in Antigua, where he owned a cricket team and sponsored numerous sporting events. Stanford's operation was just the latest variation on an old fraud scheme referred to as a "prime bank" scheme. While the scheme has taken many forms, essentially the wrongdoer sells investors on the idea that he has access to a bank instrument that is completely safe but that bears an interest rate far in excess of market interest rates. Like so many frauds, the prime bank scheme depends on a lack of sophistication by investors and a desire for risk-free returns that are not realistic.

There were obvious clues that Stanford's operation was a fraud. For instance, why would banks in Antigua, a Caribbean island that enjoys prosperity, pay interest rates far in excess of the interest that U.S. and other banks are paying? Stanford's con could not have worked without the skills of a master manipulator. Through his huge body frame and slick personality, Stanford intimidated and charmed associates and clients. As with many of these schemes, victims were taken in by the fraudster, and some continued to defend him even after he was arrested.

The troubling twist in the Stanford case? SEC examiners suspected early on that Stanford was a fraud, but they were unable to convince their enforcement colleagues to pursue the case. Examiners even wrote in a report in 1997 (12 years before his arrest) that Stanford was running a "possible Ponzi scheme."[24] However, they could not get the Fort Worth Enforcement staff interested in launching an investigation of Stanford that that would have shut the fraud down. Why? Allegedly because enforcement officials in Fort Worth worried about the difficulty of getting evidence from Antigua that might have made the case time consuming.[25] This calamitous breakdown at the SEC led to the public testimony of examiner Julie Preuitt before Congress and the world that I wrote about in Chapter 1.

Unlike Madoff's case, which dominated headlines and whose victims included many wealthy and powerful New Yorkers, the Stanford fraud was laced with the additional bitter salt that the more than 30,000 investors Stanford bilked recovered little money. Fortunately, a jury restored the scales of criminal justice with a guilty verdict, and the trial judge sentenced Stanford to 110 years in prison.

If I had to express Schapiro's approach to running the SEC in three words, it would be these: *No more Stanfords.* His colossal crime hovered over us like a dark cloud whenever another potential fraud emerged. Not only had Stanford happened, but MF Global, the investment brokerage run by former New Jersey governor Jon Corzine, was in trouble because it couldn't cover its bets on European bonds and had transferred customer funds to cover certain losses. SEC examiners were crawling all over that place. MF

Global eventually declared bankruptcy on October 31, 2011, proving that you can be a big brokerage and still fail.*

Enter Dallas-based Penson Worldwide, Inc., which handled securities trades for U.S. brokerages and also ran a futures brokerage. It was huge, trading for over a million customers. It was a publicly traded company on Nasdaq. Penson disclosed in May 2011 that "it had accepted $42 million in bonds issued by an entity that controls the Retama Park racetrack as collateral from a number of customers."[26] The bad deal became even more toxic when Penson revealed that a member of its board was chief executive of the company that managed the racetrack and owned a large slice of the bonds.[27] Not good, although the board member would later resign. Penson's filing stated, "It is possible that the value of the collateral . . . might be impaired, resulting in a write-down of a portion of these receivables that could be material in amount."

Indeed.

The racetrack bonds issue got the attention of market watchers, and Penson's shares lost 50 percent of their value.

Julius Leiman-Carbia brought Penson to my attention in May. He had started as head of the broker-dealer exam program in April and was just starting to push for change.[28] Julius gave me a call and told me he was watching this huge broker in Texas that had a big problem. I started looking at it and reached out to John Ramsay, who was deputy director of Trading and Markets (the policy division that sets the rules for brokers). The three of us realized after a few hours of analysis that Penson probably would fail.

---

*As Stephen Gandel reported in *Time*, "But what is surprising and interesting about its failure is that MF Global doesn't specialize in the credit default swaps type of derivatives that got AIG and others in trouble in the past. Instead, it specialized in more plain vanilla derivatives that are traded on exchanges. At least that was the case until March 2010, when the firm was taken over by a new leader, the former NJ governor Jon Corzine. In addition to having run New Jersey, Corzine was also a former head of Goldman Sachs . . . Corzine plunged the firm into proprietary trading—a risky business from which recent banking reforms have tried, perhaps unsuccessfully, to ban the big banks from doing." See Gandel, "Understanding MF Global: Why the Bank's Failure Matters," *Time*, Nov. 1, 2011, http://business.time.com/2011/11/01/understanding-mf-global-why-the-banks-failure-matters/.

It's very simple if you are a broker holding people's money: when all trades are netted out at the end of the day, you have to be cash positive or be able to borrow funds to be in the black. If you can't do that, you're out of business.

For a week or so we monitored whether Penson was capital positive at the end of the day for all its trades. As the movie cliché goes, I had a bad feeling about this. I got in touch with Julius and John.

"We have to get down there now," I said. "Let's reach out to the Fort Worth office and let them know."

The staff of the Trading and Markets division culturally was cautious about stepping into a company's operations and preferred monitoring the situation. But Julius and John saw how dangerous this was. So I called Fort Worth and told the staff that we had a real problem and needed a monitoring team on-site. Even after Stanford and MF Global, I could tell that the staff there were uncomfortable with a monitoring role that was not an exam.

I saw it differently. The collapse of another major trading firm could trigger a fresh episode of panic among investors, consumers, and Congress. We needed a trauma team of SEC staff watching the patient very closely. We needed to know if this massive broker-dealer was going to crash.

We had a meeting with Schapiro in early July.

"I don't care about finding violations with an exam," I told her. "I need to know every day if they're going to make it to the following day. Their customers don't know how bad this is—yet. So we don't have a huge run on capital, but it could happen."

Schapiro noted that another MF Global or Stanford could start an avalanche.

A few minutes later, she told us, "I want to do something now. This can't happen."

The Fort Worth folks still were dragging their feet. I got my own team together to monitor Penson. I assigned Valerie Bushfort, a terrific staffer, to lead the monitoring team on-site. (She has since left the commission and lives with her husband in Alaska, where they bought some land. Someone should bring her back—she's that good.) She started talking to the Penson operations people and looking at the company's accounts. Penson couldn't be one penny in the red at 5 p.m. or it was over. We started learning more facts on the ground even as Penson was saying that the firm would survive the racetrack bond disaster and the firm's lack of profitability.[29] Penson's cash position was even worse than we thought. As a publicly traded firm, its bankruptcy would be a major event.

We determined that John Ramsay and I would go to Texas and meet with Penson's management and board. Schapiro wanted us to go as soon as possible. I was in Washington that day, so instead of returning to New York, I walked over to Union Station and bought an extra shirt at Andrew's Ties, and we left for Texas that night.

We drove over to Penson in the morning. The offices are in downtown Dallas on Pacific Street, a boulevard of glass and steel corporate office rectangles and cylinders. I spotted a few nice cafés and drugstores nearby. We parked and went upstairs and joined the members of our monitoring team in the conference room. They were working well with Penson's operations people, who were feeding us everything we needed. We knew what was happening with Penson's cash pretty much minute to minute. Valerie briefed us that it was a very close call each night as to whether the company could stay open another day. Earlier she had picked up a valuable piece of intel that Penson was holding a board meeting that morning—which was part of the reason we wanted staff on-site—so we could learn these kinds of details.

So Ramsay and I started walking down the hall to the board meeting. The CEO intercepted us in the hallway.

"I want to talk to you before we go in the board meeting," he said.

I said that was fine. And so Ramsay and I sat down with him in his office.

"What's the issue?" he asked.

I told him, "As you know, Penson is barely passing its capital test every day. You are able to borrow, but people are nervous. We have a lot of issues, and we are very concerned about the firm."

Forcing a smile, he told me the firm had been through these things before and would get through this.

"Well, we're not sure you'll get through this."

Now I knew his name was over the door. Penson is an acronym of his name and the cofounder's name. I knew he had a lot of pride and built this business. I respected that a great deal.

He repeated his view that the firm would get through.

"We are not so sure," I replied. "I'm sorry. I wish it were otherwise."

"We just had MF Global," I told him, not to mention Stanford. "We cannot have you go down in a huge public flameout. The U.S. economy cannot have you go down. So we are going to talk to the board, and then we want you to get restructuring and bankruptcy lawyers. We want you to get a bankruptcy workout banker. We want you to make plans for whether you are going to have to go bankrupt or whether we can sell you to someone else."

He reacted like a guy who came to the ER with chest pains only to have the surgeon tell him he has to have a triple bypass.

"What are you talking about! You can't say that to the board."

"Actually I am going to," I said. "Look, you are our registrant. We have to hold you accountable, and we'll come under fire if we don't. We almost had a global economic depression a couple of years ago, your future is questionable, and you don't get to do just ordinary business."

So we went into the board meeting to meet with the directors of the corporation. I said all those things. I told them how we were worried about their capital and really didn't know if the company was going to make it. I told them about Lehman and the stakes for the U.S. government. While Penson's cash position wasn't as public as Lehman's, because it was a clearinghouse, many of the clients were not only leveraged day traders but small brokers on Main Street whose clients wouldn't even know the name of Penson when its bankruptcy caused their portfolios to crash.

The board members were actually much more open to us than the CEO. They were scared. They realized the senior people from the SEC were sitting there saying you have a problem and the whole world could watch you go under. The board members had reputations outside Penson. Their names weren't on the door, but their names would be in the lawsuits, the newspapers, and the prosecutorial briefs.

We could see they were uncomfortable and beginning to sweat (some of them literally). So we started calmly talking to them about what they needed to do, the next steps, how to handle this in full compliance. I told them we'll have our team to advise them. A couple of the board members made a point to reassure us: "We will get advisors. We will get lawyers. We understand."

John and I didn't want any disputes about what we said at that meeting. So we sat down afterward and drafted a letter detailing our guidance to the board members. They needed not only to obtain restructuring lawyers and bankers but to look for a merger partner. They needed to prepare in case they had to go bankrupt, they had to think about what would happen to three million accounts if they went under, and they had to coordinate with us. You can't walk out of a meeting like that and not have a written record of what was said. John and I knew that could be a nightmare. They could easily or even inadvertently twist what we said or misrepresent what we said. We knew we were vulnerable. We may have been the government, but if something went wrong, we'd take the blowback.

We agreed that the best course for Penson was to merge with a firm that had better capital. Mary, Julius, John, and I felt heartburn for investors if the brokerage behind a million customers vanished into bankruptcy. Now this wasn't about saving Penson, because a merger was going to scoop up the accounts and assets and leave not much else of value. Penson was dying, only slowly.

By the fall I stepped back from a lot of the daily maneuvering but did help with finding a buyer. Penson talked to some huge firms, most of which didn't like all the baggage that came with the company's three million accounts (some customers had multiple accounts). In the fall we connected Penson with a prospective buyer, a well-known brokerage. Talks dragged on through the holidays and ultimately broke down.

At last in April 2012, Penson sold its securities-clearing operations to a company called Peak6Investments, Ltd., and later moved its futures brokerage business to Knight Capital Group. By January of the next year, Penson had gone gently into that good night, declaring bankruptcy for its remaining business, Nexa Technologies Inc.[30] We spared investors the nightmare of the largest brokerage failure by number of customers and accounts in U.S. history. Despite the SEC's byzantine ways, the agency had managed to intervene and prevent the public destruction of a major brokerage when consumer confidence in the economy hung by a thread. We'd established new oversight for the beleaguered credit rating agencies. With the issuance of the first Exam manual in January 2012, we had national standards and process in place for the previously autonomous regional offices. Sometimes the gang could shoot straight after all.

NO ONE MENTIONED
THE WAX MUSEUM

You don't lead by hitting people
over the head—that's assault,
not leadership.

—Dwight D. Eisenhower

MY DREAM JOB

"Norm, I'd like to talk to you about something. Can you come upstairs?"

It was June 2012, and I received an unexpected call from the top. Didem Nisanci, chief of staff to SEC chair Mary Schapiro, wanted to see me. I assumed it was going to be a straightforward meeting. Perhaps Didem wanted to talk to me about a personnel issue, or maybe she needed help with a question from Congress. But when I walked into her tenth-floor office, I could tell right away that something beyond the usual was going on.

Nisanci told me that Eileen Rominger was leaving the agency.[1]

I was surprised. Rominger was the director of the Division of Investment Management, one of the most important jobs at the SEC. She'd been there only 18 months. Then I felt my pulse quicken as I realized why Didem was telling me this.

This position was now open. "Is it something you would like to be considered for?" she asked me.

On the legal side of the investment management business, the head of IM (as it is known in the business) occupies the highest office in the U.S. government. At that time the division employed just under 160 people. IM staff wrote the rules for the business, reviewed mutual fund filings, and provided guidance on asset management issues to the industry, the SEC, Congress, and the executive branch. I knew it was the kind of job in which I would have a chance to make a big difference.

When I told her that, yes, I would like to be considered, she said, "Good then. Why don't we stop by Mary Schapiro's office?"

Stop by? I'd been to many Dodd-Frank meetings and some Penson meetings in Schapiro's office, but I'd never just "stopped by." I took a deep breath to calm my nerves.

We stepped into the beautiful office with its spectacular view of the U.S. Capitol and the skyline of Washington. The corner office measured about 30 yards long with windows running down the left side as you walk its length with windows at the end as well. The chair's desk was in an "L" to the right at the far end of the office so you couldn't see it from the door. We found Mary tapping away on her computer. She stood and greeted me in her usual friendly and kind way. We chatted with no obvious agenda while my mind raced a million miles a minute thinking about what I should say to try to get the job.

Mary brought up the subject of money market mutual funds and said it was the biggest challenge facing her at that moment. These funds played a huge role in bringing the economy to a halt in September 2008. She mentioned that a reform proposal had recently been submitted by IM to the SEC commissioners for review.

I hadn't seen the proposal but blurted out that in my view the SEC should change how these funds were priced in order to make their true value more transparent to consumers. This was a bit aggressive considering I wasn't quite sure where Mary stood on the issue.

I took the elevator back down to the seventh floor to talk to Carlo di Florio. I told him that Eileen was leaving and that I was being considered to lead IM. Carlo wished me luck and offered to be a reference for me. We both laughed about the fact that when I had agreed to be his deputy, I told him that I would apply for the IM job if it ever came open. Carlo and I had only met once prior to our time together at the SEC. But over the past 2½ years, we had worked together as if we had known each other for decades. We made a dynamic duo because we combined theory and practice. As a consultant to businesses, Carlo had studied organizational theory and knew a great deal about how to construct better business processes. But like most consultants, Carlo made recommendations to firms and then moved on to the next consulting job. I had spent 10 years in a company also learning the same importance of process but on the practical, day-to-day level of running an investment management business. Carlo was excellent at thinking of creative structures, and I was good at getting them built. We made a great team.

I next discussed with Sally and our four children the possibility of staying longer at the SEC. At this point I'd almost reached the end of the three years that I had originally promised Mary

Schapiro. My family was eager for me to return to the private sector and leave behind the constant public scrutiny and endless nasty-grams. Thinking about ethics requirements was enervating in and of itself. Several times I had to analyze whether I could accept a car ride home from one of my son's baseball games from another parent who happened to be in the investment business. The anonymous notes continued to fly until the day I left the agency, so you never knew where the next salvo was coming from. A part of me wanted to be free of it all as well. I had already been thinking about what might come next.

But I made the case to my family that this would most likely be the only opportunity I would have to become the top federal policymaker for investment management. It would mean staying at the SEC at least two more years, because I always believed that you should never hold a job for less than that. I'd be traveling more often to Washington and spending more time away from home since Washington is where most of the IM staff were located—and where IM did its critical work. My family agreed to make the sacrifice of my not being around part of each week so that I could pursue my dream job. And Sally told me that I could not turn down the opportunity and that she would carry on raising the kids when I was not around. It was difficult, because I knew that each event I missed in our children's lives would never come around again. In my time as the director, I did everything I could to miss as few occasions as possible.

Back in my days on Wall Street, my job was to make sure my firm followed the rules—at home and in new offices abroad—and took care of our investors. Of course I had looked deep into myself long ago, realizing that my respect for the law and for setting expectations and limits surely had something to do with my chaotic childhood. As the son of alcoholics, I'd had a father who broke most of the rules on how you treat your family, squandered the family's money, and ran the family business into the ground. I have tried to be a better father and husband while providing a comfortable life for my family. I always traveled more than I wanted and worked longer hours than I wanted, but that can be the price of success in my business.

Mary Schapiro called and offered me the job, and I accepted.[2] I began to prep for my new role before I headed home from a Fourth of July vacation in Martha's Vineyard. I called my three predecessors— Eileen Rominger, Buddy Donohue, and Paul Roye. Eileen made time for a long call with me and filled me in on some of the management changes she'd made in IM. Paul Roye told me to never forget that I worked for the chair. I often thought of that advice as the commissioners, people on the Hill, and others would press me to advance their own agendas and power plays.

I was sad to walk away from Exam, but our reorganization was in place now, and its momentum would carry on without me. We'd brought common sense and accountability to Exam, and this would become a mission for many other fiefdoms of the SEC—a mission I planned to continue in my new role at IM. I was comforted knowing that the many talented people who had worked with me to make Exam a more effective and rational organization would remain at their posts. I said goodbye to the leadership team and Exam's now somewhat calmer waters. Then I walked into a meltdown at IM including radioactive contamination from the near failure of money market funds in 2008 that was still toxic in 2012 and nearly poisoned the U.S. money market fund industry, not to mention my career in government. As I immediately found out, some of the reasons the radiation was so lethal had to do with outdated processes and misplaced priorities at IM.

EARLY INDICATORS

Yet again my first day at the new job held portents of the larger breakdowns in accountability I would soon encounter. The day started when I found that the door to my new Washington office was locked. I dropped my briefcase and propped my rolling bag against the wall and went looking for help. No one in the division seemed to have a key. Eventually someone called security to let me in. Once I settled in, the technology adventure began. I tried to log in to the computer to get started for the day but to no avail. After about an hour or so of people unsuccessfully trying to log me in, I called Denise Green—the chief administrator from Exam—who quickly found someone to solve the problem. I soon found out that IM had no clear process for setting up new employees with their tech. Per usual, I wasted a half day working around the issue, as many others did. The experience drew yet another stark contrast to the private sector where even the most oblivious staffer would make sure that the new boss has a working computer. Common sense says, "Let's make sure the new guy coming in doesn't have a poor first impression of us."

In the SEC and the federal government writ large, union benefits and civil service protections often meant that staff members served for life protected by multiple layers of Bubble Wrap. Directors come and go, so we are viewed as helicopter bosses, soon to be out of their collective hair. It became second nature for some of the staff to let directors and managers fend for themselves as they stumbled around their new, presumably temporary digs, while hoping not to be called upon when problems arose. This wasn't good for efficiency or morale in any organization and in the SEC it discouraged motivated, hardworking staffers. As a leader and a steward of the taxpayers' precious dollars, I believed it was my responsibility to leave the organization better than I'd found it, and this was my firm intention.

YOU WISH THERE WAS A REVOLVING DOOR

Soon after I became the director, a longtime SEC staffer asked me how I was liking it at the Wax Museum.

"Excuse me. The what?"

"The Wax Museum. Didn't you know? That's what the staff call IM—because it's frozen in time and place."

I hoped he was just feeding me a funny line. But in my heart of hearts, I worried that it was true.

The first thing I did was institute a weekly staff meeting with my six direct reports. They included five associate directors and one deputy director. We had a vacancy for a sixth associate director to run the business side, such as budgets and staffing. The five associate directors and the deputy constituted one of the longest-serving leadership teams at the SEC, with head rule maker Diane Blizzard being the "baby" with a tenure of some 24 years. My first staff meetings were painfully quiet affairs. The associates didn't share much of anything that was happening and sometimes came alive only to criticize each other and argue.

"So, does anyone have any issues that we should discuss as a management team?" I began.

Silence. The only response was the sound of shifting bodies. I noticed that certain of the associates would barely look at each other.

However, when I brought up the idea of rotating staff from one associate's group to another's group to broaden people's experiences and training, they came alive.

One said, "We have tried that. I was sent the deadwood from another group, and I had to give up my best people! I'm not doing that again."

Everyone had known each other for decades, and slights and grievances had built up over that time. After all, who knew when the next anonymous complaint-writing enemy might emerge from the shadows? SEC culture made it better to trust no one and defend whatever bit of turf you had.

There were six offices in the IM division. Under SEC personnel rules, each office should have around 35 people supervised by an associate director. But with six associates and around 160 people total, I discovered that many directors were supervising offices much smaller than 35.

Two people early on were invaluable in seeing me through the transition. Luckily for me, Eileen had appointed Diane Blizzard head of the IM rule-making office. She was an experienced policy person who had also worked outside the SEC with the Investment Company Institute. The indispensable Diane offered me sage advice on managing the division and navigating the tangled web of SEC rules. I also could not have endured the first months without my counsel, Brian Murphy. Sometimes Brian and I would close my door and just shake our heads at how the disagreements among the associates hampered dealing with the everyday issues of managing their teams.

But I also saw hope. The lawyers there were among the most talented in the SEC. They found their way to this place because they wanted to make a difference, protect U.S. investors, and strengthen the economy. I believed they could do it. But first they needed a better framework that would reward them for innovation and teamwork rather than discourage it. My first step would have to be to start building a work environment that focused on processes and results, rather than judging and criticizing people. I would have to set up new systems for holding staff accountable for measurable outcomes. But most of all, I wanted everyone in our division to be focused each day on providing service to the American public.

IM MOVING AHEAD

Becoming director of IM presented a management challenge like no other. I had to bring all the skills and experience I'd gained since law school to the task. I had faith that my prior management roles in Exam and as a hedge fund partner, corporate lawyer, and litigator had all prepared me for this moment. But that didn't mean that it was going to be easy.

My first step: I asked the IM division to commit to continuous quality improvement. Top-performing companies around the world have long embraced this management philosophy, which tells us that processes—not people—are usually the cause of problems. Using the continuous improvement approach, business professionals collect performance data and then analyze it to determine if what they're doing is achieving their goals.

I challenged my folks to stop relying on "We have always done it this way." (Like Exam, IM had no written rules, policies, or procedures because "everyone knew" how to do things.) The associate directors complained that they were way too busy with their existing workloads to take on the task of learning and implementing continuous improvement. The tone of their comments added up to: How would they find the time to collect data and analyze it in the search for potential improvements? They were swamped! When I asked that letters from investment management firms requesting waivers be tracked and scheduled for decisions, one manager in the IM chief counsel's office patiently explained to me that it simply couldn't be done . . . We had to keep muddling through the letters as best we could with no system! I got the staff to create a simple list of all the incoming letters and where they stood in the process. This enabled us to track the letters and improve the division's ability to respond in a timely fashion.

This attitude toward setting up a new system wasn't surprising. Wherever I've worked, I found that people tend to resist change. It's just human nature. I sold my staff on my own conviction that by investing the effort up front to improve our processes, we'd ultimately eliminate duplication, paper pushing, and other inefficiencies, making everyone's lives so much more productive and happier in the long run. This argument appealed to my colleagues who had more external focus and wanted the SEC to change—and to those who were more resistant because ultimately this would result in less busy work for them.

The Madoff and Stanford disasters exposed the aspects of the system that had failed. Yet even after all the egg on the faces of staffers at Exam, some still resisted the program to overhaul our processes. I faced the same kind of obstructionism at IM where some staff members rejected my plans for improving the way the division should work simply because they didn't believe or agree that the financial crisis of 2008 had had anything to do with them.

I was gobsmacked at one town hall meeting when a supervisor asked why we should think about making improvements, because after all, "We didn't do anything wrong." But in fact the division *did have* a dramatic downfall during the 2008 crisis when the Reserve money market mutual fund almost collapsed, forcing the U.S. Treasury to guarantee *all* money market funds.[3] As in Exam, the staff perceived the failure as an isolated, once-in-a-century event, not a systemic problem with the way the SEC did its business.

I truly believe that always trying to do better is simply a good way to manage our lives. Businesses have so embraced this concept that they now routinely ask us to complete feedback surveys after flying on their planes, renting their cars, or buying their books. They do this so that by refining their operations to reflect the feedback, they will improve services and ensure customers want to return. It's a truism that a fish in the water doesn't see the water; but I knew way before I swam in the IM fishbowl that a government agency designed to serve the public should offer nothing less than continuous improvement.

IM does three big things: it writes the rules regulating the investment management industry, provides guidance to industry and government on how those rules are applied in practice, and reviews documents that mutual funds use to sell their shares to investors.[4] This work affects millions of lives. I always kept in mind that people invest their savings for any number of reasons, including for a down payment on a home, a child's education, or retirement. IM makes sure that the managers of mutual funds—the vehicle through which most Americans invest in capital markets—accurately disclose their investment strategies and portfolios and that they treat investors fairly. The SEC's mission is not to guarantee that investors make money. Rather it requires that investment management firms and fund managers will not act to benefit themselves and their companies at the expense of investors. These rules are vital to the savings of millions of U.S. investors and the continued health of U.S. markets, which are the best in the world. In the ever-evolving world of investing, for IM to carry out these critical tasks "same as we always did" is at best an unacceptable mindset and at worst dangerous to the country's well-being.

WHAT DO PEOPLE THINK?

When searching for the right approach for how to operate an organization, I've always found that it's best to consult the people who work there and find out what they think. Early on, people frequently asked what my "plan" was for the division. Outside of being a continuous improvement organization, I had no premade agenda. I knew well enough that if I were to come up with a plan and impose it upon the staff members without their input, they would resist it. I needed to find out the issues that the people on staff wanted to address, get their feedback on what the division did well and where it could improve, so we could figure out the changes that needed to be made.

I persuaded human resources to transfer Carolyn Grillo from Exam to help me with the process (Carolyn was very enthusiastic about the move). I had worked with her during the Exam reorganization. Carolyn was a talented organizational development executive and had been invaluable to me. She understood how to gather the right information from all stakeholders and use it to design a vision for where the organization should go. No matter how tense things were, Carolyn brought unfailing good humor to any situation and a penchant for cropping a photo of my face onto various bodies to make PowerPoint presentations more entertaining. When Carolyn pasted my headshot on a superhero's body, I was fine with it—but some of the other combinations were less appealing, like my headshot on a break-dancing Santa's elf!

We selected groups of employees in the division and representatives of other departments across the SEC and asked for their thoughts, positive and negative, on the division's strategy, structure, people, process, and technology. Some we met individually, others in small focus groups. Our initiative meant getting cooperation from local leaders of the National Treasury Employees Union.

As often happened, the union asserted its prerogatives to serve its interests. Union head Greg Gilman took the position that management could not conduct these interviews with nonsupervisory employees in the division on its own because the union was the exclusive bargaining representative of staff. The union insisted on selecting the members of the focus group sessions and having the union steward attend them as well. Since federal unions cannot have dues automatically deducted from employee paychecks, union leaders look to reward those employees who pay dues. So it was not surprising that the union picked dues-paying members.

As a manager I felt it was wrong that the union had such control over operational decisions. But to its credit, the union cooperated by setting up meetings, in addition to the focus groups, with me and the entire staff in groups of 10 that led to good discussions. Pat Copeland was the union steward for the division and was extremely helpful. Pat had been at the SEC a long time and was well aware that many of the union employees were unhappy with the status quo and wanted to work with me to make things better.

One idea was to set up a suggestion box to capture any feedback that managers or staff did not want to share publicly. This entailed another discussion with the union about what would be done with the suggestion box and who would open it. We eventually agreed that a member of management and Pat would open the box together. One of the first notes that showed up was from someone in the division who wondered how I could come from a hedge fund firm and become an SEC employee. The anonymous writer asked how the staff was to believe that I would be a "traitor to your class" and enforce the laws against investment managers. That wasn't worth a response.

Just as we were gearing up this feedback effort in the fall of 2012, I heard from a number of sources that Mary Schapiro was going to leave the agency. She had backed all my efforts to reform the SEC, and so I worried that with Mary's departure, we would lose the momentum for change in the agency. Happily, her successors Elisse Walter and Mary Jo White gave me tremendous support, and the transitions went smoothly. My daughter was captivated by the fact that a powerful federal agency that employed her dad was run by the first woman ever appointed chair.

QUICK WINS

As comments from our focus groups arrived from around the division and other SEC offices, I quickly grabbed the low-hanging fruit. One theme that emerged: employees felt stifled, not informed about what was happening in the other offices in the division. Another: that too many layers of management were frozen in place for decades in the Wax Museum, the museum where transparency goes to die.

The squabbling among the associates that I witnessed at my senior staff meetings didn't stop there: it mirrored the same tone when they went off to run their individual groups, and it kept them isolated from each other during the day-to-day. I could see immediately that this lack of exposure to each other stunted employees' professional development by preventing information sharing and cooperation. Even worse for the American people, this segregation and isolation of employees within fiefdoms meant that we had almost no chance of carrying through our mandate to uncover emerging risks from sketchy investment products or practices. I was infuriated that the primacy of fiefdoms in SEC culture at times superseded the responsibility of the agency to serve the American people.

I addressed this by throwing job listings open to everyone, for the first time giving managers and staff the opportunity to move around the division and the SEC. I undid the long-held view in the SEC that openings were reserved for the favorites of senior managers. So now when a commissioner called down looking for a new counsel, I would send an e-mail to the whole division asking who was interested. We would then screen those names and make recommendations to the commissioner. Similarly within the division we began welcoming moves by employees to different groups. Talk about easy pickin's of the low-hanging fruit!

All of this generated perhaps the one anonymous missive that I liked. We had a vacancy in disclosure review, the division's office that reviewed mutual fund filings. This can be mind-numbing work because there are literally thousands of filings to review. We filled the spot with a real go-getter, Michael Spratt, an ambitious young lawyer who had worked in the division at one time but left to assist one of the commissioners; he came back equipped to lead and bring a broader perspective to us. Almost immediately we got an anonymous nastygram saying that the position should have gone to a long-serving person in the disclosure review office who "deserved" the promotion. The theory was that this person had labored for years at a lower pay level and the position we filled, which was a grade higher in pay, should be a reward for long service. We had hired the best person for the job, not the "next person up" that the writer wanted. That was one note that I didn't mind because it showed me that the staff realized it was a new day: we were doing things differently by promoting distinction, not tenure.

We had to overcome yet another shortcoming not unique to IM: a reticence by staff members to apply for jobs for fear that they would be rejected. My sources told me that the received wisdom in the division was that the bosses who were hiring already knew whom they wanted. So applying was a waste of an employee's time and self-confidence. I told our people that I had served on many hiring panels at the SEC and that I had often seen the supposedly "anointed" candidate not get the position. Plus, even if a staffer did not get the promotion he or she applied for, simply applying might lead to another opportunity. I saw many instances where people who behaved gracefully when they did not get one job ended up being considered for another opportunity because they impressed us with their ambition and professionalism.

To address the concerns that we in the division were not transparent enough to the outside world about what we were working on, we began to publish guidance updates on the SEC website to share our opinions on certain issues with the public. These pieces give investment managers and executives a window into what we are seeing and thinking. To no one's surprise at the SEC, the industry reacted in a variety of ways. The folks in the investment world liked our updates when they conformed to their way of doing business. They weren't so pleased when we called them out in updates for conduct we found unacceptable. One particularly unpopular update reminded fund managers that it is not permissible for them to accept gifts or entertainment from anyone doing business with their fund![5] Even though it came out after I left the agency, I got an earful on that one when I attended conferences of industry folks.

My new deputy director, Dave Grim, led the effort to write and publish the guidance updates. I hired Dave in early 2013 after I conducted a search that targeted both internal and external candidates. Dave is a career public servant who joined the SEC straight out of law school in what was then known as the SEC's advance commitment program. Dave has an encyclopedic knowledge of the rules from his almost 20 years at the SEC, but he also could still spot and fight the absurdities of the bureaucracy. For two guys who at first didn't know each other, we worked together seamlessly and became great friends. Dave was instrumental in making the reorganization of the division happen. He worked tirelessly with Pat, our union steward, to make sure change actually occurred.

MANAGING THE BUSINESS

The division's workforce felt intense frustration about the slow pace of hiring and the lack of good equipment. (I had experienced that firsthand!) We had to address how to improve the business side of the division. Mary Schapiro understood the issue because she instituted a managing executive position for the bigger divisions so the director could concentrate on strategy and mission and not get bogged down in the day-to-day of budgets and administration. But when I got there, no one had filled the managing executive position, although IM did have a business manager working one pay grade level below that.

Shortly before I arrived, the business manager had hired the former director's talented executive assistant, Sandi Hult, to report to him in the administrative group. The business manager seemed almost gleeful when he kept reminding me that Sandi, who would have been my assistant, worked for him now! It was difficult starting a new job without an assistant, but it did mean I could hire Ammani Nagesh, who went on to do a tremendous job. Ammani served as the confidential assistant to chairs Christopher Cox and Mary Schapiro, so she was invaluable in guiding our policy initiatives in the commissioners' offices. The business manager's records were so confusing, it took a while for me to figure out that the division was authorized to have 187 positions; but a whopping almost 30 of those were vacant. I couldn't understand how we'd gotten to this point when I kept hearing how heavy the division's workload was.

After I questioned whether he was committed to doing the work required to fill all the vacancies, the business manager did me a big favor by finding a perch at a less demanding federal agency. I jumped at the chance to hire Denise Green from Exam to fill the job. Faced with a system that defied common sense and basic principles of management, Denise found ways to just get things done that would make any tough private-sector manager gleeful. She succeeded by cultivating relationships with the staff in the human resources and other support departments. Whenever we ran up against a cordon of paper clip–shuffling functionaries, Denise knew exactly whom to call to find a way around the roadblock.

One example comes to mind. Early on, I learned that the enforcement division's paralegals were available to help our IM lawyers with routine tasks—but it never happened. I asked the amazing Denise to investigate, and sure enough, she discovered that the requests were tangled in red tape because the paralegal contract was being renegotiated. She found the right person to reach out to and got the requests pushed through. When the paralegals arrived to relieve my lawyers in IM of many administrative tasks, it was as though a light had been switched on in the cave!

A DRAMATIC STEP

Now that the business and administrative sides were in good hands, Dave and I could concentrate our energy on our mission to the U.S. investor. But first we had to address the continuing challenge of the fiefdoms in the division. Armed with the feedback from the focus groups, we felt it was time to sit down with the associates to address the challenge: how to get people to work together on our mission, which would broaden their opportunities for growth and job satisfaction. In the summer of 2013 we held an "off-site" senior staff meeting to change the mood and put everyone at ease. Our fights in Congress over the SEC's budget meant we couldn't have any actual off-site meetings because they cost too much. Instead, we reserved a conference room located far from IM's offices to at least get folks away from their phones and computers. I opened the meeting by talking about the feedback and how important it was that we come up with a plan. Together. My theme was that staff members felt cut off from each other and the broader strategy of the division because IM was segmented in six offices that did not coordinate with one another. I was as honest with the associates as I could be.

"I need your help. You've been here for decades and know the division better than I do. We'll never make any productive changes unless you all are on board with our plan."

Eventually Doug Scheidt, chief counsel and one of the longest-serving associates, broke the ice by suggesting that maybe we should consolidate some of the offices and reduce the fiefdoms. That breakthrough was big! Everyone agreed that we needed to shrink from six offices to four. And the people in the two offices being eliminated would touch down on natural landing spots in the surviving groups. For example, the folks who reviewed prospectuses for annuities based on mutual funds joined the group that reviewed all the other mutual fund filings. A tiny office that advised the commission on whether certain funds (such as exchange-traded funds, or ETFs) should be given exemptions from the securities laws was folded into the chief counsel's office whose job is to make the calls on all the other waiver requests the industry sends into the SEC. The remaining offices: Rulemaking, Disclosure Review, Chief Counsel, and Managing Executive. Fewer and larger offices would mean two less fiefdoms and greater opportunity for employees to gain new experiences at work. And fewer offices meant fewer cracks among them where emerging risks to investors might go unnoticed.

Working in the private sector, I regarded consolidating offices and functions as a relatively routine organizational development step. In the government, where new offices and functions are often created but almost never eliminated, our reorganization was revolutionary.

Even a couple of years later, SEC commissioner Mike Piwowar marveled that I had eliminated some boxes on the org chart without being tarred and feathered!

From that restructuring plan in the summer of 2013, the next step was getting approval from the union. As if the logistics of moving so many people around weren't complicated enough, we also had to consider how we'd work within union rules such as the fact that employees could choose their new supervisors! If it hadn't been for my genial relationship with union president Greg Gilman, steward Pat Copeland, and counsel Ralph Talarico, we wouldn't have been able to get the reorganization implemented so quickly—by November. And I swear we set a land speed record from everything I'd seen in the government.

The reorganization paid immediate dividends when our merged chief counsel's office was finally able to grapple with several innovative applications from investment managers to offer new ETFs that had been languishing for years. These included new types of ETFs where the exact securities in the fund would not be revealed to the public, so-called nontransparent ETFs. Investment managers who devote resources to researching stocks and picking them for the fund do not want their picks, essentially their intellectual property, given away to the public. We sent our recommendations for approvals and rejections of these applications to the commissioners after years of delay and the prodding of Congress. And the commissioners agreed with me.[6]

Investors love ETFs because they get access to all kinds of investments in one bucket—stocks, bonds, commodities, you name it. In addition, the costs are very low, and the active investor can trade the ETFs all day long. Industry managers and lawyers applauded our team at IM for unclogging the SEC's pipeline of applications and industry requests. Even when we rejected some "nontransparent" ETF proposals, the industry credited the commission for providing detailed reasons for its actions.[7] Another benefit of the new structure: we uncovered and eliminated more head-scratching duplication. I quickly discovered that two teams of lawyers in different offices were researching the same issue regarding fees paid to brokers, and they didn't even know it. As I found time and again, the associates' insistence to me that the old six offices worked well together couldn't have been further from the truth.

HITTING THE STREET . . . FOR THE FACTS! OR WHAT I LEARNED FROM THE BIG DOGS

One day after landing at IM, I was back on one of the Exam floors, and Jon Hertzke, who had worked with me on the credit rating agency exams, was standing nearby. I was talking with someone else about how great it was to work with motivated people who took their jobs seriously. Jon turned and said to me, "You'd be surprised how attractive it is to work with people who get things done."

From that exchange I had a feeling that Jon might be the right man to help me attack a big undertaking: overhauling the antiquated and crippled data collection and analysis system. I was losing sleep worrying about this. If the SEC didn't catch up to the industry this way, it would be at a permanent disadvantage in identifying risks and preventing more scandals.

If I were going to get the division to transform our use of data, I needed to hire folks who had the chops to do it, not another phalanx of lawyers. I am no fan of the Dodd-Frank Act, but in this case it made my life better because it mandated that we hire these kinds of experts to get a better grasp of the industry we're meant to regulate. Congress had included a clause in the act that specifically required IM to hire its own SWAT team of superexaminers.

Knowledgeable staffers on the Hill slipped in the provision because they believed the rule-making offices at the SEC like IM had become too distant from Exam and were not benefiting from the "facts on the ground." I knew of the requirement, but when I got to IM two years after the law passed, I couldn't believe only one person had been hired. The division had all these open positions—some mandated by Congress—and yet it had filled only one! I quickly formed the Risk and Exam Office and set Jon the task of staffing it.

To get this done, I needed not only to hire people and find better technology, but also to get our senior leadership out in the field talking to the lords of finance running the investment management firms we regulated. Carlo and I did some of this when I was at Exam, but now IM was mandated to get better intel in the field. We began to call on the senior managements and boards of directors of investment management firms to understand what was happening at those firms.

I saw these visits as an opportunity to initiate a dialogue with the biggest names in the world of Wall Street. I had serious concerns about industry developments that were keeping me up at night. The Volcker Rule reduced risk taking on Wall Street and imposed greater capital reserve levels on banks. This meant that even the big financial supermarkets like Goldman Sachs that were now both depository and investment banks had to reduce their bond holding and trading activity. I worried that fewer bonds available for trading could produce big price declines that would hurt individual investors. Another concern that had me tossing and turning: many of these supermarket banks were switching clients from free brokerage accounts to fee-bearing investment management accounts. I had to find out how this affected the banks and the investors.

We also wanted to give leaders at these firms the chance to tell us what risks they were seeing in the markets. We visited all kinds of financial firms including mutual fund giants like Fidelity and large hedge funds similar to the one I once helped run. The senior executives at all these businesses couldn't believe that the SEC leadership had not visited before! I knew that Exam staffers had always pitched their sights to compliance personnel—mostly lawyers—and not engaged much with senior management, the folks who actually make policies and deliver the profits. I believed, and these firms' senior leaders agreed, that it was better to talk through both sides' concerns when the waters were calm rather than wait for disaster to strike to meet for the first time clasping fire hoses and pickaxes. This proved out when a high-level executive at PIMCO called me on my cell phone at the IM picnic in 2014 to alert me that the legendary Bill Gross would soon resign, news that could rattle the markets. Because he had my number and I made myself reachable, we had plenty of time to react to the news and prepare for any tumult, which thankfully didn't ensue. I used the advance knowledge of this transition to brief other federal financial services regulators and reassure them that we had an IM team at PIMCO to monitor fund flows.

At Goldman Sachs we talked to the biggest dog of all, the CEO Lloyd Blankfein. I brought up a tough question with Blankfein. I raised my serious concern that banks like his had dramatically reduced their inventory of bonds since the 2008 crisis. Fewer bonds available to trade meant turbulence in a particular industry or national economy (think China, for example, or a rise in interest rates), which would mean faster and steeper drops in the value of everyday investors' bond portfolios or bond mutual funds. Blankfein said that the Volcker Rule and the Fed's tougher requirements on how much capital banks needed to hold had led to less risk taking at the firm and thus lower bond holdings. Blankfein understood my concern about this major issue for investors. If interest rates rose, the bond market could get slaughtered because big banks wouldn't intervene the way they used to by buying up more bonds and cushioning the blow on the markets. This is in fact exactly what happened to the high-yield bond market at the end of 2015, which was among the reasons for problems at a large mutual fund called Third Avenue.[8]

I asked Blankfein about an idea that was raised by some of the investment managers like BlackRock and that we'd kicked around at the SEC. Would it reduce volatility in the bond market if corporations made fewer, larger bond issues so that bonds could trade more like stocks? I know companies use bonds a lot like the way a small business takes loans from a line of credit. Business owners are human beings wired to minimize risk. So they tend to borrow what they need, say to add more table space to their pizza parlor or more limos to their fleet, rather than get the bigger loan that could cover a lot of needs but leave a big chunk of debt on their balance sheet (even if analytically an argument could be made for the larger loan). Blankfein explained that bigger companies do the same thing. They typically issue hundreds of smaller bonds in response to a range of needs over time. The result? Bonds typically don't trade that freely, as each issuance is relatively small and sells out quickly. After about six months, institutional investors own most of a particular bond issue, and there is no ready market to trade it. Blankfein said another reason that corporate treasurers would never issue bonds in larger amounts: they don't want to have to come up with the great deal of cash they would need if all their bonds matured at once. The corporate treasurers also want to take advantage of interest rate fluctuations if they can: small issuances of bonds help them manage their exposure to higher rates.

I also got a lot out of my meeting with the CEO of Morgan Stanley, James Gorman. We discussed why Morgan Stanley had placed so much emphasis on growing its investment management business, including the massive task of integrating the broker-dealers Dean Witter and Smith Barney into its supermarket. Morgan Stanley had built up its asset management operation so that it was competing now with the independent shops like Vanguard and Fidelity.

Gorman said the asset management business was a much more stable and profitable revenue source than the broker-dealer business where Morgan Stanley only got paid if clients traded. So Morgan Stanley shifted some clients from free brokerage accounts into fee-bearing asset management accounts. The reason was pretty simple but rang alarm bells for me. I knew that brokerage clients only pay commissions when they authorize a trade, while clients with investment management accounts typically pay a fixed fee like 1 percent of assets a year. So that means lots and lots of retail brokerage clients aren't generating many fees for the management of their small, stable portfolios. Move them into an asset management account, and voilá, they're paying percentage fees on an annual basis.

As a result, I was concerned about how clients moved from brokerage to investment management accounts, a clear benefit to the bank. Gorman told me that his firm's clients preferred the investment management model because they could leave investment decisions to the investment experts who are duty-bound to put clients' well-being above their own. Charles Schwab executives as well told to me how they now make greater revenue from managing assets for clients than they do from commissions on trading stocks. This from the discount broker of the 1980s that set off a revolution based on cheap trading! I worried about whether clients really understood what they were doing when they transitioned from the brokerage model to asset management. I reminded Morgan Stanley and Schwab executives that they needed to make sure that they were disclosing everything their clients needed to know about these moves.

We visited firms both large and small. And talked with all sorts of managers, owners, and board members. Every meeting I held confirmed my view that asset management was growing at a rapid rate during the postcrash years, and I realized that the division needed to watch these developments like a perpetually hungry hawk. When we sent the intel from our meetings back to the chair, staff, and commissioners, they were blown away. They loved the information we'd shared, especially because no one before had brought them this kind of fresh reporting from the C-suites of the industry they were regulating. With these reports from the front lines, we provided the chair and commissioners with ammunition they could use in their meetings with industry representatives. It was a turning point at the SEC.

By the close of 2013, a team of us had accomplished a great deal to shake up the management of IM, instill more accountability, and break down the silo walls and get people working together. We found more opportunities for staff and opened up the dusty corners of the Wax Museum to the sunlight. We formed the Risk and Exam Office and were out meeting with the leaders of the industry. Dave, Carolyn, and I with many others drove these important changes and were thrilled to see how energetically the staff responded. But no matter how many times I spoke publicly about these organizational transformations, Congress, economists, and the media remained focused on the status of rules growing out of the crisis, including those mandated by Dodd-Frank. As director of IM, I stood at the crossroads of two of the biggest policy fights of all: new rules for money market mutual funds and the adoption of the Volcker Rule. For the public, these battles defined my stewardship of IM and are the topics of the next chapters.

BREAKING THE BUCK ALMOST BREAKS MY BACK

Success is not final, failure is not fatal:
it is the courage to continue that
counts.

—Winston Churchill

When Mary Schapiro asked me to be the director of IM, she could not have predicted that one month later the commissioners would devolve to bitter finger-pointing over how to protect the money market mutual fund industry that had nearly crashed and burned billions of investor dollars in 2008. My predecessor at IM had circulated a policy proposal on new rules for these funds earlier in the summer of 2012. Soon after taking the director job, I learned that the proposal included measures to reform money market mutual funds that would make them more like savings accounts at your local bank than the riskier securities funds and products the SEC regulated.

Money market mutual funds buy market instruments like bonds and take the risk of those investments going up and down. Bank products such as savings accounts do not fluctuate in value and are insured by the federal government. By forcing mutual funds to hold capital reserves, as banks do, IM's proposal would reduce the vital risk taking of the U.S. markets. I had a feeling that the proposal was headed for trouble; however, I was not prepared for the meltdown that followed.

On August 22, 2012, Schapiro issued a surprisingly strong-worded press release stating that she did not have the three votes needed to make the proposal public and describing the proposed reforms she supported. In part, the release read:

> One of the most critical lessons from the financial crisis is that, when regulators identify a potential systemic risk—or an industry or institution that potentially could require a taxpayer bailout—we must speak up. It is our duty to foster a public debate and to pursue appropriate reforms. I believe that is why financial regulators both past and present, both Democrats and Republicans, have spoken out in favor of structural reform of money market funds. I also believe that is why independent observers, such as academics and the financial press—from a variety of philosophical ideologies—have supported structural reform of money market funds, as well.
>
> The issue is too important to investors, to our economy and to taxpayers to put our head in the sand and wish it away. Money

market funds' susceptibility to runs needs to be addressed. Other policymakers now have clarity that the SEC will not act to issue a money market fund reform proposal and can take this into account in deciding what steps should be taken to address this issue.[1]

Then things got ugly. Another Democratic commissioner, Luis Aguilar, issued his own statement asking for more study of the problems of money market funds.[2] Newspaper reporters called every five minutes looking for comment, and I couldn't get the commissioners to engage on what path might work.

Right before the controversy exploded in the public eye, I managed to get Commissioner Aguilar on the phone. I asked him if there was anything I could do to modify the proposal that would help. He said that the proposal as it stood would not get his vote as it didn't address issues like money market business flowing to private, less-regulated funds. A few days after Aguilar's statement, Republican commissioners Troy Paredes and Dan Gallagher issued their own statement asking that the commission's economists do more work to evaluate potential reform options and their likelihood of success.[3] The whole mess was front-page news in the *Wall Street Journal* and other papers.

It was quite a welcome to the world of policy making in Washington, DC. It also illustrated the fragility of one of the most important features of the U.S. financial markets. Let's take a look back at how we got here.

THE SEC SELLS A PIECE OF ITS SOUL, LIVES TO REGRET IT

In 1980, the SEC strayed from its mission, a mission born in securities laws that became a model for free economies worldwide. It was a departure, and a rare one. In my view, when you stray from your core values and carve out a piece of your soul as an organization, it may take 30 years, but you're eventually going to regret it. That's what happened after the 2008 crash and then culminated in a bitter

Beltway cage match over how to "fix" the $7 trillion money market mutual fund industry.

When a new investor learns personal finance 101, from whatever source, that new investor will learn the same core concepts grounded in the structure of the U.S. financial industry first set down in law during the 1930s. First, it's important to save money and then take advantage of interest-bearing opportunities so that your investments grow over time. Therefore, as an adult, you no longer need a piggy bank, coffee jar, or hidden safe for your cash. Second, you can have diversified savings that include federally insured bank accounts where you can't lose a penny for amounts under $250,000; federal, state, and city government bonds that are similarly exceedingly safe (a "savings bond" is a government bond); and various kinds of securities that have higher levels of risk. The more money you can afford to lose in the short to medium term, the more you can invest in stocks, mutual funds, and other securities.

Bank accounts more or less ensure that short of a zombie apocalypse or the rise of a supremely evil army of master hackers, if you put a buck into an account, you will at least get a buck out. Bank interest rates generally don't provide much of a return on your money and since the 2008 crisis have hovered near zero. To get better returns on your money, you have the option of taking part of your savings and going to a different kind of store to buy stocks and shares in mutual funds.

You can shop at this other investing store that has been very successful but doesn't guarantee your dollar. You hand over a buck, and you're hoping that a money manager as good as Peter Lynch at Fidelity, John Bogle at Vanguard, or Warren Buffett at Berkshire Hathaway invests your money so that it does great for you—that is, earns higher returns over time than the interest that banks pay. That'll be great for your retirement, your family, and your enjoyment of life.

That's the normal bargain. But in 1980, the SEC changed the bargain with money market mutual funds, partly because bank deposit interest rates were capped by a Depression-era law (another unintended consequence). It became possible for the investing store to offer higher rates of returns than were possible at the bank store, but if you asked the shopkeeper, he'd still give you all your money back that you initially invested.

Thus you have the idea of the twenty-first century's multi-trillion-dollar money market mutual fund industry, which became the bedrock of everyday securities accounts for millions of middle-class investors. This couldn't have happened, however, unless the SEC changed federal securities rules. And that's what the SEC did in 1980—in a rare decision to cater to the industry it regulated.

That year, the SEC passed an exemption to benefit the money market fund industry. This exemption, known as Rule 2A-7, allowed these funds to seek to maintain a stable $1 net asset value (NAV) by using penny rounding and amortized cost accounting. Amortized cost essentially allows the mutual fund to count a short-term bond as worth its cost even if the market says it is worth a little less. This convention, coupled with allowing the fund to round up a 99 cent valuation of its shares to $1, enables money market funds to stay at a "stable" $1 share value. This meant these funds did not have to comply with the mark-to-market valuation standards required for other mutual funds. (If you put a dollar of cash into a money market mutual fund, no matter what happens to the fund's investments, you can get your dollar out, which is not true of other mutual funds.)[4]

In exchange, the money market mutual funds relying on Rule 2A-7 had to follow strict limitations on their investments. The SEC told them, OK, Mr. Money Market Fund managers, you need to buy lots of short-term debt so your holdings are liquid and you're not exposed to excessive long-term risk in stocks and derivatives. Like so many actions by policy makers, these limits on what money market mutual funds could invest in had an unintended consequence. They created a massive appetite in investment markets for short-term high-quality debt, or what is called "commercial paper."[5] This meant banks and other companies used commercial paper like a cash spigot to run their businesses. They issued short-term debt notes to a ready-made group of buyers in money market mutual funds that snapped them up. Thus the money market funds became a daily source of billions in cash for U.S. companies, including banks and investment houses, to run their businesses!

Many at the SEC, including my friend Commissioner Aguilar, argued to me that money market mutual funds provided a convenience and benefit for investing customers that the SEC shouldn't sacrifice as part of reform. My concern was that fund managers loved money market mutual funds because their reputation as being safe meant that customers kept their money in the managers' money market mutual funds after the customers sold stocks, bonds, or other mutual funds. Managers got to keep more of the investors' dollars in-house and collected fees when the customers again deployed their cash to buy stocks and bonds. The funds were a good deal for investment managers too, but most investors didn't realize this. I remember making these points with Commissioner Aguilar and telling him, "Yes, they're convenient for customers, but they're also good for the house because you keep your cash with the house when you might not otherwise."

With money market mutual funds, it became commonplace for small and large investors to use them as they did bank accounts, writing checks and making withdrawals as needed. Consumers with money market funds behaved at the opposite end of the spectrum from the investing gurus who advise buying stocks "for the long run" and using investment dollars to "buy and hold" over numerous market cycles. Investors treated money market mutual funds like bank accounts that they used for everyday transactions, blissfully ignoring the fact that these funds did in fact hold securities whose value could change.

Consumers liked the strong sense of stability offered by the walls of the $1 NAV. The walls might rumble in a storm but never crumble and fall. Their money market holdings were in a kind of metaphoric sealed vault with other account holders' money.

But what happens in a market downturn where the headlines are scary and people are losing their investments? The money market fund customers want to get their funds out of the vault first. "MMFs are vulnerable to runs because shareholders have an incentive to redeem their shares before others do when there is a perception that the fund might suffer a loss," stated the 2010 findings published in a report of the cabinet-level President's Working Group on Financial Markets. The report continues:

> When a fund incurs even a small loss because of those risks, the stable, rounded NAV may subsidize shareholders who choose to redeem at the expense of the remaining shareholders. *A larger loss that causes a fund's share price to drop below $1 a share (and thus break the buck) may prompt more substantial, sudden, destabilizing redemptions. Moreover, although the expectations of safety fostered by the stable, rounded $1 NAV suggest parallels to an insured demand deposit account, MMFs have no formal capital buffers or insurance to prevent NAV declines.*[6] (My emphasis)

Thus we arrive at 2008 and the financial storm of the century (so far). By this point, the money market fund industry was huge. Pension plans and endowments, following bylaws requiring them to set aside cash in safer vehicles, had parked billions in money market funds. Institutional investors were more sophisticated than retail investors and have larger investments at stake. So they responded with greater urgency when they perceived a threat to the stability of the funds.

So when the Lehman Brothers bankruptcy in September 2008 sent the floodwaters of the crash over the walls of the world's largest money market funds, the institutional investors led the frenzy of withdrawals, nearly collapsing dozens of household-name funds.

THE RESERVE PRIMARY FUND BREAKS THE BUCK

In the 30-plus years since the SEC's adoption of Rule 2A-7, money market mutual funds have rarely broken the buck. Losses on short-term bonds did not cause major disruptions to the buck and were often shored up by money market fund managers adding their own cash to the funds to mask any problems.[7] Then September 12, 2008, came, and Lehman went down. As a result, the Reserve Primary Fund, a $62 *billion* money market mutual fund, broke the buck. This fund held $785 million in commercial paper issued by Lehman Brothers. When Lehman went bankrupt, Reserve Primary Fund shareholders freaked out and started redeeming shares (withdrawing funds) to the tune of $40 billion in just two days (that's over two-thirds of the entire fund!). Adding to the panic, the Lehman debt owned by the Reserve Primary Fund was now worth zero. The fund began selling off its portfolio to pay redemptions. Unlike other funds with a mega-capitalized sponsor (say a Fidelity or State Street), Reserve had no other entity to call on, step in, and replenish its capital reserves.

On September 16, Reserve announced that the Primary Fund would break the buck and reprice its shares at $0.97.[8] A few days later, the SEC announced that investor redemptions of Reserve fund shares would be suspended "to permit their orderly liquidation."[9] Uh-oh.

Now many investors wanted their cash, particularly institutional investors, and they wanted their cash right now. I remember thinking at the time, "This is about as scary as you can get." If you have a money market fund, you are thinking, "I want my cash. I want out." Everyone wants out. During the week of September 15, investors withdrew about $300 billion (14 percent of assets) from prime money market mutual funds.[10]

Neil Irwin, who was a *Washington Post* economics editor and blogger, wrote:

> Money-market mutual funds serve as part of the bedrock of the American financial system, serving as a way for millions of Americans to save money in a financial product that (normally) offers better returns than bank savings accounts and is (normally) very safe—and then funnels that money to companies that issue short-term debt, thus funding their operations.
>
> How do we know that this system has flaws? Because they nearly brought down the financial system in 2008.[11]

You get what happens next.

To meet the flood of redemptions, money market funds burned through their cash and sold off their securities into crashed markets where no one was buying. These efforts slashed prices of short-term bonds and impacted fund portfolios, threatening the NAVs of the funds.[12] It was a near-Chernobyl money meltdown for funds as they burned away the billions in cash they could access to pay back their investors. In that terrible two weeks, fortunately only the Reserve Primary Fund broke the buck, as some fund sponsors made money transfers to their funds to prevent capital losses.

During September 2008, money market funds in the United States reduced their buys of commercial paper (the short-term notes companies used to raise cash) by about $170 billion, or one-quarter of their total holdings. Now the cash was barely dribbling out of the commercial paper spigot, and huge companies needed to pay workers and keep the lights on. So they drew down their backup lines of credit, which placed additional pressure on the balance sheets of commercial banks.[13] Suddenly all kinds of companies were in panic mode.

It only took 11 days. The U.S. Treasury and the Fed stepped in on September 19, 2008, to essentially guarantee all the money market funds in the United States. Treasury's Temporary Guarantee Program for Money Market Funds provided stopgap guarantees for shareholders in money market funds that elected to participate. The branding wizards at the Fed installed a new bailout program less than memorably entitled the Asset-Backed Commercial Paper Money Market Mutual Fund Liquidity Facility (AMLF), which extended credit to U.S. banks and bank holding companies to finance the purchases of high-quality asset-backed commercial paper from these funds. Several other interventions provided support for the money market fund industry and short-term funding markets. The Guarantee Program and the AMLF expired in 2009 and 2010, respectively.[14] All these steps had calmed the waters enough so that they weren't needed.

These events were fresh in the minds of the participants as the controversy over money market fund reform hit the fan in fall 2012.

FED UP

The SEC got hit hard in 2008 and 2009. We tend to forget the magnitude of the beatdown. The SEC was in the unenviable position in Washington, DC, of being both pitied and scorned. The front-page financial rescues of the time had sent the SEC back to the kitchen, taking out the garbage after the party was over. It was the Fed and the U.S. Treasury that had the huge budgets, palatial conference rooms, famous names, and friendships at the White House, with the media portraying Geithner and Bernanke as storming in on their white horses to save the world from financial collapse. The SEC was seen as the bureaucratic necessity that no one liked, a dysfunctional mess best kept away from the adults' table. Some of this was deserved, as I have amply documented in these pages.

The lopsided power struggle with the Fed and Treasury formed an important backdrop to efforts to pass money market mutual fund reform. The conflict later deepened during the SEC's and my wrangling with the Financial Stability Oversight Council (FSOC). This was a powerful body of interagency regulators chartered by Dodd-Frank to keep watch over the financial industry and designate institutions that were systematically important to the U.S. financial system. Being designated put these firms on the FSOC's short leash by subjecting them to additional regulations and oversight by the Fed.

The SEC's numerous failures gave the Fed and Treasury leverage in battles over issues like money market fund reform. When the SEC couldn't stop the money market fund industry from going under, Fed and Treasury had to guarantee the funds. When the global leaders of the broker-dealer industry like Goldman Sachs and Morgan Stanley nearly all collapsed at the same time, the SEC could do little while the Fed made them bank holding companies to bail them out. Then a couple of months go by and the world discovers that Madoff is a fraud and the SEC missed the chance to stop him a number of times. By the end of 2008, the SEC had taken the fall from hell. Everything it touched seemed to turn to dust.

These early fights with the Fed scarred a number of SEC personnel including a few who screamed at me during our negotiations over money market reform, saying things like "Tell the Fed to go screw themselves." I often said we have to understand the Fed's point of view. If you are a Fed person, you are thinking, I just spent the crisis cleaning up the SEC's mess. Why should I listen to the SEC?

BOILING POINT

Despite the fall from hell, the SEC emerged in 2010 with its rule-making ability intact, and it adopted new rules regulating money market funds. One rule required each fund to have more liquidity of its assets (ability to pay cash) to meet redemption demands for investors. Funds needed to be ready for a "run on the bank." They needed to be able to turn at least 10 percent of their holdings into cash in a single-day period and meet a 30 percent requirement in a weekly period. Second, the SEC ruled that the funds had to be more conservative in their investments. The new rule limited each fund's maximum holdings of "second-tier" securities, which carried more risk than first-tier securities, to 3 percent or less of their assets. Finally, the rules also required that the funds carry more short-term bonds (because this makes their assets more liquid), and said fund managers had to periodically "stress-test" their funds against hypothetical events, such as a change in short-term interest rates, to understand how much they would lose and whether they would "break the buck."[15]

Now remember how I was sitting with Mary Schapiro after Didem raised the possibility of becoming director of IM? Mary had mentioned that money market fund reform was the biggest challenge facing her as the IM proposal on the subject was on the commissioners' desks.

She said that a share price for such funds that reflected the actual market value of the securities held (thus "floating") was part of the proposal. I blurted out, "To me these are mutual funds, and we should stop hiding the risk from investors. The commission should change the $1 fixed price per share for these funds to the floating price."

This was a bit aggressive considering I wasn't quite sure where Mary stood on the issue. She nodded her head in a friendly manner and changed the subject.

By August 2012, I was starting my first days as the new head at IM. The money market fund plot had thickened, and the tension was building between the Fed, FSOC, the SEC, and Congress over who would control how the final rule would be written Schapiro was prepared to submit her proposed new rules for money market funds based on a proposal written by one of the senior officials from IM. Now that I had the new job, I read the proposal soon after I arrived and had many misgivings. It turned out I wasn't the only one.

While it was technically proficient, the policy appeared to be designed by the bank regulators at the Federal Reserve Board and not based on an analysis by the SEC's own economists. The proposal included capital requirements for money market funds and a hold-back of investors' funds.[16] These steps would turn an investment vehicle into a safe, Main Street–type bank account. Proponents claimed this was "cracking down" on the industry, but I saw it as overkill and overreach. The 2010 measures had already required fund managers to install more safeguards while not removing all the market incentives (that is, to get a better return than CDs) that made them successful in the first place.

With the SEC being punched back on its heels time and again because of Madoff, Stanford, and other scandals, the Fed and Treasury had huge clout. They were the cool people at the Beltway high school, and turning brokers into banks was the big fad. It seemed to me some people at the SEC had fallen under the Fed's influence, including the design of the 2012 money market fund reform proposal. The commissioners of the SEC wanted nothing to do with Obama's regulators at Fed and FSOC taking over money market reform. They had reservations about the Fedlike idea of watering down the risk in money markets, but Schapiro thought she could still get two out of the four of them to vote with her and autho-rize its issuance by a 3–2 vote.

She was wrong. The proposal was not brought to a vote in August 2012 because Democrat Luis Aguilar was the swing vote who, along with the two GOP commissioners, said he wouldn't vote for it. Luis knew the industry well, and he strongly believed the pro-posal was bad for consumers who didn't dabble in complex invest-ing. The next day he issued a statement arguing that any reform of money market funds should only be made after additional study of the entire U.S. cash management industry and the impact of the SEC's previous money market fund reforms in 2010. The commis-sioner worried as I did of unintended consequences: "I remain con-cerned that the Chairman's proposal will be a catalyst for investors moving significant dollars from the regulated, transparent money market fund market into the dark, opaque, unregulated market. Currently, in addition to all the prescriptive conditions applicable to SEC-registered money market funds, these funds are also highly transparent to investors and regulators in a way that other cash management vehicles are not."[17]

For my situation, as stressful as the whole lost vote was, it resulted in one important example of addition by subtraction.

The IM official who'd written the proposal took it personally when the commissioners did not vote to publish it. He was also uncomfort-able because I don't think he believed in the project to try to change the Wax Museum (although we got along well personally). When I started the new job, I sat down with him.

I said, "OK, let's say the money market funds rule passes or goes away. What are we going to work on next? What is our pipeline?"

He mentioned that he had 50 or 60 project papers on the shelf in his office. He called them "shelf projects" and he'd pull out a couple of those for IM to work on next.

"Wait a second," I said. "Is this how the U.S. is making financial policy? Have we evaluated those 60? How do we pick one?" This was a well-meaning and well-qualified official. But the commissioners and other experts within the huge agency should have more analysis to decide what policies to propose.

We all worked to count up these shelf projects. It turned out there were 72 possible rule projects on the office shelf. In a good year the Division of Investment Management maybe gets two rules through the commission, so the 72 represents a 36-year plan! To be fair, SEC culture didn't demand much rigor in setting priorities.

I told him that we were going to analyze the shelf projects for their feasibility, affordability, and strategic value. Hardly a radical idea! I wanted to get wide input from others to help us make sense of the priorities.

When the commissioners refused to vote on the draft money market fund proposal, that seemed to be the last straw, and he told me he was resigning. I accepted his resignation, seeing this as an opportunity to bring in some fresh thinking. We ultimately narrowed the shelf projects down to just a few that we could prioritize.

THE MORNING AFTER

When Commissioner Aguilar suggested the SEC should do an economic analysis of the issues remaining with money market funds, he was hit with a lot of negative spin from some Democrats and the press. The media picked up the administration's messaging that the industry needed a crackdown rather than common sense. After all, what the three commissioners who said they would vote no were saying was simply this: can we please slow down and study this some more before piling on more regulations?

Before you know it, bing-bang-bing, former SEC chairman Arthur Levitt went on a radio show and called Aguilar a "villain" for requesting further study.[18] The *New York Times* reported on August 26, 2012, "Mr. Aguilar derailed one of the most significant current efforts to tighten regulations on the financial industry. His opposition to a proposal put forward by the S.E.C. chairwoman, Mary L. Schapiro . . . put Mr. Aguilar in lock step with the powerful and aggressive mutual fund industry in which he worked as a lawyer from 1994 to 2002."[19]

In the *Wall Street Journal* one commentator labeled the SEC "toothless" and asserted "anything is better than the 'let's study this issue to death' approach taken by SEC commissioners such as Mr. Aguilar. The financial crisis proved money funds are a real risk, and the notion that their unit values are always $1 is a fiction. Action, not further study, is needed."[20]

Politico published one of its instant trend stories that made it clear the reporter didn't know how the SEC worked. "Dems Shy from Money Market Reform," *Politico* big-and-bold-typed on its front page. Why? Well, according to *Politico*, if Aguilar, a commissioner of a nonpolitical agency, voted against the proposal, then somehow Hill Democrats were behind the no vote as the consensus of a partywide view.[21] That was an insult to Aguilar and the commission. The *Washington Post* published a more balanced story, but almost no one got it right.

I liked Schapiro and Aguilar—and all the other commissioners. I worked for the chair, but my good relationships with the other commissioners meant a great deal to me. I had learned long ago in my childhood how to defuse conflict, and we needed a new start. Mary had been right to identify the money market fund industry as needing further reform, but the proposal had been co-opted by the pro-Fed elements within the SEC. She probably pushed the commissioners too hard at the eleventh hour, rather than working behind the scenes with Luis. But that was a rare miss for her.

I now had an opportunity to help out Schapiro and the commissioners and to do my job by seeing if I could get reform back on track. But I'd have to contend with the rising power over at FSOC.

F-SOC IT TO US

Commissioners Aguilar, Gallagher, and Paredes couldn't support Schapiro's proposal because it was a Fedlike bank solution, but the lack of an SEC proposal had the effect of giving FSOC an opening to take over the issue. Once the Schapiro package was stalled at the SEC, she asked the superbody of financial regulators to take up the problem, playing right into their hands.

Washington Post columnist Irwin definitely, really got it. He quoted Treasury Secretary Timothy Geithner's letter at the time to FSOC members urging them to step up oversight of money market mutual funds.

Irwin noted that the letter was "written in painstakingly formal language." He translated Geithner's message to the SEC this way: "Nice little industry you've got there. It would be a shame if something nasty happened to it, like having Federal Reserve examiners running around all the time questioning everything they do. You might want to ask your friends at the major banks, like Citigroup and Bank of America, how they enjoy that."

Irwin mused, this was a "bit more thuggish than ... ('the Council's authority to designate systemically important payment, clearing, or settlement activities under Title VIII of the Dodd-Frank Act could enable the application of heightened risk-management standards on an industry-wide basis'), but more accurate."[22]

By involving FSOC where market regulators like the SEC and CFTC are outnumbered by bank regulators such as the Federal Reserve, the FDIC, and the Comptroller of the Currency, Schapiro risked ceding SEC authority to the bank regulators. Not only did this anger many SEC folks, but it also foreshadowed another big battle in 2013 when FSOC went for a takeover of most of the SEC's functions regarding investment management.

I saw the dangers of FSOC and the Fed's power in trying to take over control of investment management firms and brokers. The Fed and Treasury regulate banks that are obligated to take care of everyone's money in the entire country, from the low-income retiree on social security to the hedge fund trader. Banks provide home and small business loans. They are a kind of financial public utility that isn't expected to get in trouble, and they don't pay huge returns on their CDs and savings accounts.

The FSOC was dominated by banking regulators who did not understand securities markets. The key to U.S. bank regulatory schemes is the "safety and soundness" of banks and their federally insured deposit accounts.* In contrast, the mission of the SEC is to "protect investors, facilitate orderly markets and promote capital formation."[23] For the banking regulators the object is the avoidance of risk, particularly for deposits. Since the Federal Deposit Insurance Corporation is the insurer for bank deposits, there is a federal interest in banks being sound to protect deposits.

The banking model is simply inapplicable to the model of risk capital in the securities markets regulated by the SEC. Investors come to markets to put their capital at risk as equity or debt investors in publicly listed companies in order to earn a return on that capital. The United States has created the most vital markets in the world through a regime based on the full and fair disclosure of all material facts about publicly traded companies and accurate presentation of accounting information on such companies. This regime proceeds from the fundamental premise that investors, armed with all the material facts, can make the best decision about where to invest based on their risk tolerance.

The U.S. securities markets are the envy of the world. I participated in the SEC's "technical assistance" missions in Saudi Arabia, Abu Dhabi, and Hong Kong, where SEC personnel shared knowledge about U.S. securities markets and how the SEC regulates those markets and their participants. Those non-U.S. regulatory authorities around the world pay all the expenses for SEC personnel to travel to their countries so that they can learn from the country that has fostered markets that are transparent and reliable for investors seeking a return on their capital.

---

*Under 12 USCA Sect. 1(a), the Office of the Comptroller of the Currency was established within the Department of the Treasury and "charged with assuring the safety and soundness of, and compliance with laws and regulations, fair access to financial services, and fair treatment of customers by, the institutions and other persons subject to its jurisdiction."

With this in mind, I knew the SEC couldn't lose the right to write the rules on money market funds.

REBOOT

In early September 2012, I sat with Mary Schapiro at the conference table in her office. Mary told me how disappointed she was about the fracas over the money market fund proposal and even apologized that it had all gone so wrong right after I agreed to head up IM.

I told Mary that, despite the chaos, I felt that there could be a path to a compromise on money market fund reform. I asked her if she minded if I approached the commissioners to see if I could find common ground, and she encouraged me to do so. Mary noted that dialogue with the commissioners had broken down and she told me to give it a try.

About a week later, I was in my New York office, now on an old law firm floor with plenty of light that the New York region expanded into, when Craig Lewis called me to talk. Craig is a professor at Vanderbilt Business School who was on loan to the SEC as the chief economist. Craig and I talked for a long time that day. We had a feeling that a "floating NAV" coupled with "gates" allowing money market funds to suspend redemptions in a crisis could be a potential solution. The floating share price would restore market discipline to the funds, and the gates would let the funds stop redemptions if the funds still got in trouble—it was a good balance. With some tweaks, that is exactly what happened two years later.

Craig and I participated in a long road of meetings and talks with commissioners, FSOC staff, SEC staff, key staff in Congress, and industry people. Craig and I first sat down with each of the commissioners to see if our idea could be acceptable, and we received generally favorable responses. In November Craig completed the economic study of the 2010 reforms that Commissioners Aguilar, Gallagher, and Paredes had called for during the August tumult and posted it on the SEC website. I worked with the tremendous IM rule-making staff led by Diane Blizzard and Sarah ten Siethoff to develop a term sheet for a floating NAV–plus–gates proposal based on these meetings and the study. Chair Elisse Walter, who had succeeded Mary Schapiro, backed our efforts to find a compromise.

While we formed consensus in the SEC building, I had to go outside to several meetings of the FSOC principals and staff to explain where the rule-making process stood to fend off an FSOC takeover of the process. One such briefing occurred in the Diplomatic Reception Room at the Treasury with its elaborate mirrors and chandeliers standing in contrast to the jammed table and side chairs packed with principals and staff. At the same time we listened to industry representatives and activists talk about their views of what money market reform should look like, and we briefed staff on the Hill about where things stood. I walked a delicate line of reassuring all these groups that we were making progress but also not sharing any details of our compromise, as such information would undoubtedly leak out to the press and could upset the applecart at the SEC.

By the summer of 2013, Mary Jo White was the new chair of the SEC. She and the other commissioners approved the proposal 5–0, and we published it for public comment and further discussion with Congress and the industry. In the summer of 2014, we had two new commissioners, Michael Piwowar and Kara Stein, to replace Elisse Walter and Troy Paredes. Mike and Kara both voted against adopting the new rules, probably because they were new to this issue and didn't want to take sides in a debate that had embarrassed many folks at the SEC. But White, Aguilar, and Gallagher did vote for it, and we got it done.

We ultimately did float the NAV—that is, apply the same rules to money market funds as other mutual funds and securities, meaning you can lose your money if the fund's investments lost money. This allowed the daily share prices of funds to fluctuate along with changes in the market-based value of fund assets. We also provided money market fund boards with new tools—liquidity fees and redemption gates—to address runs.

Luis Aguilar wouldn't vote for the package unless the fixed NAV—you put in a buck, you get at least a buck out—was preserved for funds that served retail investors. Since large institutional investors, not individual consumers, historically had rushed to pull their money out of these funds in 2008 and other times, I could live with it.

As was noted in the SEC's press release on July 23, 2014:

> With a floating NAV, institutional prime money market funds (including institutional municipal money market funds) are required to value their portfolio securities using market-based factors and sell and redeem shares based on a floating NAV. These funds no longer will be allowed to use the special pricing and valuation conventions that currently permit them to maintain a constant share price of $1.00. With liquidity fees and redemption gates, money market fund boards have the ability to impose fees and gates during periods of stress. The final rules also include enhanced diversification, disclosure and stress testing requirements, as well as updated reporting by money market funds and private funds that operate like money market funds.
>
> The final rules provide a two-year transition period to enable both funds and investors time to fully adjust their systems, operations and investing practices.
>
> Norm Champ, director of the SEC's Division of Investment Management, said, "Today's adoption of final money market fund reforms represents a significant additional step to address a key area of systemic risk identified during the financial crisis. These reforms are important both to investors who use money market funds as a cash management vehicle and to the corporations, financial institutions, municipalities and others that use them as a source of short-term funding."

While this was a gratifying victory for American investors in 2014, few of them knew how close FSOC, the Frankensteinish super-regulator designed by Dodd-Frank, nearly came the year before to taking the SEC's place by staging a hostile takeover of the SEC's role in regulating America's mutual funds, investment advisers, and other investment management firms. Nothing would have been more disastrous for America's economic growth and job creation. My tale of surviving that ordeal is in the next chapter.

EDGAR AND FRIENDS

Go right straight down the road, to do
what is best, and to do it frankly and
without evasion.

—George C. Marshall

Can systems of government be reformed to regain their fitness for mission? It's far from impossible, U.S. history demonstrates. The branches of the U.S. military, for example, have needed dynamic leadership and merit-driven shake-ups to overcome periods of bureaucratic dysfunction. They have done so, particularly when national survival is at stake.

Many of us know from history courses and movies such as *Saving Private Ryan* about the wartime leadership of U.S. Army chief of staff General George C. Marshall and the strategy named for him of rebuilding Europe after World War II. What's less well known is Marshall's success as a change agent in revitalizing a moribund bureaucracy.

As historian Dwight Jon Zimmerman has written: "On September 1, 1939, Germany invaded Poland, plunging Europe into the conflict soon named World War II. On that same day, Marshall was sworn in as the fifteenth chief of staff of the U.S. Army. He assumed command of a 190,000-man force ranked nineteenth in the world, behind Portugal and ahead of Bulgaria." As Zimmerman chronicles, President Roosevelt tasked Marshall with infusing the army with vigorous, young commanders and pruning out the careerist desk-bound officers in their fifties and early sixties, many of them aging colonels who had risen to their ranks purely on the basis of seniority. Military lore holds that Marshall kept a "little black book" during the interwar years where he recorded the names of promising officers who would be needed in the next crisis. Whether he kept the book or not, Marshall had an excellent memory for his leadership recruits that eventually included World War II's greatest generals such as Dwight Eisenhower and Omar Bradley.

Congress cleared the way for Marshall when it passed the Second Supplemental Appropriation Act of 1940 that eliminated seniority-only promotions. Wielding *congressional authority* to elevate qualified officers, Marshall began his work.[1]

He established what he called the "plucking committee," a panel of six retired officers. The committee reviewed older officers—particularly colonels in their sixties and near retirement who could not withstand the rigors of combat command—and got rid of many officers to create opportunities for promotions. As Zimmerman has written: "In the first six months of its existence, the panel removed 195 captains, majors, lieutenant colonels, and colonels. Ultimately 500 colonels were forced into retirement."[2] Marshall's approach led to the military's up or out policy where officers must meet standards to be considered for promotion over the years. If they don't the brass reassign them or arrange for retirement.

World War II remains one of the greatest tests of national survival faced by the United States and its leaders. It required a federal mobilization program throughout civil society that would be difficult to implement in the America of the twenty-first century where consensus is so elusive. Its lessons for the untapped potential of our government agencies are important, however.

The challenges faced by the SEC since 2008 pale in comparison to the operational scope of those faced by the military and President Roosevelt in World War II. But the SEC *was* in a war to assure its own existence and to protect the free functioning of financial markets. Many sectors of the U.S. economy *did* face fundamental questions about their survival.

Mary Schapiro was charged to lead the SEC from a sleepier, clock-punching "peacetime" operation to a modernized and energetic "wartime" organization. That's why she hired me and other veterans of the financial sector. It's why she knew that we had to address many glaring shortcomings at the SEC including its yawning technology gap.

For too long, the SEC had practiced unilateral disarmament with its underfunded, out-of-date technology and data analysis. Systems and equipment were decades old. The agency had paid too little attention to its IT and data analytics operations that didn't care about the SEC's existential need to close the efficiency gap with the sector it regulated. In fact, before Schapiro, the SEC in most cases lacked the processing capacity to review and use the data it collected from the financial services industry. What's worse, many of the SEC's managers resisted efforts to make progress because they feared obtaining and using industry data would make the SEC liable for indicators of fraud and mismanagement in the data that they'd miss and later be blamed for. So the outdated technology systems and failure to deploy analytics reinforce one another.

Washington's struggles with tech meltdowns such as the Obamacare website and China's hacking of government employee information from the Office of Personnel Management (including mine!) are seen by some critics as evidence that the public sector will never work. From what I saw at the SEC, that fear is well grounded. However, I knew the application of a modicum of smarter management could make the agency work better. In the same way lax standards discourage individuals from standing out as top performers, higher standards create a space for employees with ambition and smarts to step up and do more.

THE DATA SILOS

By 2017, the SEC's capacity and capability to analyze the data it collects and use intelligently mark one of its greatest areas of progress since the dark time of 2008. But when I first encountered SEC technology, I wouldn't have believed that was possible. It began with a call to Doug Scheidt, IM's chief counsel, about an issue the examiners in my group in New York found.

"Doug," I said, "it's Norm Champ in the New York office. We found a problem with a manager running multiple types of investment products, including funds, and not allocating opportunities evenly. It looks like they're favoring some accounts over others, which means they're violating their duty to some of their customers."

The exam team and I then had a great conversation with Doug, who was very helpful. He told me I needed guidance from Enforcement, and later I decided to actually bring Enforcement staff to meetings with the fund manager in question rather than send over our whole exam file to Enforcement and hope someone got to it soon enough. We made it a regular practice to get Enforcement officials involved early when examiners found major issues so we could see if Enforcement agreed with Exam's analysis.

But as we hung up with Doug, another concern immediately struck me. Here I was in one of the 12 SEC offices talking to Doug about an issue that came up in our region. But examiners in other regions might be seeing the same questions, and we'd never know, plus they would not have the benefit of Doug's advice. The SEC didn't have the tech infrastructure to do searches of internal exam reports to glean trends across regions. Examiners were like air traffic controllers who couldn't track their jets outside of local airspace. We lacked a simple system for tracking exam red flags outside of each regional silo.

Geez, I thought, this must be pretty basic. I asked my team about it at our next Tuesday meeting.

"Guys," I told them, "I'm finding out there's no way for us to communicate what we learned from Doug, which was pretty darn good. We can't capture this and spread it around to anyone else in the country. There must be a way to post exam findings online, make them searchable."

I talked to Jim Reese, an Exam assistant director in headquarters, who along with Brian Snively, worked tirelessly to try to screen the massive data coming into the SEC to determine where examiners should look. When you entered Jim's office in DC, you saw reams of paper with the lists of firms, and the phone rang constantly as Jim was the go-to guy for information on brokers and investment firms registered with the SEC. Jim explained that there had been an attempt to set up a system to track risks that examiners saw when they visited firms. The effort terminated when examiners input so many risks in the system that managers couldn't draw anything meaningful from the information. I couldn't help but think that the SEC could do better. We did have a system called STARS that tracked what exams were under way, but it contained little of substance about what the examiners found. Jim told me that the STARS system operated on outdated technology that could no longer be supported by IT and would be shut down soon.

During the national effort to resuscitate the Exam program, Jane Jarcho from the Chicago regional office emerged as a leader on improving technology for the Exam staff. Jane and a team in Chicago had an idea for a new exam tracking system that would also generate reports based on staff members' input as they examined a firm. I hoped we could use the widely available Salesforce system when I learned that the SEC actually owned some licenses for the software (making visits to firms for exams is not that different from making sales calls). However, IT informed me that no one knew how to use the software (despite the fact that we had licenses!), and so we would have to let a consulting contract, a process that could take years. Jane and other Chicago staff forged ahead and built the system themselves. Now exam reports were online in the system and could be searched by examiners nationwide. What a huge jump from reports in paper form filed in each office and not accessible nationwide.

Someone in our weekly staff meeting suggested that we could try EDGAR to automate exam processes. Based on what I had seen of how EDGAR operated, I had no confidence in that route.

THE EDGAR MAFIA

EDGAR (which stands for electronic data gathering, analysis, and retrieval) is the SEC's online data system for corporate and fund filings. About 4,000 staffers depend on data from EDGAR, which was state-of-the-art in 1988 but hasn't changed much since then. While EDGAR's antique operating system and print-only output make it extremely secure, it would have been laughed out of any private-sector operation long ago.

EDGAR and I had our awkward meeting during my first year in Exam.

One of the many Dodd-Frank rules in the SEC's court required individuals and firms that advise municipal governments about investments to file registration papers with the agency. We searched for a system to handle these filings and considered whether EDGAR would be the one. My assistant set up a meeting with one of the EDGAR specialists, which I expected to last about half an hour. It was a little bit like the dinner party where your nephew brings all his buddies and doesn't tell you beforehand. About 10 people showed up for the meeting, both SEC IT people and external EDGAR consultants, and filled up all the chairs in the conference room. Everyone was friendly and appropriate, all button-down shirts, polos and khakis, a scattering of white Venti Starbucks cups. A few folks took notes as I described the filing system we would like, the top manager assured me it would be no problem, and before you knew it, the entourage moved off to the next meeting.

I came to learn that like most long-running government programs, EDGAR had spawned an ecosystem that lived off EDGAR and fended off any attempts to replace it. The outdated system continues to be used and, in fact, "upgraded" at costs of tens of millions of dollars even though Google and other corporations have far more effective data storage systems. The SEC still hires numerous outside consultants to keep EDGAR running despite its tremendously outdated technology. Perhaps worst of all, different divisions in the SEC have different versions of EDGAR, one being used by Corporation Finance, one by IM, and others. All these different varieties of EDGAR had to be maintained separately, providing numerous contracts for an army of consultants while reinforcing the silo walls between divisions.

At the same time, a cottage industry of consultants outside the SEC repackaged EDGAR filings for private subscription sale.[3] Even at the SEC, taxpayers ended up paying the R&D costs for more Beltway bandits to get rich. To cap it all off, EDGAR embarrassed the SEC when an outside study found that the private contractor running the EDGAR filing feed allowed traders who subscribed to get access to EDGAR filings before they posted on the SEC's website and potentially exploit the time advantage.[4] In addition, fraudsters used fake EDGAR filings to spread false reports on public companies and, presumably, to trade on such reports.[5]

Soon I referred to this technology-consultant complex as the "EDGAR mafia" because it was so tight-knit and resistant to change. Whenever there was a meeting with the EDGAR staff to discuss improving the system, I sat and listened as the members of this

EDGAR mafia said that they could easily program whatever techno-logical or analytical requirement we requested. However, throughout my time at the SEC, somehow all of that easy programming never happened.

FROZEN IN PLACE

As with EDGAR, the New York office's laptops had been industry standard many years before my arrival, but they would no longer be confused even by a sixth grader for state-of-the-art personal com-puting technology. It was another way the SEC had been bringing the equivalent of a cavalry with spears to a twenty-first-century battle-field. This was most dramatically exposed when Dodd-Frank passed in the summer of 2010.

Dodd-Frank reregulated the entire securities industry, so the SEC had a ton of new rules to write (remember, regulators write the rules that figure out all the details for how each provision of a law will be carried out). The proposals for new rules ran into the hun-dreds of pages each, usually at least 800 pages. As the head of the policy effort for Exam, I regularly reviewed the draft rule proposals and worked with my indispensable partner Judy Lee to give feedback based on the input of the expert examiners. There was one big prob-lem. The technology system in New York couldn't handle that many pages. The laptops we used as desktop computers were so under-powered that my system crashed the minute a long release arrived by e-mail. The frustration of tapping keys while your screen refuses to change a single pixel can make the most even-keeled managers grind their teeth.

It took me a while to figure out that the long release drafts were causing the computer to freeze up and crash. The urban legend held that during some prior regime, management ordered that the lap-tops have the least amount of memory possible to save money. I don't know if that was true, but I do know that the SEC had laptops that couldn't even handle an everyday task such as rule writing—or even e-mail storage, as we learned in Chapter 3.

Despite these storage shortcomings, in New York my personal computer did work from day one. I was impressed by our regional head of technology, an incredibly talented guy named Ed Fallacaro. Ed had managed technology in the private sector, and he knew how to make stuff work. Ed was commuting to work in New York from Philadelphia. Even with that terrible schedule, he managed to run an excellent IT function in New York. Ultimately, he got hired in the Philadelphia SEC office to be the regional managing executive. I know that Philadelphia management was thrilled to have him, and he was doing a great job when I left.

BATTLING BACK

None of this was lost on Schapiro as she fought to upgrade the SEC. In 2010 she hired Maris Technology Advisors' CEO Tom Bayer as her chief information officer,[6] and she pushed for funding for the SEC's technology budget in the Dodd-Frank Act. She charged Bayer with modernizing and transforming the SEC's infrastructure and data processing, and over his four-year tenure Bayer made good progress. Tom moved the SEC to cloud-based data storage and computing capacity and, in my view, stepped up the professionalism of the IT function.

Tom called soon after he started and made an appointment to see me in New York. When he called, I wasn't exactly sure who he was, but just a few minutes into our meeting, I realized he was an ally who didn't think much of EDGAR either.

Tom's hiring was the first step. Schapiro and the commissioners lobbied hard during the debate over what would become Dodd-Frank to allow the SEC to set its own budget instead of Congress deciding its budget despite the fact that the SEC was largely self-funded through industry fees.

Schapiro argued that the agency found it extremely difficult to establish and fund priorities when appropriations fluctuated so much each year based on political considerations in Congress. This argument was particularly powerful in the area of technology, where both poor management within the SEC and the constantly changing budget meant that long-term technology projects were extremely difficult to establish, maintain, and fund. In practice this meant that as the SEC lurched from one technology project to the next, the project would either get delayed, canceled due to lack of funding, or ultimately forgotten in the mishmash of spending on technology. As Schapiro testified in June 2009 (and would testify in similar terms again):

> I believe additional resources are essential if we hope to restore the SEC as a vigorous and effective regulator of our financial markets. . . .
>
> Although expanding our workforce is a critically important step, I believe we also must give our staff better tools to conduct oversight of vast financial markets. That is why the President's request for FY 2010 also contains funds for additional investments in our information systems. Investments in new systems have dropped by more than half over the last four years, and as a result the SEC has a growing list of technology needs that have gone unfunded. . . .
>
> The SEC also plans to improve our ability to identify emerging risks to investors. We have many internal data repositories from filings, examinations, investigations, economic research and other ongoing activities. But the SEC needs better tools to mine this data, link it together, and combine it with data sources from outside the Commission to determine which firms or practices raise red flags and deserve a closer look.
>
> Finally, we would invest in our multi-year efforts to improve the case and exam management tools available to our enforcement and examination programs. These systems would give our senior managers better information on the mix of cases, investigations, and examinations, so they can apply resources swiftly to the continually evolving set of issues and problems in the markets. In addition, these tools will provide better support for line staff in these programs, so they can be more productive and better able to match the sophisticated systems used by the financial industry.

Schapiro hammered this message every time she could, and she got a bigger budget. The advocacy began to work. It improved our ability to do a number of things during my years of service to upgrade the SEC's capacity to understand and use its storehouse of data about financial firms.

Show Me the Numbers   First, we stopped making things up when it came to writing policy rules. Schapiro and chief economist Craig Lewis published a document that laid down the law. It required that SEC policy experts use real-world economics to show how a new policy would affect investors, consumers, and businesses. For a policy to be adopted, the officials writing it had to show an understanding of the risks and an analysis of the financial consequences—a kind of economic impact statement.[7] I was thrilled because this was a check against the power of anyone—commissioners, directors in IM or any other division—deciding on his or her own the direction of financial regulations in the United States. Requiring that regulators run the numbers makes an effective balance against officials making policy based on their own views.

One problem: This slowed down analysis of market risks because the Economic and Risk Analysis division now had to perform more work to sign off on the economic impact of a rule. When new policy documents started going through the door at that division it meant that analysis of industry data to spot risks slipped lower on the priority list. Schapiro's directive was brilliant for policy making but diverted economists' resources away from analyzing data both to help Exam know where to look and to help IM and the other policy divisions identify emerging risks. For Carlo di Florio and me, even before this development, we weren't going to wait.

We saw the opportunity to strengthen and mobilize Exam's own Risk and Surveillance Unit. We started collecting our own data from field audits and doing our own risk reports. We bulked up Jim Reese's staff and harnessed data to identify risky firms for examination. Soon other divisions followed suit—including IM later on under my leadership when we formed the Risk and Exam Office. In some ways, this looked like the duplication of services that drives people including me crazy about the SEC. But the satellite units helped keep the agency looking out the window at the real-world trends in the financial industry.

Secret Meetings   Sharing data and information across tech silos was sometimes easier than doing so across human ones. Here's an example of how old-school intel sharing should work, where government operatives working toward the same goal trade information, but in this case did not.

While I was in the hedge fund business, I sat down quarterly with two SEC staff members from the Division of Trading and Markets about observations on the market. It was a good idea on their part. Why not learn more about the hedge funds that are the big customers of broker-dealers such as Goldman Sachs that Trading and Markets regulates? Hedge funds had billions of dollars of securities held by those brokers.

After I started at the SEC in January 2010, I ran into one of those Trading and Markets guys in the hallway, and the lightbulb went on over my head. I fast-walked back to my office, thinking "Great idea, Norm!," got a meeting set up, and sat down with him and his partner later that week.

"Hey, you know I really enjoyed meeting you guys when I was on the outside," I told them.

"You, too, Norm; we really enjoyed it!" they chimed back, relaxed, even a smidge jovial. To me, the subtext was "It's Norm the new guy. My fresh coffee's hot, and he's not a problem."

And I didn't want to be one.

"Now I am in charge of Exams," I went on. "By the way, I am a little nervous because there are a lot of firms that haven't been examined. I have this list of hundreds of firms that we could examine, but I could use your help to decide where to send my examiners."

I continued, "Listen, you're out talking to hedge funds all the time. Do you see any red flags in any of them? Do you see any hedge funds you think may be superaggressive? Do you see any that you didn't think had great internal controls, anyone that said anything that might worry you? Let's talk. Tell me who those might be. Then I can go out and examine them."

A long pause.

"Well . . . uhhh . . . what do you mean?" they asked. Less jovially.

"You're out at hedge fund firms. I was in one for a number of years, and I am involved in the industry, so I have some view of the whole industry. But you guys are Trading and Markets. You are going and visiting a bunch of hedge funds. Were any of them you thought better than others? Were any of them worse than the others? Were there any that were riskier? I am after some color so I know where to send my examiners."

They explained that they didn't write anything down.

I said, "Do you have a report on these people?"

"No."

"Do you have any sense about any of them?"

"No."

"Well, do you have a report or something you can put out about them?"

They repeated that they never generated anything like that.

For the next 2½ years I never got any information from these guys about the funds they met with, and I could never get a straight answer about why I didn't get the information. We all worked for the U.S. government, and we were there to fulfill the agency's mission, and yet they wouldn't share the most basic information with examiners.

I saw that my two friends did a lot of good work. But they didn't budge on this one, nor at first did senior leadership in Trading and Markets. Why? Perhaps they thought that if they gave information to us that they learned from speaking with hedge funds or, for that matter, included Exam in conversations with the brokers they regulated, the hedge funds and brokers would clam up and no longer be candid with them. I didn't view it that way, of course. My friends were taking a huge risk if they believed they were having off-the-record conversations with these firms. First of all, nothing in this world is off the record anymore. Second, if my friends learned about wrongdoing at a firm and didn't follow it up, their own careers would be in jeopardy. We all took the oath that I reproduced in Chapter 2 requiring us to faithfully discharge the duties of our offices, including investigating any irregular or potentially illegal actions. If you see something, yes, you say something.

But my two Trading and Markets friends knew *I knew* that busting fund managers wasn't the purpose of their meetings. I later confirmed in my own get-togethers with top broker-dealer and fund managers that people at these firms know the laws and rules, aren't planning on breaking them, and definitely wouldn't in front of you. So they're happy to learn from the SEC and vice versa. But they cannot be told that the conversations are "off the record." No such thing.

Arming IM with Analytics It wasn't until I took over IM in 2012 that I'd face the most resistance in carrying out Schapiro's call to become "more productive and better able to match the sophisticated systems used by the financial industry." IM was at a great disadvantage in the SEC's dealings with the Fed and its analytical firepower. The Fed used its deep bench of economists and analysts to trample over the views of the SEC on policy disputes.

I learned from my time in Exam that IM lawyers weren't that informed by industry data Exam had when they wrote rules. (I also found out they didn't want too many inquiries from the public and industry because IM's website featured instructions in blaring font for every type of website visitor to contact another division of the SEC—anyone but IM! Fortunately we fixed this.)

The SEC's examiners appreciated the data findings from Exam's Risk and Surveillance group because they became tools to point them toward trouble spots, to find the securities firm needle in a haystack that most warranted attention.

But the silo between Exam and IM as well as Exam's structure blocked examiners from sharing data found in their exams with the policy makers in IM. No mechanism existed for Exam to convey its findings to rule makers in IM. This left staff members at IM writing rules based partly on their own views and meetings with consumer activists or industry lobbying groups. This opened them to the real risks of helping carry out interest-group agendas without giving due consideration to the impact of their decisions on investors whose well-being we swore to protect. Without data, regulators lacked objective criteria for highlighting risks that required action and tended to revert to their own long-held views. IM was like the Oakland A's without Billy Beane or a cargo ship without a navigation system—hoping the old scouts and salts knew best.

I needed a better way for IM to understand what was happening in the industry. We didn't have an office or specialists dedicated to industry intelligence or analysis. So I decided in the fall of 2012 to see what industry data materials we might have that had been overlooked. I took a look at the division's Disclosure Review Office.

The 60 attorneys in disclosure review spend their days evaluating hundreds of filings by mutual funds each year to make sure that the disclosure in fund documents is adequate for investors to understand. For instance, if a fund manager does not state exactly what investment strategy the fund will pursue, the lawyers in the group will return the document and ask for changes to be made.

The disclosure attorneys sat at their terminals wading through a blizzard of documents that never stopped piling on. I'm sure after a while it wasn't good for their mental health. They were dedicated public servants doing work that had to be done, and their diligent reviews weren't being utilized effectively.

They lacked any tools to manage how they reported their findings. The laws required that the disclosure office gather and publish their comments on the filings so future filers could see the correspondence. But none of that could be automatically done in EDGAR or a shared server workspace as basic as a G-drive. It wasn't like the lawyers were writing up the comments in calligraphy on parchment—but it was close. The reviewers sent in their comments to one poor sod who had the job of assembling the comments via cut and paste into a document that was uploaded to the EDGAR system. If this person took a long vacation or went on sick leave, the public postings fell months behind. Fortunately, my predecessor Eileen had reassigned some folks to help the disclosure office catch up, but it was hardly a solution. Happily some of the paralegals that Denise Green obtained from Enforcement helped shoulder the burden of publishing the comments.

I realized the filings offered a vital stream of information about newly launched funds, their strategy, and their operations that none of us were tracking. So I sat down with Barry Miller, the head of the office.

"We're seeing the development of the industry through these filings," I said. "I'll bet we can mine them for trends and hot spots. You know, are there more of certain kinds of filings? Are there issues with disclosures? What fees are you trying to get people to disclose that they don't want to disclose?"

Barry told me that disclosure didn't keep anything like that. I remember Barry saying. "We have so many filings."

"The attorneys don't need to reexamine every filing," I said. "We can use triage and spend more time looking at amendments because the registrant actually has to say in the amendment filing if there is a material change or not."

"We don't have to take Vanguard's word every time," I continued. Maybe we will take Vanguard's word 99 out of 100 times. We will sample a filing and make sure that the fund is telling the truth. It could be a start."

Barry went away, and he talked to a lot of his people. When he came back to me, he related that they found an uptick in managers' filing papers for "alternative" mutual funds that market themselves as pursuing hedge fund investing strategies. In fact, the growth was big—from zero to more than 30 percent of new inflows in one year.[8] These funds gave the ordinary investor access to the riskier, "hedging" strategies used by the likes of John Paulson without needing the $5 million to invest that his fund requires. We highlighted this filing trend at the SEC Speaks conference in early 2013 well before the financial press noticed the trend in these filings. Since hedge funds often pursue strategies involving illiquid securities, I gave several speeches emphasizing that these new funds would have to be able to redeem investors on a daily basis as required by the law.[9] This became our first effort at capturing industry information on a systematic basis for use by the policy makers at IM and the SEC in general.

It was an example of what IM could do with the most rudimentary considerations of the data that was passing right under our noses. And a refutation of the fear that it's not worth it. To institutionalize the effort of gathering data from the filings, we assigned Mike Spratt, the talented IM lawyer who had come back from a commissioner's office, to compile data on filings on a routine basis in order to inform the division.

Closing the Quant Gap   As we were ramping up our disclosure office operation in the fall of 2012, I decided to ask my team: Where are the examiners? Dodd-Frank, the sweeping national law reconfiguring the entire financial industry, said IM must hire its own examiners—a sound policy.

Remember that by 2012, IM had only hired one analyst, two years after the law ordered them to. Someone said to me, "Oh, we haven't done much about it."

I fumed a bit. I had to stare out the window to go to my Zen place. Congress told us to hire examiners, and we haven't done anything?! If I am asked about this during a hearing up on the Hill, it will get ugly. What's worse, we're wasting an opportunity to continue to modernize.

I also didn't see the value of hiring a few examiners to replicate what Exam was doing with 450 investigators looking at investment firms. IM's people needed better processes to work with the entire Exam Division. I feared having a few examiners down the hall would become an excuse for folks to stay in their silo. I chewed it over with my team, and we gave the whole situation a few days. What we did next became one of those very few times in life that I had an idea that took off right away and worked beyond expectations.

I put together a proposal to start a Risk and Examinations Office (REO) in IM and recommended that we hire Jon Hertzke to run it. Mary Schapiro approved it immediately. We chartered REO, as the SEC's website says, to monitor industry trends, manage and analyze industry data, and gather and analyze operational information from the asset management industry, including "the risk-taking activities of investment advisers and investment companies."

So we went out and recruited data analysts and quants (such as a risk manager from BlackRock and two science PhD holders) who know how deal with massive amounts of data and tell you what it means. We hired some traditional examiners, too, because I wanted to be able to go to Congress and tell them that I had examiners. But we used those examiners in a much different way. We used them more to find something out for the policy writers rather than to check on firms' compliance.

One early example of the role of these new examiners: we wanted to understand how firms value the securities held in their funds, which is the basis for calculating NAV (which we discussed in Chapter 6). So we took the REO examiners and sent them out to collect valuation policies from different firms. If you need to know something from a policy perspective, they can go do it. We even had the REO examiners piggyback on exams of firms that Exam was already conducting so that our data gathering efforts were invisible to the industry. We ended up hiring about 20 experts in the office.

Having the new office turned out to be exquisitely timed and perhaps saved the SEC from being relegated to the second tier of regulators. In 2013 and 2014, a number of crises rocked the United States markets. The Puerto Rican debt crisis surfaced, Russia invaded Ukraine, and the Nasdaq went dark off and on for two days.

We sicced our team of quants on all these issues. In years previous the government's pressure for answers would have forced SEC leaders into a defensive crouch, such as during the 2008 money market fund crisis when IM could not provide any real-time analysis. Now we had a math geek squad of our own that helped us anticipate questions such as if Puerto Rico is going to default on its debt, what does that mean for the many muni bond mutual funds that own bonds issued by Puerto Rico?

A number of financial executives and media appreciated that we had these new assets. But that didn't stop the star chamber at FSOC from attempting a takeover of the SEC's core function. In September 2013, FSOC's Office of Financial Research published a report, "Asset Management and Financial Stability," that was essentially an act of war against the SEC.[10]

The report announced that FSOC thought the investment management industry was too risky and should be regulated like banks by FSOC instead of the SEC. This was the bureaucratic equivalent of the U.S. Army trying to take over the U.S. Navy's ships.

The commissioners and many others at the SEC started to freak out. Commissioner Michael Piwowar gave a number of speeches taking on FSOC that were characteristic of how SEC commissioners and leaders felt. In a chamber of commerce speech in January of 2014, Piwowar said:

> The second threat to our core mission is banking regulators trying to impose their bank regulatory construct on SEC-regulated investment firms and investment products. Yet the Commission— not the banking or prudential regulators—is responsible for regulating markets. My concern is that the banking regulators, through the Financial Stability Oversight Council (FSOC or Council), are reaching into the SEC's realm as market regulator. . . .
>
> The FSOC, within which the banking and prudential regulators exert substantial influence, represents an existential threat to the SEC and the other member agencies. Last September, the Department of Treasury's Office of Financial Research (OFR) published a study—and I use the term "study" loosely—prepared for the FSOC on the asset management industry. The study sets the groundwork for the regulation of asset managers by the FSOC. . . . I vehemently believe that before the FSOC decides whether further study or action is warranted, the collective voices of the public and the SEC should be heard by the members of the Council. This is all

the more important because the vast majority of asset management firms are SEC-regulated entities.[11]

Piwowar argued that the bank regulators had three seats at FSOC (Fed, OCC, and FDIC), and the SEC had only one; what's worse, the banking members restricted meeting attendance to maintain control of FSOC: "One of the responses I received to my request [to attend] was that, if the SEC started bringing multiple people to the Council meetings, then every agency would want to do the same. My answer to that concern is that the FSOC should get a bigger table."

Later in 2014 at the American Enterprise Council, Piwowar said the FSOC releasing its own recommendations on money market funds—including instituting capital requirements similar to what banks face in order to prevent investor panics similar to bank runs—was "the most obvious example of the Council's much-discussed hubris." He said his complaints about the FSOC made "the Colonists' 27 grievances against King George III and Martin Luther's 95 Theses protesting clerical abuses seem remarkably terse."[12] Among the terms Piwowar used to describe FSOC during the speech included "the firing squad on capitalism," "the bully pulpit of failed prudential regulators," "the Dodd-Frank politburo," and the "unaccountable capital markets death panel."

Could this have been the end of the SEC as we know it? Even worse, were we witnessing a federal government takeover of America's investment sector!? As we've shown, FSOC was driven by bank regulators who distrusted the risk-reward trade-offs that characterized investing in mutual funds, the stock market, bonds, and other instruments.

But Jon Hertzke and his quants in REO and the IM rule-making staff, along with economists Christof Stahal and Giulio Girardi from Craig Lewis's Division of Economic and Risk Analysis, saved the day. FSOC formed staff working groups to look at designating Fidelity and BlackRock as "too big to fail," and I insisted that our staffers be on the working groups. Our quants and lawyers provided the data showing that these two firms did not present significant risk because they managed money based on investor mandates for their funds. Each time an FSOC official would say to me that if these firms sold all their securities, the markets would crash, I responded that these managers had a legal obligation to invest in the securities stated in their fund documents. Selling everything violated that obligation. One frustrated FDIC official finally said to me, "I don't care about the facts of how they work. I want to designate a few." At least he was honest.

IM's team shredded FSOC's dangerous arguments that American investors couldn't handle the risk of open markets. We argued that forcing mutual and hedge funds to eliminate risk to investors by running only highly conservative, low-return funds would cost far more in U.S. and global job creation, wealth creation, and productivity than would be gained by minimizing investor losses through market cycles. The squabbles with FSOC continued through 2014, but their attempt to capture these two firms ultimately fizzled out because our SEC was getting stronger and faster to respond. In Chapter 9, I'll share the interesting conclusion to this part of the SEC's continuing existential war with FSOC.

Fortunately the SEC finally had started to understand the power of big data and how to use it. The financial media began to notice our defense against FSOC.[13] We were a littler meaner and leaner. We were getting more comfortable standing up to the FSOC star chamber and fighting for the core mission of the SEC. Our newfound confidence would be needed as we tackled the next big challenge—making sure the Volcker Rule for banks didn't wipe out vital risk taking in U.S. markets.

THE VOLCKER RULE AND ME

The best way to get a bad law
repealed is to enforce it strictly.
—Abraham Lincoln

Some call the Volcker Rule "Glass-Steagall Lite"—and considering the political and lobbying firepower that lined up over the Volcker Rule, I think that's the closest Washington will ever get to restoring Glass-Steagall no matter which party is in power. Senator Elizabeth Warren, Senator Mitch McConnell, President Obama, the Tea Party caucus, Citigroup lobbyists, Secretary Geithner, Secretary Lew, and what Senator Maria Cantwell called "the Armies of Wall Street": all the major powers had a stake in passing the Volcker Rule or trying to stop it. Named after former Fed chairman Paul Volcker who championed the issue, Congress and the White House included the rule in Dodd-Frank to limit the ability of "depository institutions" (banks as classified by the Fed) from taking part in investments solely for their own profit, including stocks, bonds, derivatives (mortgage-backed securities), and foreign exchange. Why? Because this kind of trading exposes the banks' own capital reserves to risk. The rule also prevents banks from retaining significant ownership interests in, sponsoring, or having certain relationships with hedge funds or private equity funds.

I ended up being one of the few guys who had to find a way to actually implement it.

A Democratic Congress and the president included the rule in the final Dodd-Frank legislation in 2010 over the objections of many who saw it as unworkable. By 2012 when I got to IM, the rule moldered in the regulatory netherworld between the law passed by Congress and adoption of the rule itself by regulators. The uncertainty over what the rule would do weighed on the banking and financial services industries.

The battles over the Volcker Rule related to the money market mutual fund crisis in interesting ways. Remember, a main reason Lehman—a global broker-dealer—ran out of money in 2008 was that it sold short-term debt like commercial paper to money market mutual funds for its everyday cash flow. When panicked institutional investors began a run on the money market funds, the funds stopped commercial paper purchases, and the broker-dealers had nowhere to turn for cash. They weren't banks. But the lucky ones (at that point!)

soon became banks. Soon after the death of Lehman, the Fed permitted Morgan Stanley and Goldman Sachs to become banks over a weekend, instantly giving them access to Fed loans, which they desperately needed.[1] Bear Sterns effectively became a bank earlier in 2008 when J.P. Morgan bought it.

So even though the SEC had some fine print in its rules about how broker-dealers needed to keep a certain amount of cushion against a crisis, the broker-dealers had long since figured out how to be technically compliant with the rule without holding so much cash. When the financing provided by money market funds dried up in 2008, the broker-dealers were in deep trouble. That was another part of the Volcker Rule: how do we deal with the business of broker-dealers that are now part of large banks? (This was not an academic exercise, as Bank of America bought Merrill Lynch during the crisis to stave off its default.)

The new debate in Congress over Volcker was more about larger, more traditional banks such as Citibank that needed bailouts to survive. (These were not hypothetical concerns on Congress's part. Citigroup had massive housing-related liabilities in 2008 carried off its books that it ended up bringing back onto the balance sheet—thus absorbing the losses and forcing itself closer to insolvency.[2]) Volcker had to say how risky lending would be curtailed for hybrid behemoths such as JP Morgan Chase and for Main Street community banks.

"Banks" such as JP Morgan Chase, Morgan Stanley, and Goldman Sachs had massive broker-dealer units trapped inside them. So how would the Volcker Rule address the spectrum of investing going on inside all these different parts of a "bank"? While FSOC supervised JP Morgan Chase as "systemically important," for one example, the firm still engaged in destabilizing nonbank practices such as the trading that caused its May 2012 multibillion-dollar "London Whale" loss. Jamie Dimon, J.P. Morgan's chief executive, had to concede that the fiasco "plays right into the hands of a bunch of pundits out there."[3]

In the end this made it hellish for the five agencies trying to turn Volcker into a rule that could separate out all the risk taking going on at these bank behemoths. The SEC also wanted to make sure the rule wouldn't crash the financial sector. The Volcker Rule needed to draw a line between what risks traditional banks could and could not take and what risks broker-dealers located in those banks could and could not take.

The five agencies published the first draft of the Volcker Rule in October 2011. The 298-page proposal included more than 1,300 questions for affected banks to consider during the comment period that ended February 13, 2012. The proposal generated over 17,000 public comments providing answers to some of those 1,300 questions! "The Treasury assigned 15 staffers to comb through them," Scott Patterson and Deborah Solomon reported at the time in the *Wall Street Journal*. "They assembled a 100-page 'heat map' outlining how many times particular issues were raised and by whom. The outpouring was so huge it led two commissioners of the SEC, Daniel Gallagher and Troy Paredes, to suggest scrapping the proposal and going back to the drawing board." While about half of Dodd-Frank had been formalized in regulations, the Volcker Rule remained in limbo.[4]

It was known around the SEC how dysfunctional the Volcker process had become. The agencies all had different constituencies and interests and lacked political leadership. The staffers couldn't get together on the big issues. They debated where to hold meetings, how to define common terms, and so on. It all got a lot worse before it got better.

INTRODUCTIONS

It was September 2012, just before the presidential election, when Mary Schapiro brought me to my first meeting on getting the Volcker Rule unstuck. I met Treasury secretary Geithner and the other agency heads working on the rule. Geithner didn't seem to be driving too hard to get Volcker done. Most SEC folks and I thought that lack of movement on the rule worked just fine because we worried the rule would prevent brokers from playing their vital role in making markets for the trading of securities.

Then Schapiro and later Elisse Walter asked John Ramsay, acting director of the Division of Trading and Markets, and me to represent the SEC in the interagency meetings that had been taking place at offices around town—including the Fed, OCC, FDIC, SEC, CFTC, and the U.S. Treasury. (Robert Cook, the director of Trading and Markets, left the agency soon after Mary.) Now if Investment Management involved mutual funds, hedge funds, and related structures, how did I get so involved in a banking law? Well, the Volcker Rule impacted IM because Congress wanted to restrict the ability of banks to channel their investment dollars into private hedge and equity funds.

For example, JP Morgan Chase could make Volcker-triggering risky investments through efforts of its own employees, or it could create a private fund or find one to its liking and shunt its risk-taking deals through this "nonbanking" entity. The architects of Dodd-Frank didn't like this possibility. Banks could circumvent any kind of risk restriction the Volcker Rule clamped on them by funneling investments through a private fund. Let's say the bank wanted to buy collateralized mortgage obligations. Instead of buying them itself, it could sponsor or invest in a hedge fund that would buy them. This major issue brought IM and me into the negotiations.

John Ramsay and Trading and Markets fought the other half of the battle to make sure that Volcker didn't harm U.S. markets by stopping broker-dealers inside the banks from performing their usual functions to keep markets active and liquid. As Scott Patterson of the *Wall Street Journal* wrote in February 2013, "One area that continues to befuddle regulators is how to distinguish between a firm's own risky trading, commonly called proprietary trading, and the buying and selling of securities on behalf of clients, the people say. SEC officials have taken an interest in the issue since the agency directly oversees broker dealers that conduct such 'market making' activities."[5]

By the time the interagency work was fully under way, it was early 2013. Geithner had resigned, and President Obama had appointed Jack Lew as his successor. I knew that most of the chattering classes assumed Volcker was in effect. In fact, its implementation was well overdue, and Bernanke had to testify to that in front of Congress in late 2012.

THE REGULATORS

The Dodd-Frank law assigned the heads of five different agencies to write the rule: the SEC, FDIC, CFTC, OCC, and Fed, with Treasury in the class-minder role. When they met on the rule, it was usually in the Treasury secretary's small private conference room right off his office and next to his private elevator. These officials and staff would determine the Volcker Rule's role in the economy. I got to know them all:

- **U.S. Secretary of the Treasury Jack Lew:** Lew demanded action on finishing the rule and was proactive in pushing for it. While I disagreed with his policies, I appreciated his businesslike approach to getting things done.
- **Federal Reserve chair Ben Bernanke:** Bernanke retired in October 2013 and was succeeded by Janet Yellen. Neither played much of a vocal role during the Volcker debates. However, their most influential staff member, Scott Alvarez, had the most clout.
- **Scott Alvarez, the general counsel of the Federal Reserve Board:** Alvarez is a long-serving government employee who wields immense power at a Federal Reserve Board where chairs and governors come and go. Quiet, trim, buttoned up, with short pewter-gray hair and silver-rimmed glasses, Alvarez has been the Fed's chief lawyer for more than 20 years. I would not want to play poker with Scott Alvarez. He has kept his counsel and navigated to a position of almost unchallenged power in the Fed. As noted by reporters Alan Katz and Ian Katz on *Bloomberg*, Alvarez was "the power behind the throne, the backroom officer who, while prominent appointees come and go, quietly makes himself indispensable to them through dedication, mastery of detail and unparalleled knowledge of the Fed's secrets."[6]
- **Dan Tarullo, a governor of the Federal Reserve Board:** Tarullo is a former professor at Harvard Law School where he apparently met then law student Barack Obama. Again, I had

no stomach for Tarullo's desire to have the Fed take over regulation of asset management, but I enjoyed discussions with him. I admired Tarullo's incredible knowledge although we disagreed on many issues.

- **SEC chairs Mary Schapiro, Elisse Walter, and Mary Jo White:** I've written about Schapiro and White in these pages. I worked for Elisse Walter when she served as SEC chair from December 2012 until April 2013. President George W. Bush appointed her a commissioner in 2008. One of the smartest and warmest people I have ever known, Elisse played a large role in forging the money market fund compromise proposal in early 2013.

- **FDIC chair Martin Gruenberg:** Gruenberg remains FDIC chair as of this writing, receiving Senate confirmation on November 15, 2012, for a five-year term. As is described on the FDIC's website, Gruenberg served as acting chair from July 2011 to November 2012 and also from November 2005 to June 2006. He came to the FDIC from top staff positions on Capitol Hill working for Senator Paul S. Sarbanes (D-MD) and on the staff of the Senate Committee on Banking, Housing, and Urban Affairs. As with many political appointees from the Hill that I knew, Gruenberg sat back and kept quiet in the regulatory meetings I attended.

- **Bobby Bean:** On the other hand, Bobby Bean, who was Gruenberg's staffer, had his sleeves rolled up at every meeting and wasn't afraid to push the FDIC's agenda including making banks formally commit to having a Volcker Rule compliance program. Meeting with Fed officials was like visiting the White House with the embossed chocolates, the waiter service, the map room, and the official photographer. When you sat down with the FDIC, these guys came across more like street brawlers or hard-bitten fraud investigators. They weren't in the Beltway bubble. Their mission was to protect the savings of everyday people who used community and regional banks. Their targets were struggling banks. When a local bank was in financial trouble, the FDIC knew how to shut it down over a weekend and make sure it was open under new management for customers on Monday. Bobby was a genial southerner well known for his love of fried chicken, and during negotiations of the rule, SEC staff were able to lure Bobby to the SEC's building over by Union Station by serving Bojangles' chicken that was sold at a counter in the train station. (That's how desperate the process could be!)

- **Commodities Futures Trading Commission chair Gary Gensler:** Known as a driven, meticulous micromanager with big public-service ambitions, Gensler was not your typical agency head. A superliberal Obama and Clinton supporter, Gensler made partner at Goldman Sachs at the age of 30, joined the U.S. Treasury at the age of 40, and eventually became undersecretary of the Treasury. He also tragically lost his wife to cancer in 2006, making his public service all the more admirable. Slight of frame and slender, Gensler liked running marathons—good training for making public policy. Gensler fought hard to make sure Dodd-Frank had sharp-enough teeth, and he was credited with making the CFTC a player in national policy.[7] He was a force of nature to tangle with in debates, but I believe I held my own.

- **Comptroller of the Currency, Thomas Curry:** The OCC administers the federal banking system; this includes over 1,600 national banks and federal savings associations. During the fall of 2012, Curry took part in a number of agency head meetings to move Volcker forward, but substantial progress didn't begin until 2013. He mostly kept his head down and let staffers advocate for OCC positions. I didn't find Curry rolling up his sleeves on Volcker again until the negotiations were further along in 2013.

Now that we know the lead players, let's find out what happened.

My behind-the-scenes battle forging agreement on the Volcker Rule encapsulated so much of what I learned about going public since I started at the SEC. John Ramsay and I tried to prevent the Volcker

Rule from doing too much damage to the SEC's regulatory architecture for broker-dealers and private funds. First I was outmaneuvered by the consummate career bureaucrat. Then the secretary of the Treasury blasted through the passive resistance with his orders. Now with the call to action, I soon found myself in the bureaucratic ivory tower of bickering and debating over esoteric details such as what size banks the rule would cover or what types of private funds the banks would be prevented from owning. Then when I couldn't take it anymore, a few of us including the secretary of the Treasury smashed the ivory tower and freed the staff to begin serious work on a real deadline for a final compromise. It produced the moment when our messy government reaches a result. Finally, the leaders take over the precooked agreement, iron out their final differences, get the credit, and take it to the public.

MEETING OZ AT THE FED

Soon after I was brought into the Volcker Rule meetings in 2012, I sat down with Scott Alvarez for the first time. It felt more like meeting the Fed chair than meeting the actual Fed chair, which I'd done many times over the years. As I mentioned above, Alvarez had been general counsel of the Fed for more than 20 years. His office was larger than that of the SEC commissioners, with a huge desk, white couch, real fireplace, luxurious red carpet, and oak bookcases.

Scott always looked great—thin, fit, and energetic. He writes the minutes of the Fed's Open Market Committee meetings, which are closely watched by the entire world for hints on U.S. interest rate policy.

If you don't know much about how the Fed works, it goes like this. In brief, the president appoints and the Senate confirms seven members of the Federal Reserve Board of Governors who each serve a 14-year term. The United States is divided into 12 Federal Reserve Districts. Only one Board member may be selected from any one of the Districts. The president must by law make appointments that select a "fair representation of the financial, agricultural, industrial, and commercial interests and geographical divisions of the country."[8]

The seven Board members make up a majority of the 12-member Federal Open Market Committee (FOMC), the group that sets interest rates and makes other decisions affecting the cost and availability of money and credit. The five other members of the Open Market Committee are the regional Federal Reserve Bank presidents, one of whom is the president of the Federal Reserve Bank of New York. The other bank presidents serve one-year terms on a rotating basis.[9]

At Fed meetings, Alvarez was in charge of the minutes. He wrote them line by line. He exerted total control of this document that has such impact on the financial markets. If you go on the Fed website, it lists something like 12 lawyers in Scott's office. But no one else ever came to a meeting. I didn't meet anyone who was Scott's deputy with authority to represent him when he wasn't available.

When we went to a meeting, it was always Scott. When we needed to schedule a meeting, it was always Scott. Everything ran through Scott to the extent that his power spawned a phrase around the federal government called "OSD," meaning "on Scott's desk." If something is not happening and you can't get an answer from the Fed people, the problem is likely OSD. Scott didn't delegate much that I noticed. Every time FOMC had federal Open Market Committee meetings to talk about interest rates, he was buried for a week or two. He had to get ready, he went to the meeting, he wrote the minutes, and then they had to be published and distributed. So we regularly had blackout periods where we couldn't move an inch without Scott.

I'd kid him about his juice with the Fed, where I'd say something like, "Can we meet next week?"

He would say, "No, Open Market Committee." Then I'd respond, "Scott can you tell me, are you guys going to raise interest rates? It would be great to know ahead of time." He'd shoot me a quizzical, are-you-nuts? kind of look. Scott was a nice guy, very courteous in a way that many power bureaucrats were not. He was a gentleman who was willing to listen. I believe that's a major reason he survived at the Fed for more than 20 years.

The first big issue I tackled with Scott during the fall of 2012 had to do with a Volcker Rule requirement that was a controversy among Congress, financial regulators, and industry people but was utterly unknown anywhere else in the entire universe. Remember that Dodd-Frank required IM to take part in the Volcker Rule because Congress essentially said, "Hey banks, you can't do risky trades and endanger your principal in ways you did before the crash. You can't act like a trader with government-insured money. Nor can you circumvent this by shifting your investments to hedge and private equity funds that take these same risks in their investing strategy." Now, here's where it gets pretty wonky. Beginning in the 1980s, Congress began passing exemptions for hedge funds and private equity funds (until then these funds were really and truly private operations and not well known at all) that said, "OK, you can have more investors (the old limit was 100 per strategy) if you meet certain conditions" that included the investable assets of investors and other criteria.

Over the decades, as private funds became more popular, Congress kept adding exemptions over the years and labeled these structures 3(c)1, 3(c)7, 3(c)6, 3(c)5, and so on. Think of it like a local government setting rules on how folks build home extensions to preserve local character and sight lines for neighboring homes. The local government might pass zoning rules that say, "OK, you can't have an extension that's more than one-quarter of the size of the existing house," and then it passes exemptions allowing a larger extension, such as if your surrounding property is of a certain size, or you build some of it underground, or your architect is Michael Graves.

Many of us in IM were concerned that the narrow definition of private funds used in the Volcker Rule (it defined private funds as those organized under just *two* of the many exemptions) would encourage banks and fund managers to evade the rule by forming fund vehicles under exemptions other than these two, another instance of a law leading to unintended consequences that undo its very intent! (Sure enough, even before the rule was adopted, Goldman Sachs and others formed funds called business development companies that were perfectly legal because the private fund definition was so narrow.)[10]

The Volcker team at the SEC didn't like the "covered funds" provision because it limited banks' investment in two of these exempted funds and not the others. My colleagues and I knew exactly what would happen. Private fund managers can work around federal rules on structure. They can do that all day and all night long if they have to. They're like surgeons with appendectomies. They can tweak their operating rules to get around structure with their eyes closed. At the SEC, some of us thought it would work much better to prohibit banks from using funds that deploy certain types of *investing strategies*. Private funds aren't going to change their *core investing philosophy* too easily. So, for example, the Volcker Rule could prohibit banks from investing in hedge and private equity funds that have more than 10 percent of their assets invested in collateralized debt obligations and other asset-backed securities (these CDO types of investments were the ones betting on tranches of real estate debt, and most collapsed in the 2008 crash).

I made this argument to Scott.

In his mellifluous, voice, he said, "That is OK with me, Norm. The only problem is that you have to get the FDIC to go along."

By shoveling me off to the FDIC, the tough-as-nails G-men types who love to crack down on banks and *hated* watering down the Volcker Rule, he knew I wouldn't get anywhere but he wouldn't have to say no to this new guy from the SEC he barely knew. The good part of the story is that I got into the mix early with the FDIC folks and we got to know each other. (We eventually got some of what we wanted when the final rule was passed in 2013, but the narrow definition of private funds stayed.)

I joined other senior staff from the Volcker agencies in a few meetings during the final months of 2012, but we needed more direction about what was truly important. The months wore on, and the meetings were going in circles debating a lot of arcane stuff like the cutoff point for the size of banks that would be subject to Volcker.

The truth is, for the SEC the Volcker stakes were higher. The rules we pass have to be submitted for comment to the public where they get commented on by financial industry types, academics, media, powerful lobbyists, and even Congress. For the FDIC, the OCC, and the Federal Reserve, they write a rule and vote on it internally and that's it (I'm generalizing a bit, but that's the idea). The banking bureaucrats were accustomed to making up regulations along the way.

THE LEW IMPERATIVE

On February 28, 2013, President Obama held the ceremony swearing Jack Lew into office as the successor to Timothy Geithner as U.S. Secretary of the Treasury. That same day[11] the FSOC principals of agencies working on Volcker were called to a meeting in the Treasury secretary's office. Elisse Walter was the chair at the time. She headed over before Ramsay and I, because first there was a full FSOC meeting of the heads of all 10 FSOC agencies. John and I arrived at Treasury, were cleared at the guard booth outside, went inside through the metal detectors, headed up the ornate marble stairway, and met an assistant who ushered us into the secretary's private conference room. Alvarez, myself, and a few other staffers were crowded into the chairs against the wall, balancing our bottles of water, computers, and notepads on our laps. The Volcker principals arrayed around the table: Fed chair Bernanke (Yellen was sworn in early in 2014), Fed governor Daniel Tarullo (the Fed's most engaged governor on these issues), Treasury's undersecretary for domestic finance Mary Miller (who became a major staff player in the Volcker group meetings), Martin Gruenberg, Thomas Curry, Gary Gensler, and Elisse Walter.

Secretary Lew walked in and introduced himself and made some friendly chatter around the table. He bared a half-friendly, half-menacing smile under his owlish glasses.

Lew called the meeting to order and said this Volcker thing had dragged on way too long. He pointed out he had just come over here from the White House, and intended to get going on Volcker. The basic message was "the statute appoints me the shepherd dog for this project, and you people have got to get your butts in gear."

So Bernanke called up Alvarez to the adults' table. I'll admit I was glad I wasn't the one on the spot. Alvarez wasted no time spinning the secretary a fanciful timetable.

"Well, you know, the rule was put out for proposal in 2011," I remember Alvarez said. "The working group has had several meetings over the last few months. We should be able to get this done by the summer, like maybe June or July."

I literally almost fell out of my seat right there in front of the secretary. We couldn't meet that deadline under any circumstances. It had taken two years to get to this point, and we hadn't talked about one substantive issue in what ended up as almost a thousand-page rule with this working group or the principals. I had a better chance of flying to the moon than our finishing the Volcker Rule by June.

But respectfully Alvarez outmaneuvered the whole group. He couldn't say to Lew that it's going to take a year; he couldn't blame the rest of us publicly. But by giving the secretary a public commitment to an unachievable date, he ensured we'd all share the blame when we failed to meet the schedule. Or perhaps his experience with Fed rule making (the governors apparently vote by e-mail based on the recommendation of the governor leading the project) gave him no sense of what it would take to get five federal agencies to agree on a rule.

For the SEC and CFTC, we don't tell our regulated industry, "Oh this is what you do; have fun with that." We have to get comments, we have to have the commissioners agree and vote on it. Ramsay and I just stared at each other with "Can you believe it?" faces. We looked at Scott and then around at other staff, who were looking back at us. It's quiet. The air is heavy in there. We just wanted to get out of there and start working.

Then the secretary asked Scott for the next steps in the process. Scott said that the staff will continue to meet and will give a progress report at the next FSOC meeting if not sooner. Secretary Lew thanked Scott and wrapped up the meeting.

PICKLE IN THE MIDDLE

As the Vocker principals' meeting broke up, I chatted with other staffers in the hallway, and we agreed to a series of conference calls to start identifying key issues. Some people seemed less concerned about the July deadline than others, a response that started to make more sense to me as the negotiations continued. Many smart and dedicated public servants at the SEC became entangled in the Volcker talks and did heroic work. It was a time when the SEC worked together effectively as a team because we all knew that the Fed and Treasury could write a bad rule and make our lives miserable in the process.

A key ally in this battle: John Ramsay, who not only was a pleasure to work with but fought hard to keep the negotiations moving toward an actual resolution. John has a dramatic shock of white hair and Elvis Costello–style black glasses that make him look a little eccentric, but he is a smart and practical guy.

A lawyer named Dan Townley had contacted me in the summer of 2012 just after I took over IM about coming aboard at the SEC as a change of pace after more than 20 years at Davis Polk, my old law firm. I could have jumped through the phone to hug him. A lawyer with his knowledge of investment management and experience in getting things done? Someone I knew and respected? We hired Dan as part of an SEC attorney fellow program, which, since the position lasted four years max, allowed us to get around the laborious hiring procedures at the SEC.

Dan's work became a blessing to me personally. Far more important, he performed the bureaucratic equivalent of the 12 labors of Hercules to make the Volcker Rule better for investors. Dan sat right next to me in New York and worked like a madman, calling on all his experience to push Volcker over the finish line.

Of all the people I met at the SEC, the one I worked most closely with was Diane Blizzard, the IM head of Rulemaking. With the title of associate director of the Rulemaking Office, Diane supervised two offices (one for public mutual funds and one for private funds) that developed recommendations for rule making and other policy initiatives. Her mastery of policy and her ability to use data analysis in the context of changing economic and political events became a game changer during our stealth warfare with the Fed and Treasury over Volcker and FSOC's power grab to designate asset management firms as systemically significant. She more than held her own with lawyers and accountants from these agencies.

These two players among others at the SEC helped keep me sane during the next few months after our meeting with Lew. We proceeded to a series of conference calls with the Volcker agencies that made little progress. It was troubling to the SEC and CFTC staffers, who wanted to put the rule out for public comment, that the Fed might be holding back because its process allowed it to write what it wanted and pass it by e-mails from the governors. We could tell from conversations that there must have been drafts of parts of the rule, but the bank regulators weren't sharing them.

And we had some big worries about Volcker. Congress's broad outline of the rule limited purchases of securities on the part of "banks" because these banks got caught holding massive amounts of collateralized mortgage obligations and other complex instruments when the markets crashed in 2008. All of a sudden bank balance sheets looked a lot worse, and some banks needed to sell equity to the government to survive. But bonds and other securities represented a massive chunk of the investing economy. This isn't something to get wrong. Broker-dealers within the big banks needed to buy bonds for their clients. They needed to have the bonds to make markets. But now that Goldman Sachs and the rest were banks, they couldn't operate the same way. We negotiated so that brokers in the banks could buy securities if they were held to meet "reasonably expected customer demand."

We also had to address what to do about banks holding trusts-preferred securities (TruPS). These are not your daddy's blue-chip stocks for sure. They create a trust, issue debt to the trust, and then issue preferred securities from the trust to investors. Banks like them for accounting purposes, as they're treated as capital for regulatory compliance purposes.

The FDIC was on fire to ban banks from holding these. We had our corporation finance people look at the draft language, and they pointed out that if you do this, you are going to kill the market. If you suddenly say that the banks can't hold these, the value of the securities will plummet because all the banks will try to sell them at the same time! The SEC's Corporation Finance division accurately predicted that if you ban banks from holding TruPS, those securities are going to collapse and take the banks with them.

But the secrecy and lack of urgency we sensed among our banking regulator brethren made me feel more and more like the kid playing pickle in the middle. The Treasury, FDIC, and OCC seemed content to let the Fed have the pen in revising the proposal to be the final rule. They wouldn't commit to much, which sure read to many of us that they were keeping their options open for their final draft. That raised a number of problems including the truth that apparently only one lawyer could do anything at the Fed. That was Scott. We thought at the time that Scott had some people somewhere helping revise language, but it all had to pass through Scott. Volcker was OSD because Scott had to go to Fed interest rate meetings. He had to go to our meetings. He was never at his desk. I will say one thing. The guy worked hard. He was in control of all the issues, and that must have been another reason he survived for so long at the Fed.

Meanwhile, Diane was trying desperately to get all this stuff done, as she was the lead rule writer in IM. Townley was running down all kinds of issues from his new desk. But soon April arrived, and we didn't have much progress to show, and there was a new FSOC meeting coming up with Secretary Lew. Mary Jo White was sworn in as the new SEC chair on April 10, 2013.

I was thrilled to be working with White, one of the most respected and accomplished prosecutors and private attorneys of the last 20-plus years. She was also a leader. White specialized in prosecuting securities fraud and international terrorism cases as the U.S. attorney for the Southern District of New York from 1993 to 2002 (beginning just after I clerked there for Judge Haight). As her bio notes, "under her leadership, the office earned convictions against the terrorists responsible for the 1993 bombing of the World Trade Center and the bombings of American embassies in Africa."[12]

MARY JO WHITE GETS IN THE GAME

So by April we had a new boss. We had Jack Lew scheduling a meeting on April 25,[13] and many of us were still stuck playing in the middle wondering if we'd ever get the ball. Once again John Ramsay and I headed over to Treasury for the meeting on April 25. The principals of the Volcker agencies met in Lew's private conference room, and Lew reiterated that he wanted this Volcker Rule done.

As Ramsay, Mary Jo, and I left the room, she offered us a ride with her back to the SEC. We agreed of course. We left the building via the secretary's private elevator (only one of two times I rode it), which, after you exit a side door, empties you out facing the side entrance to the White House. We got in the car where we got to talk and get to know each other a little bit. She was always incredibly nice to me. She remarked that people on both the left and the right had told her good things about me, saying something along the lines of "I am not sure how you pulled that off."

Even better, Mary Jo agreed that the Volcker discussions weren't getting anywhere. She knew that Lew (and therefore the president of the United States) would become increasingly impatient. I explained how we thought the banking regulators were protecting their own draft.

Mary Jo essentially said she had our back to try to force this process out into the open.

On one of our next calls with the staffers, I made my move.

"When are we going to get to look at something?" I asked the banking regulators. "You guys say you are in charge of running the proposal. It's time to share! If you guys have a polished draft, maybe that's why you were telling the secretary that you could make July. We don't want to be blindsided again."

Next I called Scott.

"Scott," I said. "I don't think this is happening by summer, number one. Number two, we have got to stop having a dial-in once a week where people wander in and out, argue for a minute, and go back to reading their e-mail."

"We need a schedule," I said. "We need meetings in person. We need to get in rooms and start hashing it out. The Treasury secretary is telling us to get it done. I don't really agree with that, but if that is what it is and that is what is going to happen, then we've got to start moving. We have to start treating this like a corporate deal with a deadline. I don't want to go up there and have the Treasury secretary yelling at us. He is mad. He wants the thing moving."

"Scott," I said, "let's get in a room with your draft to look at. You control it; that's fine. But we need to sit there, we need to hash out the problems, and we need to make a list of what the issues are. If there are a thousand issues, let's start with number one and start crossing them off the list. Then when we get that list down to a shorter form, we can present this to the principals."

Many of my colleagues hadn't worked in the private sector on huge projects, but that's how I cut my teeth in private practice and the hedge fund world. Finally, we scheduled a more intensive series of working sessions to identify the big points, created a timeline, held feet to the fire, and ultimately made Volcker happen.

By the summer of 2013 we started hashing out details. We actually started looking at drafts. By July we had produced at least a partial joint draft with input from the SEC, the CFTC, the OCC, and the FDIC.

But at the FSOC meeting on July 16,[14] Lew said something to the effect of, "Well, you said June or July and here we are in July." He did thank us for the new intensity behind our push and asked for a Labor Day deadline. After all our hard work, the group had an easier time speaking up and setting a realistic deadline of October. Lew seemed comfortable with it.

As our work continued, the SEC remained worried about only limiting the banks' ability to invest in funds formed under the exceptions of 3(c)1 and 3(c)7 that I described earlier. Our team, including Mary Jo, argued that writing the rule this way would encourage banks and fund managers to restructure their operations to create funds that don't rely on those exceptions but rely on other exception not covered by the Volcker Rule. Admittedly this was selfish. It would have put enormous pressure on the SEC, which lacked the resources to police all the funds that would get created to comply with other exceptions. Would they really meet the criteria for those other exceptions? Who would check? Earlier in the year Goldman Sachs had formed a business development company that relied on one of the exceptions that was not 3(c)1 or 3(c)7, as this was permitted under the Volcker Rule. This seemed to be an effort to restructure trading activities into a kind of fund that the Volcker Rule still let the banks invest in. It might not have been a 3(c)1 or 3(c)7 fund limited by Volcker, but it certainly could take a lot of risk on debt securities. Despite this being just the kind of work-around that allowed the biggest banks to take just the kind of proprietary risks Volcker sought to prohibit, this example wasn't enough to change my colleagues' minds.

Overall, by October the group was moving, getting through a lot of our issues. The principals got more involved, and we started having meetings with them with the more complete draft language and lists of open issues. I could see by this point that I wouldn't get everything I wanted in the rule, but by late 2013 (one year after we started) I knew that it was going to be passed and that it was going to be promulgated to the industry, at least ending the uncertainty.

When I briefed the commissioners, Troy Paredes and Dan Gallagher weren't interested. They saw the whole thing as political and not a substantive SEC concern. I kept the Democrats Elisse Walter and Luis Aguilar up to date, but Walter and Paredes were leaving by the end of the summer, as their terms were expiring.

Obama nominated Kara Stein and Mike Piwowar to replace them (one Democrat, one Republican), and they were confirmed and sworn in during early August. They arrived as Volcker was reaching its final stages. They knew it was a high-profile issue.

They really also represented a major change, because they were both former Senate staffers trained and wired to see these issues politically—to advance their respective parties' ideas and agendas. They came into the SEC with preconceived notions. It's true that someone who has been in the industry will also have preconceived notions. It's true that we all have preconceived notions. But Stein and Piwowar had different preconceived notions more based on politics that were new to the commissioners' offices, because the vast majority of commissioners were from industry or the law.

Kara Stein was all in for Volcker and wanted it as strong as possible, while Piwowar didn't want it at all, so he wasn't going to vote for it no matter what we did. Piwowar had more investing industry experience, both because he'd been at the SEC and because he was an experienced economist. On the flip side, he was coming straight off the Hill, and so was Kara Stein. It was fascinating. Stein worked on Dodd-Frank, and she helped out on a Senate hearing on how terrible ETFs were. Piwowar never had supported much of Dodd-Frank.

While getting them briefed was different because they didn't have the background in the industry, I found it fascinating to watch two people with political backgrounds at work. I love watching politicians and political people and I learned a lot from both of them. They came to the SEC with agendas they wanted to fulfill, with a different bent than I had seen in other commissioners. Piwowar's walk-away position amounted to, "Well, I'm not voting for that." While Stein's was, "Oh yes, no risk taking by the banks; we've got a terrible Wall Street; we have to make sure it's all buttoned up." So as we worked day to day, hour to hour, and then minute to minute to finish Volcker by late October, I briefed these commissioners and particularly Stein, because in the end Chair White is going to need her vote to pass it.

During this year of Volcker and FSOC, the Republicans in Congress were threatening a government shutdown. (It's also a fascinating side note to the story that after the GOP won huge landslide margins in the House of Representatives in 2010, we never got much pressure from the House to move Dodd-Frank rules or the Volcker Rule forward. Our little drama played out in the executive agencies, unlike the Bernie Madoff and Stanford days when the blasts of political heat from the Hill made everyone at the SEC dance faster.)

When the Volcker agencies met again on September 30 after an FSOC meeting in Lew's conference room, the principals agreed to add a Volcker Rule compliance program for banks, a program supported by the FDIC's Bobby Bean.[15] At the September meeting, Jack Lew charged us to finish the rule as soon as possible. Most of us agreed with the secretary. We were exhausted, as well. We'd negotiated solutions to hundreds of issues.

At the last minute, the two most powerful Democrats, Gensler and Stein, pushed for more changes including provisions that further clamped down on the extent to which banks could invest on behalf of clients. Stein circulated a document outlining dozens of changes she wanted. I didn't agree with many of them, of course, but Mary Jo, Ramsay, and I did everything we could to accommodate her.[16] I understood why the media at the time highlighted Gensler's and Stein's role in further "toughening" the final rule, but in reality their last-minute efforts affected just a few isolated provisions. Ultimately, this was a Democratic bill pushed by a Democratic Congress and a Democratic president, and for better or worse it reflected their priorities.

On December 10 the banking agencies signed off, and at the SEC Stein, Aguilar, and White provided the three yes votes. We held a gaggle with the media after the vote and then started briefing members on the Hill where they were already getting blowback from the banks in their districts about the TruPS ban. We were in our first day of briefings on the Hill after the rule was passed, and a Hill staffer raised his hand and called out, "Hey, we heard that you're not allowing banks to hold TRuPS, and what's the story with that?"

That's the final, final ironic twist to the saga.

What do we know about any good deed done by government with the best of intentions? There's always collateral damage. As soon as the rule passed and during the 2013 holidays, banks all across America grew more and more alarmed about the TruPS provision because the banks already owned billions of dollars of them. If the banks had to sell all these TruPS immediately, the price of TruPS would plunge, and the lower value of the securities would reduce their required bank capital to a level that might violate Fed rules. The SEC with the Fed, FDIC, and Treasury shifted into crisis mode, and I was in the thick of it. I worked every day of the 2013 holidays except Christmas and New Year's Day. My family had a hard time understanding how the "work-life balance" offered by the government meant working nonstop over Christmas break. (Fortunately I was already staying in town with one of my sons, who was in the Nutcracker at Lincoln Center, while Sally took the other kids on a trip.) By early January the rule was revised to permit banks to gradually decrease TruPS holdings over time, and everybody got some rest.

Later on in the spring of 2014, when we were back over at Treasury for some discussion about money market funds, I got a chance to talk to Lew. I told the secretary that his leadership was appreciated and definitely what got us kick-started. Even though I wasn't in favor of the Volcker Rule, I said, I was favorable to how he managed the process.

REPORT CARD

Begin—to begin is half the work, let half still remain; again begin this, and thou wilt have finished.

—Marcus Aurelius

On March 6, 2014, I attended a conference at the Practicing Law Institute in New York. I was sitting in the faculty room right off the main conference room at a rectangular table with pitchers of ice water, waiting in the wings for my turn to speak. As IM director I had to speak about once a month at various industry events, which I always enjoyed. Five years earlier I spoke at a PLI conference and had my fateful lunch with Tom Biolsi. Tom died in 2013 at age 57 from cancer, and I always thought of him when I found myself at PLI (although now in a different location). Then Paul Roye, an old lawyer friend and one of my predecessors who had been so helpful, walked in and joined me.

He stopped. "Norm! Great to see you. How are you?"

"Great, still with the SEC and IM, speaking in a little while."

He noted that I had been there for years and asked if it was driving me crazy.

"Most days, but it's still a great job; you know that firsthand. Director of IM? It's been exciting."

"Have you been able to change anything?"

I paused. It was a funny question you didn't hear in the private sector. Memories of the past four-plus years fast-forwarded, a blurry newsreel in my head.

I jerked my thumb over my shoulder and then shook his hand. "I have to get inside. Stay for the speech. You'll get some answers."

Paul thanked me for sticking with it as long as I had.

While those of us at the SEC had to live with the grim reputation of 2008 stamped on the agency in the minds of many, by 2014 I was giving speeches with a lot of good news. Under three terrific leaders, we had started to close the SEC's credibility gap with the media, Treasury, and the Fed. We had broomed out a lot of the bureaucratic cobwebs, put people in better jobs, got closer to industry trends, fixed the worst of the tech problems, and started turning paper files into searchable data. We now had set a more modern direction that could be sustained for more than a couple of years. As I thought further about Paul's question, I realized that so many talented and motivated people in Exam and IM had worked hard to change the agency for the better.

PRESERVING MARKET INTEGRITY

Remember FSOC? As 2014 turned to late summer, the SEC turned back the last gasps by the bureaucrats at FSOC to control the fate of mutual funds and other bulwarks of personal investing. We successfully asserted the SEC's leadership as the primary regulator for the asset management industry and managed to prevail against FSOC's effort to designate any fund or broker it chose as "systemically significant"—that is, have the Fed crawling all over a business it doesn't really understand.[1] However, as recently as April 2016, FSOC continued its quest to regulate "activities" of asset managers (as opposed to designating firms) by looking at private fund leverage.[2] The advent of a Trump administration seems likely to quiet down the FSOC considerably.

Many meetings with the FSOC folks left me feeling frustrated that they so cavalierly ignored the Investment Company Act and Investment Advisers Act signed into law by Franklin Roosevelt, both of which had worked exceptionally well since 1940. FDR had announced to the world his hope that the law would enable the asset management industry "to fulfill its basic purpose as a vehicle to diversify the small investors' risk."[3] With the success of the mutual fund industry for the middle class, particularly in retirement funds, it certainly accomplished that goal. That history didn't curb FSOC's appetite for designating new firms.

Many of us at the SEC could relate to the classic story about FDR's friend, Winston Churchill. Once Churchill walked into the men's room in Parliament to find Clement Attlee, leader of the Labour Party, relieving himself at the marble trough urinals. Churchill took a position at the other end.

"Feeling standoffish today, are we, Winston?" Attlee asked.

"That's right," Churchill responded. "Every time you Socialists see something big, you want to nationalize it."[4]

Mary Jo White was our Churchill during that year of living dangerously with the FSOC takeover. She spoke publicly about why the SEC has the authority and expertise to monitor, address, and enforce systemic risk issues posed by asset managers. Because IM had started our Risk and Exam Office led by Jon Hertzke, we backed up her arguments with credible analysis that punched holes in FSOC's assertions. Fortunately, we had already put the Risk and Exam Office (which we referred to as "REO") up on its feet before the FSOC takeover got much momentum. I remember talking to Ken O'Connor, now one of the REO stalwarts, about this in the fall of 2014.

"We ended up really needing the REO," he said to me. "How did you ever have the vision to do that?"

"We needed it; that's all I knew," I said. "The timing was lucky. I never thought they'd come gunning for us. Thank goodness we dissuaded them."

By upgrading data collection and analysis, we made sure the SEC had the tools that would help it keep up with the future fraudsters of America. Mary Jo White placed the capstone on these reforms in May 2015 when the SEC formally released proposed rules that required a fund to submit information on a fund's risk profile, explanations of how it calculated fund performance, and more transparent communications. The SEC adopted these rules in October 2016 and they go into effect in 2018 and 2019.

"These recommendations will vastly improve the type and format of the information that funds provide to the Commission and to investors," Mary Jo announced on May 20, 2015.[5] "Investors will have better quality and greater access to information about their fund investments and investment advisers, and the SEC will have more and better information to monitor risks in the asset management industry." I'd left the SEC a few months before, but the chair and the commissioners were kind enough to acknowledge my role in starting these proposals on their way while I was the director of IM,[6] although the real credit goes to David Grim, Sara Cortes, Diane Blizzard, and all the talented IM rule makers.

NOT MAKING UP OUR RULES

As part of how we dragged the SEC into the twenty-first century, I also worked with the associates at IM to end our ad hoc approach to rule making. For decades, the SEC wrote and published rules because the commissioners or one of the IM directors decided it was a good idea. There needed to be more due diligence and analysis.

Early on in my tenure, IM instituted a four-factor approach to analyzing policy initiatives, and we asked leaders to vote on rules based on the following four criteria:

1. Review the risk or risks to be mitigated by the proposed rule making. The commission and division are built on the fundamental principle of protecting investors.
2. Consider the urgency associated with a particular initiative.
3. Analyze the potential impact of an initiative on investors, registrants, capital formation, efficient markets, and the division's and the commission's operational efficiency.
4. Review the available resources associated with a policy initiative or freed up by the initiative.[7]

With this process in place, IM could provide SEC leaders like the chair and commissioners with a coherent rationale for putting forth a new rule. The more the SEC made itself transparent this way, the less leverage the FSOCers had.

We memorialized how IM operated in an IM manual issued in early 2014 that laid out the division's mission and described how IM would carry out that mission. Superstaffers like Parisa Haghshenas worked hard to document the roles and structures of the various IM offices so that all staff new or old had a place to look for guidance on how to do their jobs.

ENGAGEMENT

But for all my misgivings about the power of the Fed and FSOC, by the wrap-up of the money market fund and asset management clashes, we had gotten the bank regulators' attention and started to consult more frequently with the Fed. Because the SEC speaks for investors, having the chance to regularly brief the Fed about market issues was great news overall for the American people.

By mid-2014 IM's leaders—including Diane Blizzard, Jennifer McHugh, Dave Grim, me, and many others—were meeting regularly with Fed analysts and economists to compare our intelligence on market and investing trends. The first briefing covered leverage and occurred at the Fed. We even persuaded the Fed to bring its asset management experts located in Boston whom we hadn't even met. I remember the Fed players seeming a bit stiff and formal as we showed them data on leverage used by funds to help achieve investment results for their investors. As we left, we walked a couple of blocks to a cabstand near another federal agency. As we all climbed into cabs to go back to the office, Jennifer McHugh, a longtime IM staffer and my invaluable senior advisor on policy, remarked that the SEC hadn't ever before had that kind of contact with Fed leaders.

The next briefing took place at our shop, and we explained securities lending because some elements of FSOC worried about the incredibly routine practice. We of course could offer no coffee or tea in our conference rooms as we had no budget for it. (I once requisitioned a water pitcher for the main IM conference room, but the bureaucrats let me know that was not allowed!) Nonetheless, commission staff continued working together with the Fed and Treasury on answering questions both on technical issues relating to Volcker and on supervision and examination issues.

We also implemented our new senior engagement program of meeting with the senior management and boards of top mutual and hedge funds and large multiservice financial services firms like Goldman Sachs. Remember when my friends liked to have off-the-record visits to funds but wouldn't share any of its insights with me, even though it couldn't be more obvious that doing so was the letter and spirit of the law? Not only did Carlo and I start our own engagement program at Exam, but once I got to IM, we incorporated IM staff into the effort. We had 8 to 10 sit-downs a year with the likes of Lloyd Blankfein and James Gorman. We had frank, open conversations. SEC lawyers like Aaron Schlaphoff and others wrote reports on each visit and compiled our insights to be shared regularly with commissioners and SEC senior staff. This made a fantastic resource for anyone meeting with an executive from the industry or informing Congress about trends.

I was discussing this program early in 2014 with a friend from several battles at the SEC, and mentioned that part of the motivation was because the well-meaning Trading and Markets guys wouldn't share their notes with me no matter how nicely I asked.

"Their boss told them to put these visits down in writing or discontinue the program," I said. "And he told me he shut it down when they didn't produce reports."

"Hmm, not sure about that," this person said.

Huh? What?! A familiar frustration began to burn.

I have seen their reports around the office, my friend told me. My friend believed they prepared reports but kept them confidential.

Ergh. I was so ticked off. And dismayed. Maybe there really were written reports, but no one would share them with us. You can't have the SEC holding off-the-record meetings with the industry! Ever! Is it off the record if you write the memo but no one ever knows about it? If the tree falls in the forest and starts an avalanche that crushes you in your car, it did fall in the forest, didn't it? Think how much more we could have accomplished by sharing data. I'm not sure what the truth is about the reports, but I certainly never saw any.

I needed to let go, though. I didn't have any leverage. I also knew IM was better off having its senior-level engagement program, and I was proud of how well our reports were received. We used our observations in the senior-level engagements to go back to firms and learn more about issues we wanted to address with policy steps. For instance, one firm we visited did its own stress tests, so I sent the IM rule makers back afterward to talk to the people there about what they did as we thought about how to implement stress tests required by Dodd-Frank.

I was also proud of many of the good hires I made during my tenure, including more than 60 new people in IM. I'd hired two analysts for the IM Risk and Exam Office who held PhDs, one in physics and one in neuroscience. These quants turned out to be quite skilled at sorting through the large amounts of data collected by IM. We were also able to place many of our IM stars in great jobs around the commission, including Brent Fields who became secretary of the SEC. Mary Jo White promoted Drew Bowden, who replaced me as deputy director of Exam, to head of Exam. Not long after I left the SEC, Exam hired Jennifer Duggins, my old chief compliance officer at Chilton, to help with exams of private funds.

What about some of the other players from the post-2008 crisis? The courageous Stanford whistle-blower Julie Preuitt was returned to her position as assistant regional director of the Fort Worth, Texas, office. Despite testifying about the SEC before Congress, she loved her work and wanted to spend the rest of her career in service of the commission.* We got her back focused on fraudulent oil and gas partnerships sold by shady broker-dealers, where she had a real talent for finding wrongdoing.

The always-clutch Diane Blizzard continues as head of rule making at IM as of this writing, where she is ably assisted by Sarah ten Siethoff and now Sara Cortes whom we got from Chair Walter's staff.

Erozan Kurtas, the first analytics quant we hired at Exam, left the SEC and as of 2017 works as senior vice president and head of advanced data analytics at FINRA.

My great friend Carlo di Florio now works at FINRA in 2017 as well, serving as the chief risk officer and head of strategy.

I don't know FINRA's CEO Richard Ketchum very well, but I'll say this: he had a fantastic eye for talent. Ketchum retired at the end of 2016, and his replacement is Robert Cook, who headed Trading and Markets when I first became director of IM. Robert remains one of the good guys and now returns to a regulatory role.

Mary Schapiro is serving on various boards as of 2017, including as a trustee of her undergraduate alma mater, Franklin and Marshall, and giving the occasional speech.

---

*From Julie's testimony: "Many have asked me why I haven't left the Commission over the course of the last several years. My answer has always been the same. I believe passionately in the mission of the SEC. I am proud to have devoted most of my professional life to the service of the investing public. I have tried to serve with honor and integrity. I am grateful for the many strong relationships I have developed with managers and staff throughout the Commission, which have kept me going through this difficult period. I am proud of the many accomplishments of the examiners and managers with whom I have worked all of these years. I hope I am fortunate enough to spend the remaining part of my career in the service of the Commission."

Of the FSOC gang, Gary Gensler became CFO of Hillary Clinton's campaign; Martin Gruenberg, Thomas Curry, and Jack Lew remained in their posts with Lew leaving at the end of the Obama administration. Under Chair Janet Yellen, Scott Alvarez brushed off a few salvos from Congress and continues to control the paper flow through the Fed.

I count many of these folks as allies and friends, but not everyone misses me, that's for sure.

ABLATION

It wasn't lost on me that the way I did my job meant disrupting some of my colleagues, even forcing some into new positions and taking away responsibilities from others. Some people had left the SEC on my account, and I wasn't an enabler of the folks who used anonymous notes for revenge, wanted service time credit for coming to work 10 minutes early,* or hid behind a fictitious arbitration ruling in order not to find out what telecommuters did all day. But I'd also learned how to compromise with FSOC and the Fed, and I collaborated with the union president Greg Gilman, counsel Ralph Talarico, and steward Pat Copeland who supported our reorganizations of Exam and IM as well as other reforms. When union president Greg Gilman found out I didn't have horns or a forked tail and I realized the same about him, we were able to find common ground. He wanted his people to be happier and better trained in their jobs, and I give him huge credit for that. I don't agree with President Obama about most things, but I do like what he said during a 2016 commencement speech to Howard University, that "democracy requires compromise, even when you're one hundred percent right." I just wish he had followed that maxim occasionally.

Democracy also requires understanding Lincoln's famous point about not making all the people happy all the time. At the end of 2013, I chose medical intervention to deal with my atrial fibrillation,

*One SEC staffer actually had the guts to ask Chair Mary Jo White about this during an SEC town hall meeting.

a long-running condition of irregular heartbeats that was well controlled by a medication that I found difficult to tolerate. I decided on having a surgical *ablation*, which involves a surgeon inserting a wire in your groin and running it up your blood vessel to your heart, where the doctor applies an electric shock to burn and scar the precise area in your heart that is responsible for the A-fib (as it's called), thereby ending my A-fib for the foreseeable future. The procedure worked for me and stabilized my heart so I was no longer in danger of a stroke or rapid heartbeat.

Sometimes an ablation is like what a manager has to do to help heal a larger organization—leaving a few scars where necessary but restoring the larger organism to health.

ANONYMOUS STRIKES BACK

By mid-2014 I had started thinking seriously about what I would do next. I figured I'm likely going to leave. On Wall Street I think I have earned a reputation as an honest and open policy maker who will listen to the industry but also protect investors. Nonetheless, I was still getting anonymous notes about other employees and spending a lot of time doing due diligence.

I look back and wonder if one of the old guard in the New York office served up one dish of revenge when a highly misleading story about my family's farm business receiving subsidies was whipped into a froth by a blogger soon after I joined the SEC. The story included my slightly altered home address and claimed I am a billionaire (which of course is not true). It is awful to think of my family being put in jeopardy by such massive irresponsibility. The story faded away though the IG had to run the traps of an "investigation," which revealed nothing at all to support this claim. Worst of all, this is all too typical of the anonymous leaks and smears that are used to discredit whistle-blowers, reformers, or simply effective public employees who tread on the wrong turf in the SEC and other taxpayer-funded bureaucracies.

PICNIC

By fall 2014, I'm thinking about the timing of my resignation. The year before, we revived the annual picnic IM used to hold for all the staffers in the division. I liked the picnic because it was the rare event that brought everybody—not just one favored group—together to celebrate our work and get out in the sunshine.

In 2014 my assistant Ammani Nagesh found a wonderful park in Virginia where we could reserve a cookout area and had access to a beach volleyball court and football field. Watching staff play Frisbee in the sun and eat food prepared by Janet Grossnickle, a talented and hardworking assistant director who took time from her demanding schedule to cook, was relaxing.

During the picnic, a number of IM staff thanked me for bringing more openness, flexibility, and teamwork to the agency and for encouraging them to take on new challenges and opportunities within the division. I reminded them that Dave Grim, Carolyn Grillo, Pat Copeland, and so many others were the ones who worked to improve the division on top of their day jobs. One veteran staffer asked me how we have been able to attract so much talent to the division to improve its operations, and a couple of visually impaired attorneys thanked me for getting them software that reads e-mails for them. In both cases, Denise Green unstuck the bureaucracy and got job postings up at the same time she made sure software got delivered! More than once I heard about a staffer who wasn't so sure about me in the beginning but came to realize that I meant to put together a team that could improve the division for all employees.

10 POINTS OF PROGRESS

Yes, we'd improved the SEC's capacity to serve the taxpayer and investor by restructuring the division to be faster and more responsive, getting important new reforms off the shelf, bringing the SEC's expertise where it was needed to inform the Fed and FSOC, and engaging top management at the major investment banks and brokerages. In fact, by the end of 2014 the Division of Investment Management could attest to 10 points of progress that occurred on my watch:

1. Strengthened IM's workforce to keep pace with a changing legal and regulatory landscape by hiring new quantitative experts, portfolio managers, economists, and experts in derivatives, ETFs, and money market funds.
2. Expanded IM's collaboration across SEC divisions and with outside stakeholders.
3. Enhanced IM's capacity to monitor and understand risk trends by creating the Risk and Examinations Office.
4. Ramped up and sharpened data gathering and analysis for use in making rules and issuing industry guidance.
5. Provided greater transparency into IM's workings through regular guidance updates and a more user-friendly website.
6. Fostered innovation where appropriate through rule exemptions such as IM's waiver of certain requirements for exchange-traded managed funds, a hybrid of a mutual fund and an ETF.
7. Supported and enforced fund compliance programs passed by the SEC in 2004, including the imperative for funds to hire chief compliance officers and other compliance executives and give them the authority to do their jobs. We made the SEC's support for compliance abundantly clear, for example, when in 2013 the commission brought an enforcement action that resulted in a "portfolio manager being banned from the securities industry for five years for misleading and obstructing a chief compliance officer."[8]
8. Committed to open and constructive communication between the SEC and the industry through the senior-level engagement program, analysis of public comments, and public statements.
9. Instituted an "early warning" approach to protecting U.S. investors by monitoring events—such as geopolitical, natural disaster, and market occurrences—that may impact funds and advisers. When such incidents occur, IM will focus on

maintaining communication with affected asset managers and funds, reviewing disclosures to investors, and assessing the impact on the ability of investors to access funds or trade securities. I'm proud that we changed IM to get out in front of significant industry developments as a key element of our mission of investor protection.

10. Expanded employee recognition awards and incentives to acknowledge outstanding performances by IM staff. At the SEC, as with all other government agencies, management is limited in recognizing outstanding performance financially. Therefore we built on the SEC annual achievement awards by creating IM directors' awards to recognize outstanding contributions by individuals in the division.[9]

MARY JO'S SPEECH

By December 2014, I decided I would give notice soon to the SEC and return to private life. We had accomplished substantial change in Exam and IM, change that many thought impossible. We turned back FSOC's takeover attempts, but the SEC needed to demonstrate the effectiveness of its regulation of asset management. IM worked with the chair's office to develop a set of policy proposals to do just that. With a new slate of policies to develop, I would need to either stay for a couple of more years to work on those proposals or leave and let someone else pick up the baton. I realized that if I left at the end of January 2015, I'd have completed five years at the agency, and that seemed like a logical stopping point.

Mary Jo White was scheduled for a major speech outlining these policies to be held December 11 at One World Trade Center in New York at the Dealbook Opportunities for Tomorrow Conference. I'd worked hard on the ideas for the speech and helped Mary Jo's office with the drafting, and so I planned to meet her there and stay for the speech.

When I showed up early the morning of the speech, I saw that the high-floor conference location at One World Trade Center was still under construction. Dealbook and CNBC had built a temporary pro-scenium, platform, and stage for the conference, blocking the bare cinder blocks, stacks of drywall, and pallets of marble slabs from the televised image although visible to the live audience. Mary Jo stayed in the greenroom as I listened to several prominent speakers includ-ing Treasury secretary Lew.

By the end of Mary Jo's speech, I knew I could give notice. It was great. She encapsulated our many accomplishments and the SEC's modernization, but more importantly she made the case-closed argument about why the SEC must remain the regulatory guardian of the nation's investors and citizens. "Over the years," she said, "the Commission and the staff have taken important steps to recalibrate its program to better match the current facts on the ground." And the tools given the SEC by the Investment Company Act and Investment Advisers Act remain effective in "responding to the evolution of the asset management industry."

She detailed how we had upgraded the SEC's capabilities to meet its responsibilities in controlling conflicts of interest, reporting, reg-istration and disclosure, fund portfolio composition, and operational risk. The SEC was readier than it had been in many years to meet its mission.

Best of all, she concluded by reinforcing the SEC's absolutely essential role in managing the " risk" in asset management that drove so much controversy since 2008:

> One of the most fundamental post-crisis changes for all of the finan-cial regulators, including the Commission, has been an empha-sis on addressing risks that could have a systemic impact on the securities markets or the financial system as a whole. This renewed emphasis, in my view, complements our long-standing mission to protect investors; maintain fair, orderly, and efficient markets; and facilitate capital formation.
>
> The program that I have just outlined is designed to serve our historic three-part mission. But, at the same time, the measures we

take will necessarily have a broader impact on the financial system. Asset management is a significant segment of our financial system—and, as we all know, the nature of finance means that changes to *any* significant segment has consequences for the others.[10]

Becoming director of IM was the greatest professional honor and most interesting work experience in my life. While many dragons remained to be slain within the bureaucracy of the SEC, I knew we had reinvigorated the leadership culture and the SEC's processes and commitment to better handle the next market meltdown. I really enjoyed working with Mary Jo because of her incredible smarts and kind approach.

In mid-January 2015 I convened the IM division's monthly town hall to provide updates to the staff in the division. The presence of my friend Commissioner Dan Gallagher may have tipped the staff off that I would be discussing something more than the new policy initiatives from Mary Jo's speech. At the end of the meeting I said that I would be stepping down in two weeks. My voice choked up with emotion, but I got the words out. I was surrounded by so many people who work so hard for investors, people like my then deputy and successor David Grim, senior policy advisor Jennifer McHugh, counsels Marian Fowler and Rich Rodgers, rule makers Diane Blizzard and Sarah ten Siethoff, Jon Hertzke and his REO team, Carolyn Grillo who helped reorganize Exam and IM, and too many others to name. I would miss the people. I gave it my all and made significant changes while setting a new policy course. Others could steer the ship from here. I promised the staff that while I would no longer be at the agency with them, I would be cheering their efforts from the outside.

After a government snow day canceled the first try at a farewell party, we held the party in early March and had a wonderful celebration of my five years at the SEC. The older kids had school (including my oldest son who was a freshman at his new high school), but my wife, Sally, and my youngest son came down with me to attend. Mary

Jo, Dan Gallagher, and former chair Elisse Walter all spoke, and my deputy and friend David Grim added a few remarks. Dan Gallagher summarized my efforts at the agency with such kindness:

> Norm is a consummate professional, a motivational leader, and someone who is not scared to run the flag up the hill to pursue rational regulatory policy. Norm and Carlo di Florio, then Drew Bowden, did a fantastic job revitalizing OCIE [Exam] after some rough times in 2008 and 2009, and Norm carried that mission into IM. Norm, along with Craig Lewis, made it possible for the Commission to navigate the rocky shoals of the money market fund rule making, and he's left us with a blueprint for future oversight of the asset management industry that will, if properly implemented, transform the agency's efforts in that space.

The SEC didn't make me a cynic; in fact I left more convinced than when I came that a sound financial system and a strong federal investors' watchdog are fundamental to the economic growth that the United States needs to ensure the health and happiness of our citizens in the twenty-first century.

As I transitioned out of the SEC, I began a period of thinking about the crash and what would strengthen our entire financial system and the personal financial security of everyday American households. How could we avoid such a catastrophe in the future? After more than 25 years in law, finance, and government, I have a few ideas that I will share in the next chapter.

PREVENTING THE NEXT CRISIS

Facts are stubborn things.

—Ronald Reagan

My experience at the SEC strengthened my belief in the U.S. markets and financial system as an unprecedented engine for wealth creation for American citizens, particularly as we suffer through slow economic growth since the Great Recession.

During my time, we improved the SEC's capacity to serve the taxpayer and investor by restructuring the IM division to be faster and more responsive, getting important new reforms off the shelf, bringing the SEC's expertise where it was needed to deter the Fed and FSOC, and engaging top management at the major investment houses and brokerages. While these are significant changes, much more remains to be done at the SEC and other regulatory agencies to make them transparent to taxpayers and to the hundreds of professionals who work diligently within the ranks.

Major private-sector unions such as the United Auto Workers and the United Steelworkers have compromised to some degree with management to restructure work rules and benefits that had gone too far in reducing competitiveness and productivity. They made the existential choice to keep their industries and jobs and potentially their children's and grandchildren's jobs in their communities. The leaders of those unions know that the consequence of a company failing in the private sector is no more jobs. The issue in the government context is that there is no such consequence, as the government never goes out of business. I urge that the new president empanel a bipartisan group of elected officials and labor and management representatives to tackle the work rules and well-meaning practices that have mutated into disasters such as the use of unlimited telework, the rampant anonymous notes from supposed "whistle-blowers," and the guarantee of lifetime employment. These dysfunctions wear down even the hardest-charging new employees and create the cracks that financial scandals can fall through.

No, I'm not saying my former colleagues should lose their pay, retirement, or health benefits. I'm saying let's look at the facts and economics of the rest of our U.S. economy and run the SEC and other agencies in a more productive manner so they can afford to do more and do better.

I know I've been fortunate in my life to have gone to good schools and built a career as a successful lawyer. I know things could have turned out differently without the support of my uncle, my wife, my friend Rod Krause, and many mentors and friends through the years. I was able to join the SEC knowing I could return to the financial services sector and had a strong safety net for my family if things went wrong. My career in the private sector trained me in using the right tools to cut through red tape and get things done. Even with these advantages, it was brutally difficult for me to solve problems because the SEC's culture lacked accountability and discouraged open collaboration across silos, much less across separate agencies.

But as I've written here, I had many, many colleagues in government who are smart, serious, and passionate about their jobs. They depend on their positions for their family's security and also want to make a difference as career public servants. I admire their dedication, but we need better processes at the SEC and other agencies to reward new ideas, smart risk taking, and innovation. The quality professionals in our federal agencies deserve a system that rewards their initiative rather than smothering it.

These thoughts occupied my mind as I transitioned out of the SEC in early 2015. I began to deliberate about what would strengthen our government, our financial system, and the personal financial security of everyday households in the United States. How could we prepare to avoid such a catastrophe in the future? And how can we all change our personal and political relationship with money?

Free, deep, and transparent markets are the best path to restore growth in the United States as we endure the slowest recession recovery in post–World War II history. Whether you are on the left, right, or in between, more U.S. economic growth means more opportunities and jobs. Full stop.

I've read about recent marine archaeology work that shows that at certain spots the bottom of the Mediterranean is virtually carpeted with amphorae that once contained wine or olive oil being shipped between North Africa and Europe and were lost during storms and disasters at sea.[1] There were undoubtedly pricing and hedging strategies used by those long-ago traders to account for the potential loss of cargo on the seas. The "risk premium" in the prices charged for those goods enabled the traders to use the profits from the high percentage of ships that got through to offset the lost revenue from the ships that sank. (Keep in mind that a modern shipment of grain from the United States to China has almost no chance of sinking but still needs a similar hedge against loss, this time more likely in a derivative that pays the shipper in the event of grain price moves that would make the shipment unprofitable.) If the ancient traders hadn't accepted the risk, they would have not opened new markets and earned more to reinvest in their olive groves and vineyards. It may have taken decades or even centuries more before other cultures enjoyed the glories of the Mediterranean harvest and other fruits of global trade. Those amphora jars are the relics of a long-ago time of vibrant global trade and bold entrepreneurship. If we promote that spirit of free market entrepreneurialism symbolized by those jars, we can preserve the United States as the financial capital of the world. Not coincidentally, our nation was founded by men and women with a strong self-reliant and entrepreneurial spirit.

But too many politicians and pundits have villainized the entrepreneurial, risk-taking spirit of American capitalism—with troubling consequences. Some political leaders have found it convenient to foster this pernicious myth rather than admit the crash was the result of specific bad judgments on the part of specific members of Congress and housing regulators as well as certain specific financial services institutions. If current trends continue, the archaeologists of tomorrow may find artifacts of our age that are far more disturbing than amphorae. They may find the remains of entrenched deepening poverty and a failed financial system: communities with vast tracts of abandoned houses, boarded-up Main Street shops, shuttered banks, burned-out buildings. Future recessions could easily break the back of fragile communities that have just barely recovered from the crash of 2008 and must have functioning markets and sources of credit to rebuild.

We have been having documented financial bubbles certainly since the Dutch tulip boom in the 1600s and undoubtedly much farther back. Yes, we can survive future setbacks if they are few and if we are smart. But to do that, we need to undertake a number of policy changes that would help the United States better prepare for the inevitable next crisis. Consider these four pillars of commonsense reform.

1. Change FSOC to a coordinating board that is only activated by severe economic crises.

I don't have a large problem with the Fed monitoring traditional banks, which have federally insured deposits. The charters of the FDIC and the Fed require these regulators to examine banks and to keep consumers' deposits safe and sound.[2] The mindsets of the banking regulators were formed by the Crash of 1929 when ordinary people suffered the financial nightmare of having their banks run out of money to pay their deposits, leaving millions destitute. Bank regulators are trained to derisk banking, and to some extent the federal oversight of banks makes sense in that context. Those deposits are insured, and as I've written, your standard bank is a kind of public utility for safe money storage.

But we don't live in the 1930s. The repeal of Glass-Steagall, the rise of derivatives, and the redesignation of global investing companies as banks in the 2008 crisis have made regulating these firms much more complex and dangerous. The regulators at the Fed and FSOC are viewing the financial landscape through the wrong end of the telescope. They view these complex financial institutions managing billions of investors' dollars through a narrow lens of traditional banking behavior.

I watched with some amusement during the 2016 presidential campaign, as many Americans—not only in the Bernie Sanders camp but across the political spectrum—denounced federal lawmakers for being too soft on "big banks." None of the presidential contenders either wanted to talk to voters about or knew enough to talk about the great irony behind these headlines. Under Dodd-Frank, any U.S. bank holding company with more than $50 billion in assets is automatically subject to stricter rules, and FSOC "designated" four nonbank companies as systemically significant—that is, subject to government control: AIG, Prudential Financial, MetLife, and GE Capital, the financing arm of General Electric Co. However, a federal judge threw out the MetLife designation on March 30, 2016, because FSOC failed to make the case, although the order is sealed.[3] Later in 2016 GE Capital got out from under designation by selling significant financial services businesses.[4]

Dodd-Frank is also changing the character of community banks and credit unions. Members of Congress are very familiar with the frustration of community banks over the burdens of Dodd-Frank. Community banks remain a vital source of credit in thousands of communities, particularly those far from our sophisticated cities. "Community banks are a fixture across the nation. Many have served their communities for decades. They are particularly important in rural areas," Hester Peirce, a senior research fellow at the Mercatus Center at George Mason University (and 2015 Republican nominee for SEC commissioner), noted in congressional testimony. She continued:

> They are also key providers of small business loans. By one measure, $1 out of every $2 lent to small businesses comes from community banks.
>
> Community banks are known for offering personalized service and meeting the needs of the local residents and businesses in ways that a larger, nonlocal bank, which does not know the unique characteristics of the community, cannot.[5]

Dodd-Frank threatens the role of small banks by adding to their compliance costs and staff, raising concerns about legal vulnerabilities, forcing more stringent capital and mortgage-lending requirements (which sounds good but ignores the unique character of small banks), and introducing regulatory uncertainties. As one community banker testified in 2013, "The business of banking can't just be an exercise in meeting regulatory requirements."[6]

We also know FSOC continued in 2016 to seek designation powers over not only banks, but money managers as well—and *as an end in itself, not as a response to a temporary emergency.* Many folks believe they're protecting taxpayers, I know that. But I was in those rooms long enough to know this: their decisions amount to a war of attrition against the ability of banks and investment companies to perform their duties for account holders and investors and still survive.

FSOC was created by a Democratic president and Congress during the financial crisis and leveraged its emergency powers to grow and consolidate power. But as recently as April 2016, FSOC released another report challenging the independence of the asset management and broker-dealer industries. It raised purported red flags about asset managers having sufficient liquidity to pay investors if there's a massive run on a particular fund. It questioned complex uses of hedge fund leverage.[7] The report worried me because FSOC's stated concerns have been repeatedly addressed since 2008. Yet FSOC keeps coming back for more bites at the apple. Even if the Trump administration keeps FSOC out of the asset management area, FSOC's ambitions could re-emerge in a future administration.

The asset management industry already meets tough disclosure and reporting requirements. Hedge funds are going to use leverage. Mutual funds' holdings vary in how liquid they are, in order to provide investors with good returns. That's the nature of financial markets. FSOC is failing at its duty by trying to regulate every conceivable risk out of investing, which by its nature means cyclic and variable returns.

I understand that in times of economic crisis, forcing financial agencies to sit in the same room and make decisions may be necessary. But the Federal Emergency Management Agency doesn't go around the country handing out funds or calling in the National Guard in case an emergency occurs someday. It does its job when needed and returns to the status quo. Congress needs to repeal the Dodd-Frank provisions creating FSOC or, at the least, amend Dodd-Frank to get FSOC out of the "designation" game except in circumstances of severe crisis. If it is repealed, I would support creating a coordinating committee of the top federal financial regulators but not one with the power to "designate" firms and activities.

2. Force government to look at the facts underlying proposed policies and analyze the consequences before instituting new regulation.

We must adopt a more fact-based approach to policy to reduce government interference in the economy. This means that when legislatures or agencies propose a new policy or law, they are required to provide outside, objective evidence supporting the benefits of the proposal. The research must be performed by credentialed experts without vested interests in the result. Some call this "evidence-based policy making" an extension of the practice of evidence-based medicine. Evidence-based policy is about making the process of lawmaking less ideological through the use of economically rigorous studies to identify programs and practices capable of improving outcomes.

This is what we did in the SEC, what governments have done in Britain and Australia, and what many state legislatures are doing successfully in the United States. A study by the liberal-leaning Pew Charitable Trusts and the MacArthur Foundation documented that 100 state laws across 42 states that were passed between 2004 and 2014 supported the use of evidence-based programs and practices. Between 2008 and 2011, 29 states reported using cost-benefit analysis to inform policy or budget decisions.[8] I like how states are experimenting successfully in this area, but the innovative spirit hasn't caught on in Washington.

Witness the roller-coaster effects of federal housing laws since the early 2000s. Washington decision makers cannot resist the seductive economic boost of artificially lowered interest rates for first-time and marginally creditworthy homebuyers.[9] The government policy of encouraging homeownership sprang from a well-meaning notion that homeownership was good for Americans, particularly low-income and underserved families. On the surface that might sound like an appealing policy goal. But it would be tough to find many people who lost their homes to foreclosure in 2009 and after who would look favorably on the benefits of those decisions to make mortgages as easy to get as a high-interest credit card.

The Obama administration's reckless 2014 decision to resume guaranteeing home mortgages with down payments as low as 3 percent is a return to the policies that created the housing bubble and distorts the economy toward the housing sector.[10] We have to start learning from policy failures instead of repeating them.

This is the kind of boring but enlightened change that can bring more reason and reality to our policy making. Policy makers acting on their own view of what sounds like a good idea rarely get it right. I see cities starting to ban plastic shopping bags, and I wonder if households that use plastic shopping bags for trash bags (like mine does) will simply buy more plastic garbage bags and defeat the supposed purpose of the ban. In the meantime, a ban could hurt sales at brick-and-mortar stores as consumers buy online because they don't want to carry a reusable shopping bag around with them. Policy makers should be forced to take a look at available studies and evidence before acting in ways that harm the economy.

3. Reduce the number of regulators of financial services by merging the two securities regulators, the SEC and the CFTC. We also need to merge the OCC into the Federal Reserve so only one agency grants bank charters.

We do not need all this alphabet soup of agencies or the resulting gaps that occur between them. The strongest lever for making government more responsive, accountable, and cost effective is to merge agencies serving the same "customers" and stop creating new agencies, divisions, and special offices with every new management team or change in political party. We merged offices at the SEC under my leadership and improved not only our efficiency but our morale. Congress has attempted agency mergers in the past. Some have passed such as the creation of the Department of Homeland Security, and many have failed. They're not a panacea. But Americans should expect better results considering how much is at stake. For all the cynics among us, both parties have proposed ideas for mergers for more than 20 years.

In 1995 Congressman Ron Wyden of Oregon (now a senator) called for the SEC-CFTC merger in the Markets and Trading Reorganization and Reform Act. When I read the following expert testimony given from James L. Bothwell, the director of Financial Institutions and Markets Issues at the nonpartisan U.S. General Accounting Office—well it was déjà vu all over again:

> The current U.S. regulatory system, however, is a patchwork quilt of federal and state agencies that has not kept pace with the dramatic and rapid changes that are occurring in domestic and global financial markets. The principal components of our regulatory system date from the 1930s. Today, we have 10 different federal financial regulators, not including the Treasury Department or the various self-regulatory organizations, such as the stock and futures exchanges. . . . [We] support the merging of some of these regulators and functions to improve the effectiveness and efficiency of the financial regulatory system.[11]

And that statement was more than 20 years ago!

The 2008 crash also raised calls for a merger of the SEC and CFTC from many in Congress and on Wall Street. In late 2012, liberal lion Barney Frank made one last push for a new merger before his retirement. Frank's politics are way left of mine, but I always enjoyed policy discussions with him because he is smart and engaged. When Frank and Democrat Michael Capuano introduced a bill for the merger that was also backed by many Republican House members, Frank noted that a merger would have helped avoid regulatory blindspots and gaps that contributed to the scandal at MF Global. "The existence of a separate SEC and CFTC is the single largest structural defect in our regulatory system," Frank said in a statement. Frank said he wanted the merger in Dodd-Frank but postponed it because the provision would have killed the overall bill.[12] I fear that if the 2008 crisis couldn't motivate this simple reform, nothing will.

Then as recently as 2015, Paul Volcker's think tank issued a report calling for an SEC-CFTC merger as part of a financial regulatory overhaul. The Volcker Alliance suggested bridging the jurisdictional divide by giving both the Senate Committee on Banking, Housing, and Urban Affairs and the House Committee on Financial Services joint oversight of the merged super agency. The Volcker think tank proposed that the merged agency be funded solely through fees and assessments, a great idea I support because it solves the problem of wildly unpredictable congressional budgets preventing technology planning.[13] Volcker also called for dissolving the OCC and absorbing it into the Fed, another good idea. But in the big picture Volcker called for combining most of the agencies *under the Fed* and further empowering FSOC, both of which, for the reasons discussed in these pages, already have far too much power.

Historically, merger proposals failed for three other reasons. One, the CFTC as the much smaller agency had the most to lose. "Many at the CFTC have maintained a 'hell no we won't go' stance with regard to merger, for some good and sound reasons," CFTC commissioner Bart Chilton testified in October 2008. "Merging a smaller agency like the CFTC with a larger one like the SEC normally means only one thing—the smaller agency ends up in the other's basement and the issues of the smaller agency (in this case, the one with responsibility for oversight of futures) become less of a priority."

But even as a commissioner defending his agency, Chilton agreed that "the issue of merger should [not] be off the table. Things have changed since the last time the issue was debated. We have an ongoing economic meltdown, particularly in the credit markets, and the SEC has been one of the key targets of those who say lax regulation is one of the primary culprits of the financial fiasco."[14]

Two, as noted above, different committees have jurisdiction over the agencies: Agriculture has jurisdiction over the CFTC, and the House Financial Services Committee and the Senate Banking Committee oversee the SEC. The Agricultural Committees fiercely resist losing the CFTC, and many of their farming constituents agree.

Three, the GAO and other independent analyses did not find great cost savings in the various proposals put forth over the years.[15] I disagree because a merger would mean one general counsel for the new agency instead of two, one inspector general instead of two, and so on. While this makes the merger a harder sell around the Hill, the economic and productivity benefits for the industry and the taxpayer are what matter.

Proposals to merge OCC into the Fed have failed similarly because the smaller agency feared being the junior partner, and stopping change in Washington is always easier than starting it.

Whether conservative or liberal, American citizens can find a lot to like in merging financial regulatory agencies. If you're concerned about the reckless risk taking—ahem—of the big banks and asset management firms, virtually every management expert will testify that eliminating duplication and improving coordination and accountability by combining agencies will mean they will do a better job of focusing on their regulated industries and enforcing violations. If you want transparent rules and accountable regulators, and some cost savings to boot, mergers will move in this direction if for no other reason than that the crucible of change management during merger activity forces managers to make tough decisions.

These commonsense principles point to the wisdom of restoring the Glass-Steagall Act to separate traditional insured banking activities from risk-taking activities. While a Glass-Steagall world likely would not have stopped Lehman Brothers from going bankrupt, other disastrous losses would have been more contained to the risk-taking sector. Most important, Glass-Steagall would reduce the federal government's control of the financial industry and make agency consolidation easier, faster, cheaper, and less political. Instead of parsing through the almost 1,000-page Volcker Rule and its myriad provisions, Wall Street firms and banks could return to a solution that worked well for decades. If a firm wants to play in the brokerage and asset management sandboxes, it's not a bank, it's not federally insured, and the Fed and Treasury won't be involved. The SEC and CFTC would be able to do what they do best.

Ultimately under a Glass-Steagall regime, the asset management sector would never be too big to fail. If a firm is undisciplined, unwise, or unlucky enough to sustain lethal losses, it won't be bailed out.

4. Eliminate government sponsorship of lotteries and casinos that cost Americans billions in lost savings with minimal chance of reward. Use the money currently dedicated to lottery advertising to encourage savings and financial literacy.

If there's a Hall of Shame for government, I nominate the role of state and federal laws in sponsoring and profiting from lotteries and casinos. This development boggles the conscious mind. In the early years of the republic, the federal government ran various lottery games until they were revealed to be corrupt. As noted in the final report issued by the National Gambling Impact Study Commission formed by President Bill Clinton in 1997, "Most gambling, and all lotteries, were outlawed by several states beginning in the 1870s, following massive scandals in the Louisiana lottery"—a state lottery that operated nationally—that included extensive bribery of state and federal officials. "The federal government outlawed use of the mail for lotteries in 1890, and in 1895 the government invoked the Commerce Clause to forbid shipments of lottery tickets or advertisements across state lines, effectively ending all lotteries in the United States."[16]

No government body touched a lottery game until Puerto Rico in 1934 and New Hampshire in 1964 (which lacking a state income tax stood in need of revenue). New York State followed New Hampshire in 1966. New Jersey introduced its lottery in 1970 and was followed by 10 other states by 1975. Currently, 44 states, Puerto Rico, the U.S. Virgin Islands, and the District of Columbia have operating lotteries, the Gambling Impact Study and other studies note.

Since the beginning of the modern lottery, lawmakers have dedicated lottery net revenue to social and educational programs.

By "doing good," lotteries have maintained sufficient public support while becoming one of the leading sources of revenue for governments—an invisible tax paid *voluntarily* by their citizens. According to the National Gambling Impact Study, in virtually every state, "the introduction of lotteries has followed remarkably uniform patterns: the arguments for and against adoption, the structure of the resulting state lottery, and the evolution of the lottery's operations all demonstrate considerable uniformity." The report goes on to say, "The principal argument used in every state to promote the adoption of a lottery has focused on its value as a source of 'painless' revenue: players voluntarily spending their money (as opposed to the general public being taxed) for the benefit of the public good."[17]

What's really upside-down about all this? Lottery dollars at least in part are *replacing* tax dollars, not adding to them. The states are selling the PR appeal, not the reality of lottery dollars doing good.

Since the Clinton Gambling Impact Study, many skeptics and studies have exposed the role of lotteries in gambling addiction, revealing that lotteries are disproportionately purchased by poor and low-income residents, that states vary widely in the accountability of how they spend lottery revenues, and that state advertising does a terrible job of making the poor odds of winning transparent (more on that in a moment).

The brilliant Pulitzer Prize–winning tax reporter and analyst David Cay Johnston wrote in 2009: "Because gambling is voluntary, there is little organized opposition to levies on gambling winnings. Contrast that with the ferocious, well-organized and well-financed opposition to income taxes, especially corporate income taxes. In 11 states, lotteries provided more revenue than the state corporate income tax in 2009, Tax Foundation data show."

As Johnston argues, that tax rate on lottery tickets is far higher than any other state tax: "Overall, lotteries pay out only about 62 percent of their revenue as winnings, an implicit 38 percent tax rate on lottery tickets. On top of that, people who win $600 or more . . . must pay income taxes of up to 45 percent on their windfalls."[18]

In New York State, taxpayers in the lowest quintile of earners pay more for the lottery on average (about $1,000) per year than any other form of taxation, according to analysis by data experts Jeff Desjardins and Max Galka.[19] Galka highlights that playing the lottery is voluntary—yes—but what we pay for the pleasure is not: "Choosing to play the lottery is voluntary. But much like sales taxes, the inflated price of lottery tickets is not. It is illegal for anyone but the state to run a lottery. So unlike casinos, which face competition from other casinos, lotteries operate as a monopoly, so they can set their pricing artificially high, or equivalently, their payout rates artificially low."[20]

Another heavily quoted study found that poor folks—households earning under $13,000 per year—spend about a tenth of all their income on lottery tickets.[21] Lottery gaming also depends for a disproportionate share of sales on people with gambling addictions. A closer look reveals the most corrupt aspect of all: the states' saturation advertising and marketing campaigns.

If you've wondered as I have for years why lottery advertising says less about the odds of actually winning money than you hear about in other ads, here are a few reasons why:

- Lotteries are not bound by the Federal Trade Commission's truth-in-advertising laws. Instead, the states are self-regulating, allowing lotteries to get away with misleading and predatory advertising far beyond what private businesses are allowed.[22]
- Lottery campaigns are outsourced to top marketing and communications firms with state-of-the-art tools for manipulating consumer behavior.[23]
- As the novelty of lottery games wears off after they are introduced—and the drain on our wallets becomes clear—states constantly invent new games and new marketing strategies, thereby driving up costs as well as artificially stimulating demand in ways that remind me of penny stock brokers hard-selling from a boiler room.

Lotteries are not only a way we're all paying more taxes and our low-income citizens are being exploited. *They're siphoning millions of dollars we could be saving or investing wisely. They're undermining the already notoriously poor savings rates of Americans, leaving us exposed when the next economic crisis hits to tighter budgets, bankruptcy, fore-closures, and poverty.* What starker individual lesson could we have from the 2008 crash? We can't exert control over the global economy, Wall Street, or Washington—nor have we ever—but we can control how we use our own dollars. We can have a stronger financial safety net and retirement plan. We can empower ourselves to understand how money works and how to make it work for us, not against us.

That's one of the most powerful changes we could make as a society. Let's use lotteries and other mass media and social media tools to teach financial literacy in early working years after high school or college to prepare Americans for the current system where they will be expected to handle their own retirement savings through 401(k)s and IRAs.

I don't expect lotteries to be repealed. But let's ask our state and federal lawmakers to impose commonsense changes such as reducing the number of new games introduced each year, holding state lottery advertising campaigns accountable to federal truth-in-advertising laws, improving disclosure of risks and odds, and best of all forcing state lotteries to set aside a share of their marketing dollars for savings and financial literacy promotion (and no gaming the rules!).

It's tragic how little is understood about the tax advantages of IRAs, 401(k)s, and similar tax-advantaged investment accounts. Let's ask our brilliant marketers and advertising agencies to raise awareness and engagement with the opportunities that tax-free retirement savings accounts provide. Not only are these one of the few ways the government supports investing activities through the tax code, but the government allows you to tap your IRAs and 401(k)s for first-time homeownership and college savings.

I love the success of prize-linked savings accounts (PLSAs), an innovative program that combines the appeal of playing the lottery with incentives to begin and continue saving that never risks the principal or earned interest in these accounts. A few U.S. states have seen good early results. PLSAs seem to have no enemies except state lotteries!

Michigan's program is the oldest and most established. Eight Michigan credit unions launched PLSAs in 2009 and expanded quickly to 36 in 2010. The participating credit unions rewarded savers with cash and raffle prizes tied to a savings account they titled "Save to Win."

The results? Nearly 6 in 10 Michigan participants had never opened a savings account before. Savers with median incomes below $40,000 maintained an average account balance of $634 the first year. By 2014, 34 credit unions in 10 states were participating. Nearly 11,000 account holders had saved over $15 million, with an average account balance of more than $3,000. Half of Save to Win account holders in 2014 were nonsavers or financially vulnerable.[24] Similar programs have demonstrated results in Great Britain, Sweden, and the Middle East.[25] States benefit when their citizens carry less debt. They save more, strengthening local banks. They pay their bills to local and state vendors. And they enjoy higher confidence and self-esteem. Plus, their savings will provide them with a financial cushion for the next downturn.

Commonwealth (formerly the Doorways to Dreams Fund) and other groups are working to great effect with Congress and state legislatures to pave the legal way for Save to Win and other initiatives such as mobile game apps for savings and Save Your Refund.[26] The IRS now offers federal tax refund filers Form 8888. This allows taxpayers to split their refund into two parts, one for spending, one for savings. They can be entered into various raffles and contests.[27]

Much of the credit for this movement goes to then Harvard (now Oxford) Business School professor Peter Tufano who conducted early research on the topic along with the then Doorways to Dreams Fund (where Tufano is a director), the Filene Research Institute, and the Michigan Credit Union League.[28]

I also admire the work of Professor William Birdthistle of Chicago-Kent College of Law. Professor Birdthistle has produced his own financial and legal literacy video series for his law students and posted the videos on YouTube. William plays himself as well as a less-informed but curious millennial in a hoodie and sunglasses. Check out his videos such as "What Are Taxes? Financial Aid with Professor Birdthistle," https://www.youtube.com/watch?v=MYp5gWkDIGI.

In every speech I've given, I've talked about how investment management is rooted in the daily lives of people, from their rainy day funds to college savings to retirement needs.

If we, the people, are better educated, we'll handle risk in better ways. We'll be a better-educated populace and just a little harder to deceive or swindle. I know from my experience going public that even our smartest lawyers and regulators have blind spots. I remember in one FSOC meeting a Fed regulator exclaimed, "Well, Norm, what if Vanguard sells all its holdings at once! The economy will tank!" Most any citizen with even the scantest knowledge about a mutual fund knows this will never happen. It simply goes against everything that has ever been known about markets. Yet it was far from the only time I heard similar comments from the best and brightest.

While it was Alexander Hamilton who became the patron saint of a national banking system, we are wise to keep Thomas Jefferson's skepticism in mind, as well. In Jefferson's letter to Albert Yancey of January 6, 1816, he wrote about the risks inherent in a market economy. He told us not to kid ourselves. There will always be bubbles and crashes, and he saw the threat to democracy:

> The American mind is now in that state of fever which the world has so often seen in the history of other nations. We are under the bank bubble, as England was under the South Sea bubble, France under the Mississippi bubble, and as every nation is liable to be, under whatever bubble, design, or delusion may puff up in moments when off their guard. We are now taught to believe that legerdemain tricks upon paper can produce as solid wealth as hard labor in the earth.

Jefferson hated that the paper currency of the time was under-mined by debt and could collapse at any time. Indeed, 200 years ago, Mr. Jefferson feared that the banks might be too big to fail:

> The thing to be aimed at is, that the excesses of their emissions should be withdrawn as gradually, but as speedily, too, as is prac-ticable, without so much alarm as to bring on the crisis dreaded. Some banks are said to be calling in their paper. But ought we to let this depend on their discretion? Is it not the duty of the legis-lature to avert from their constituents such a catastrophe as the extinguishment of two hundred millions of paper in their hands? The difficulty is indeed great: and the greater, because the patient revolts against all medicine. I am far from presuming to say that any plan can be relied on with certainty, because the bubble may burst from one moment to another; but if it fails, we shall be but where we should have been without any effort to save ourselves.

But he believed as he always had that we could only be directed by the people and their elected representatives:

> If the legislature would add to that a perpetual tax of a cent a head on the population of the State, it would set agoing at once, and for-ever maintain, a system of primary or ward schools, and an uni-versity where might be taught, in its highest degree, every branch of science useful in our time and country; and it would rescue us from the tax of toryism, fanaticism, and indifferentism to their own State, which we now send our youth to bring from those of New England.
>   If a nation expects to be ignorant and free, in a state of civiliza-tion, it expects what never was and never will be.[29]

The United States has been and can continue to be the financial capital of the world, but that status, as Jefferson says, cannot be pre-served if we think we can be ignorant and free. The steps outlined above will reduce the amount of government interference in our economy and empower individuals to take control of their own economic futures. I hope if this book has shown anything, it is that government does not generally allocate resources efficiently. The more we educate our citizens to manage their own financial affairs, the better off those citizens and the nation will be.

NOTES

CHAPTER 1: FISH OUT OF WATER

1. Dennis Cauchon, "Some Federal Workers More Likely to Die Than Lose Jobs," *USA Today*, July 19, 2011.
2. NTEU Chapter 293 Collective Bargaining Agreement Article 32.
3. David Hilzenrath, "Preuitt Says She Paid 'Heavy Price' for Protesting SEC Handling of Stanford Probe," *Washington Post*, May 13, 2011.
4. Ibid.

CHAPTER 2: TAKING MYSELF PUBLIC

1. See "Norman B. Champ Jr. Was Political Activist," *Vineyard Gazette*, Feb. 17, 2005, https://vineyardgazette.com/obituaries/2005/02/18/norman-b-champ-jr -was-political-activist.
2. See Patricia Rice, "Jimmy Carter Slept Here," *St. Louis Post-Dispatch*, Jan. 14, 1977.
3. Managed Funds Association, "Managed Funds Association Board Elects Eric Vincent of Ospraie Management Chairman, Members Elect Six New Directors Representing Amber Capital, Arthur F. Bell, Cantillon Capital Management, Chilton Investment, D.E. Shaw and S.A.C. Capital Advisors," Press Release, Oct. 4, 2007, http://www.managedfunds.org/wp-content/uploads/2011/06/10.4.07 -10.4.07-MFA-Board-Elects-Eric-Vincent-Chairman-2007.pdf/.
4. See Subhamoy Das, *Perspectives on Financial Services*, Allied Publishers, 2009, p. 4.
5. See Matthew P. Fink, *The Rise of Mutual Funds: An Insider's View*, Oxford University Press, 2011, p. 11.
6. See Securities Act of 1933 (48 Stat. 74, 15 U.S.C. 77a-77mm), Securities Exchange Act of 1934 (48 Stat. 881, 15 U.S.C. 78a-78kk), Revenue Act of 1936 (49 Stat. 1655), and the Investment Company Act of 1940 (54 Stat. 789, 15 U.S.C. 80a-1-80a64).
7. See generally Alice Schroeder, *The Snowball: Warren Buffett and the Business of Life*, Bantam Books, 2009.

8. See Karen W. Arenson, "Staggering Bequests by Unassuming Couple," *New York Times*, July 13, 1998.

9. See Danny Hakim, "Hedge Fund Industry Creates a Dinosaur: The Macro Manager," *New York Times*, May 6, 2000.

10. See Daniel A. Strachman, *Julian Robertson: A Tiger in the Land of Bulls and Bears*, Wiley, 2004.

11. SEC, "Norm Champ Named Associate Regional Director for Examination in SEC New York Regional Office," Press Release, Nov. 3, 2009, https://www.sec.gov/news/press/2009/2009-231.htm.

12. 5 USC 3331.

CHAPTER 3: PUNCHING THE CUSHION

1. See Securities Exchange Act of 1934, Section 4.

2. *Id.*, Section 4E.

3. SEC Office of Investigations, "Investigation of Failure of the SEC to Uncover Bernard Madoff's Ponzi Scheme," August 31, 2009, pp. 97–98.

4. SEC Report of Investigation, "Investigation of the SEC's Response to Concerns Regarding Robert Allen Stanford's Alleged Ponzi Scheme," March 31, 2010, p. 33.

5. Telework Enhancement Act of 2010, Pub. L. 111-292.

6. See U.S. Office of Personnel Management, "2013 Status of Telework in the Federal Government," December 2013, https://www.telework.gov/reports-studies/reports-to-congress/2013reporttocongress.pdf.

7. *United States v. United Mine Workers*, 330 U.S. 258, 312 (1947).

8. "SEC Attorney Salaries," Glassdoor, https://www.glassdoor.com/Salary/SEC-Attorney-Salaries-E8027_D_KO4,12.htm.

CHAPTER 4: POSTCRASH TRIAGE IN THE SEC EMERGENCY ROOM

1. John Kotter, "Leading Change: Why Change Management Efforts Fail," *Harvard Business Review*, January 2007.

2. Rao LaClair, "Helping Employees Embrace Change," *McKinsey Quarterly*, November 2002.

3. See, for example, Satish Subramanian, *Transforming Business with Program Management*, Auerbach Publications, 2015.

4. Michael Frömmel, *Portfolios and Investments*, 3rd ed., Books on Demand, 2013, p. 164.

5. Rebecca Marston, "What Is a Ratings Agency?," *BBC News*, Oct. 20, 2014, http://www.bbc.com/news/10108284.

6. See "Stars of the Junk Yard," *The Economist*, Oct. 21, 2010, http://www.economist.com/node/17306419.

7. "Adoption of Amendments to Rule 15c3-1 and Adoption of Alternative Net Capital Requirement for Certain Brokers and Dealers," Exchange Act Release 34-11497, June 26, 1975. See also "Removal of Certain References to Credit Ratings Under the Securities Exchange Act of 1934," Exchange Act Release 34-64352, April 27, 2011, pp. 5–6.

8. SEC website, "Credit Rating Agencies and Nationally Recognized Statistical Rating Organizations (NRSROs)," https://www.sec.gov/answers/nrsro.htm.

9. SEC, *2011 Summary Report of Commission Staff's Examinations of Each Nationally Recognized Statistical Rating Organization*, September 2011, p. 5, https://www.sec.gov/news/studies/2011/2011_nrsro_section15e_examinations_summary _report.pdf. See Office of Credit Ratings, SEC, for a current list, https://www.sec.gov/ocr.

10. Jeanette Neuman and Jean Eaglesham, "SEC Eyes Ratings from S&P: Regulators Scrutinize 'Dummy' Assets in Investments Marked as Triple-A," *Wall Street Journal*, Sept. 27, 2011.

11. Valentin Dimitrov, Leo Tang, and Darius Palia, "Impact of the Dodd-Frank Act on Credit Ratings," *Journal of Financial Economics*, April 2014. *Harvard Law School Forum on Corporate Governance* (blog), October 2014, https://corpgov.law.harvard.edu/2014/10/09/impact-of-the-dodd-frank-act-on-credit-ratings/.

12. *2011 Summary Report of Commission Staff's Examination of Each Nationally Recognized Statistical Rating Organization*, pp. 1–4.

13. See David S. Hilzenrath, "SEC Budget Increase Voted Down in House," *Washington Post*, June 23, 2011, https://www.washingtonpost.com/business/economy/sec-budget-increase-voted-down-in-house/2011/06/23/AGCornhH_story.html.

14. *2011 Summary Report of Commission Staff's Examinations of Each Nationally Recognized Statistical Rating Organization*, p. 4.

15. See Damian Paletta and E. S. Browning, "U.S. Warned on Debt Load," *Wall Street Journal*, Apr. 19, 2011, http://www.wsj.com/articles/SB1000142405274870400400457 6270693061767996.

16. Binyamin Appelbaum and Eric Dash, "S.&P. Downgrades Debt Rating of U.S. for the First Time," *New York Times*, Aug. 5, 2011, http://www.nytimes.com/2011/08/06/business/us-debt-downgraded-by-sp.html.

17. Zachary A. Goldfarb, "S&P Downgrades U.S. Credit Rating for First Time," *Washington Post*, Aug. 6, 2011, https://www.washingtonpost.com/business/

economy/sandp-considering-first-downgrade-of-us-credit-rating/2011/08/05/
gIQAqKeIxI_story.html.

18. "S&P Downgrades U.S. Debt Rating—Press Release," *Wall Street Journal*, Aug. 5, 2011, http://blogs.wsj.com/marketbeat/2011/08/05/sp-downgrades-u-s-debt -rating-press-release/.

19. Appelbaum and Dash, "S.&P. Downgrades Debt Rating of U.S. for the First Time."

20. "Judge May Allow Standard & Poor's to Seek Information from Geithner," *Bloomberg News*, Mar. 11, 2014.

21. Matt Levine, "Is S & P Being Sued Because It Downgraded the US?" *Bloomberg*, Jan. 21, 2014.

22. Toni Reinhold, "SEC Looks to Reassure Investors," *Reuters*, Feb. 7, 2009, http:// www.reuters.com/article/us-sec-idUSTRE51620H20090207.

23. See Clifford Krauss, "Stanford Sentenced to 110-Year Term in $7 Billion Ponzi Case," *New York Times*, June 14, 2012, http://www.nytimes.com/2012/06/15/ business/stanford-sentenced-to-110-years-in-jail-in-fraud-case.html.

24. SEC Office of Inspector General, "Investigation of the SEC's Response to Concerns Regarding Robert Allen Stanford's Alleged Ponzi Scheme," Mar. 31, 2010, p. 18.

25. Aruna Viswanatha and Sarah Lynch, "Blamed over Stanford, SEC's Texas Office Plots Comeback," *Reuters*, July 20, 2012.

26. See Jacob Bunge and Joseph Checkler, "Penson Files for Bankruptcy, Capping Years-Long Decline," *Wall Street Journal*, Jan. 13, 2013, http://www.wsj.com/ articles/SB10001424127887324235104578240140214121754.

27. See Andrew Osterland, "Three Clearing Firms Face Uncertain Future," *Investment News*, July 17, 2011, http://www.investmentnews.com/article/20110717/REG/ 307179998/three-clearing-firms-face-an-uncertain-future.

28. "Julius Leiman-Carbia Named Head of SEC's National Broker-Dealer Examination Program," *SEC News Digest*, Issue 2011-76, Apr. 20, 2011.

29. See Theresa W. Carey, "Clearing Firm Rattles Investors," *Barron's*, May 21, 2011, http://www.barrons.com/articles/SB50001424052970203869804576327382200 170672.

30. "Pension Files for Bankruptcy, Capping Years-Long Decline."

CHAPTER 5: NO ONE MENTIONED THE WAX MUSEUM

1. SEC, "Director of Division of Investment Management Eileen Rominger to Retire," Press Release, No. 2012-114, June 15, 2012, https://www.sec.gov/News/ PressRelease/Detail/PressRelease/1365171482626.

2. SEC, "SEC Names Norm Champ as Director of Division of Investment Management," Press Release, No. 2012-129, July 5, 2012.

3. Diana B. Henriques, "Treasury to Guarantee Money Market Funds," *New York Times*, Sept. 19, 2008, http://www.nytimes.com/2008/09/20/business/20moneys .html.

4. See "Division of Investment Management," SEC, https://www.sec.gov/divisions/ investment/investment_about.shtml.

5. IM Guidance Update, "Acceptance of Gifts or Entertainment by Fund Advisory Personnel," No. 2015-01, Feb. 2015.

6. Todd Shriber, "Eaton Vance Lands Approval for Non-Transparent ETF," *ETF Trends*, Nov. 6, 2014.

7. Jackie Noblett, "Precidian Not Giving Up on Non-Transparent Active ETFs," *Ignites*, Nov. 17, 2014.

8. John Gittelsohn, "Investors See Third Avenue Fueling More Bond Market Carnage," *Bloomberg*, Dec. 13, 2015.

CHAPTER 6: BREAKING THE BUCK ALMOST BREAKS MY BACK

1. SEC, "Statement of SEC Chairman Mary L. Schapiro on Money Market Fund Reform," Press Release, Aug. 22, 2012.

2. Luis A. Aguilar, "Statement Regarding Money Market Funds," SEC Public Statement, Aug. 23, 2012.

3. Daniel M. Gallagher and Troy A. Paredes, "Statement on the Regulation of Money Market Funds," SEC Public Statement, Aug. 28, 2012.

4. SEC, "Statement of SEC Chairman Mary L. Schapiro on Money Market Fund Reform."

5. SEC Proposing Release, "Money Market Fund Reform," Release No. 33-9408, June 5, 2013. p. 306.

6. "Report of the President's Working Group on Financial Markets: Money Market Reform Options," October 2010, pp. 2–3.

7. SEC Division of Risk, Strategy, and Financial Innovation, "Response to Questions Posed by Commissioners Aguilar, Paredes and Gallagher," Nov. 30, 2012, p. 3.

8. SEC Proposing Release, "Money Market Fund Reform," p. 32.

9. SEC Adopting Release, "Money Market Fund Reform," Release No. IC-29132, Feb. 23, 2010, p. 6, note 12.

10. SEC Proposing Release, "Money Market Fund Reform," p. 32.

11. Neil Irwin, "The Hidden Cost of Bailouts," *Washington Post*, Sept. 28, 2012.

12. "Report of the President's Working Group on Financial Markets," p. 12. See also SEC Proposing Release, "Money Market Fund Reform," pp. 32–33.

13. "Report of the President's Working Group on Financial Markets," p.12.

14. SEC Proposing Release, "Money Market Fund Reform," p. 34, note 91.

15. SEC Proposing Release, "Money Market Fund Reform," pp. 35–37.

16. Gallagher and Paredes, "Statement on the Regulation of Money Market Funds."

17. Aguilar, "Statement Regarding Money Market Funds."

18. Former SEC Chair Arthur Levitt talks reform on Bloomberg Radio, *Bloomberg: Surveillance* show radio broadcast, Aug. 23, 2012, transcript available at https://advance.lexis.com/api/permalink/b5e83e2f-b6d9-49e0-8bc5-e7f8cdb0 fabf/?context=1000516.

19. Nathaniel Popper, "A Regulator's Key Role in Failed Mutual Fund Reform," *New York Times*, Aug. 26, 2012.

20. David Reilly, "Toothless SEC Caves on Money-Market Funds," *Wall Street Journal*, Aug. 24, 2012.

21. Zachary Warmbrodt, "Dems Shy from Money-Market Reform," *Politico*, Sept. 11, 2012.

22. Irwin, "The Hidden Cost of Bailouts."

23. http://www.sec.gov/about.shtml.

CHAPTER 7: EDGAR AND FRIENDS

1. Dwight Jon Zimmerman, "Gen. George C. Marshall Eliminates the 'Dead Wood,'" DefenseMediaNetwork Sept. 1, 2015, http://www.defensemedianetwork.com/ stories/eliminating-the-%E2%80%9Cdead-wood%E2%80%9D/.

2. Ibid.

3. SEC Announcement, "Edgar Public Dissemination Service (PDS) System Contact Information," available at sec.gov. ("This privatized PDS System is managed by Attain, LLC and is the primary source to receive a dedicated feed of all public EDGAR filings.")

4. Gina Chon, "High-Frequency Traders Said to Get SEC Filings Early," *Financial Times*, Oct. 29, 2014.

5. James Willhite, "The Ease of Fooling the SEC's 'Edgar,'" *Wall Street Journal*, May 15, 2015.

6. U.S. Securities and Exchange Commission, "Thomas A. Bayer Named SEC Chief Information Officer," http://www.sec.gov/news/press/2010/2010-201.htm (last updated Oct. 20, 2010).

7. *Current Guidance on Economic Analysis in SEC Rulemaking,* Mar. 16, 2012, http://www.sec.gov/dera/current-guidance.

8. "Remarks to the Practising Law Institute," Private Equity Forum, New York, June 30, 2014.

9. "Remarks to the Practising Law Institute," Hedge Fund Management Seminar 2014, New York, Sept. 11, 2014. "Remarks to the SIFMA Complex Products Forum," New York, Oct. 29, 2014. All three speeches are available at sec.gov.

10. Office of Financial Research, "Asset Management and Financial Stability," Sept. 2013, https://www.treasury.gov/initiatives/ofr/research/Documents/OFR _AMFS_ FINAL.pdf.

11. Michael S. Piwowar, "Advancing and Defending the SEC's Core Mission," SEC Speech, Jan. 27, 2014, https://www.sec.gov/News/Speech/Detail/Speech/ 1370540671978.

12. Michael S. Piwowar, "Remarks at AEI Conference on Financial Stability," SEC Speech, July 15, 2014. See also Matthew Zeitlin, "An SEC Commissioner Just Gave the Most Aggressive Speech on Financial Regulation Ever," BuzzFeedNews July 15, 2014, https://www.buzzfeed.com/matthewzeitlin/an-sec -commissioner-just-gave-the-most-aggressive-speech-on?utm_term=.vdMAAj A8z#.qoO00a0jM.

13. Dave Michaels, "Money Funds Embrace US SEC's Rules to Escape FSOC," Bloomberg July 24, 2014, http://www.bloomberg.com/news/articles/2014-07-24/ money-funds-embrace-u-s-sec-s-rules-to-escape-fsoc.

CHAPTER 8: THE VOLCKER RULE AND ME

1. Jon Hilsenrath, Damian Paletta, and Aaron Lucchetti, "Goldman, Morgan Scrap Wall Street Model, Become Banks in Bid to Ride Out Crisis," *Wall Street Journal,* Sept. 22, 2008.

2. Eric Dash and Julie Creswell, "Citigroup Saw No Red Flags—Even as It Made Bolder Bets," *New York Times,* Nov. 22, 2008.

3. William Alden, "War of Words over the Volcker Rule: A History," *New York Times,* Dec. 10, 2013, accessed June 1, 2016, http://dealbook.nytimes.com/2013/12/10/ war-of-words-over-the-volcker-rule-a-timeline/?_r=0.

4. Scott Patterson and Deborah Solomon, "Volcker Rule to Curb Bank Trading Proves Hard to Write," The Wall Street Journal Sep. 10, 2013, http://www.wsj .com/news/articles/SB10001424127887323838204579000623890621830.

5. Scott Patterson, "Volcker Rule Could Be Delayed Again," The Wall Street Journal Feb. 27, 2013, http://www.wsj.com/articles/SB10001424127887324662404578330 563892792982.

6. Alan Katz and Ian Katz, "The Most Powerful Person at the Federal Reserve You've Never Heard Of," *Bloomberg*, June 10, 2015.

7. Ben Protess, "Regulator of Wall Street Loses Its Hard Charging Chairman," *New York Times Dealbook*, Jan. 2, 2014.

8. 12 USC Section 241.

9. Federal Reserve website, "The Board of Governors of the Federal Reserve System," http://www.federalreserve.gov/pubs/frseries/frseri.htm.

10. Matthew Goldstein and Emily Flitter, "Goldman Finds a Way Past Volcker with New Credit Fund," *Reuters*, Jan. 25, 2013.

11. Secretary Lew's Calendar, February 2013–July 2013, https://www.treasury.gov/FOIA/Documents/Secretary%20Lew%20Calendar%20FebruarytoJuly2013.pdf.

12. SEC, Mary Jo White biography, https://www.sec.gov/about/commissioner/white.htm.

13. Lew Calendar, https://www.treasury.gov/FOIA/Documents/Secretary%20Lew%20Calendar%20FebruarytoJuly2013.pdf.

14. Ibid.

15. Ben Protess and Peter Eavis, "At the Finish Line on the Volcker Rule," http://dealbook.nytimes.com/2013/12/10/regulators-vote-to-approve-volcker-rule/.

16. Ibid.

CHAPTER 9: REPORT CARD

1. U.S. Treasury, Office of Public Affairs, "Financial Stability Oversight Council Meeting, July 31, 2014," Press Release, July 31, 2014.

2. Jesse Hamilton, "Hedge Fund Leverage Faces New Scrutiny by Top U.S. Regulator," *Bloomberg*, Apr. 18, 2016.

3. Franklin D. Roosevelt, statement on signing two statutes to protect investors, Aug. 23, 1940.

4. See Richard Langworth, "Urinal Humor: Churchill & Attlee," RichardLangworth.com, Aug. 23, 2015.

5. "SEC Proposes Rules to Modernize and Enhance Information Reported by Investment Companies and Investment Advisers," SEC Press Release 2015-95, May 20, 2015.

6. Daniel M. Gallagher, "Statement at an Open Meeting on Investment Company and Investment Adviser Reporting," SEC public statement, May 20, 2015.

7. Norm Champ, "Remarks to the 2012 ALI-CLE Conference on Investment Adviser Regulation," SEC speech, Dec. 6, 2012.

8. In the Matter of Carl D. Johns, Investment Advisers Act Release No. 3655, Aug. 27, 2013, http://www.sec.gov/litigation/admin/2013/ia-3655.pdf.

9. Norm Champ, "Remarks to the 2014 ICI Securities Law Developments Conference," SEC speech, Dec. 10, 2014.

10. Mary Jo White, " Enhancing Risk Monitoring and Regulatory Safeguards for the Asset Management Industry," SEC speech, Dec. 11, 2014.

CHAPTER 10: PREVENTING THE NEXT CRISIS

1. Nick Romeo, "How Archaeologists Discovered 23 Shipwrecks in 22 Days," July 11, 2016, available at news.nationalgeographic.com.

2. See 12 USCA Section 1817 (FDIC), 12 USCA Section 248(n) (Fed Examination power).

3. Barney Jopson and Alistair Gray, "MetLife Ruling Vindicates Lonely Decision to Fight," *Financial Times*, Mar. 31, 2016.

4. Ted Mann and Ryan Tracy, "GE Capital Sheds 'Systemically Important' Label," *Wall Street Journal*, June 29, 2016.

5. Hester Peirce, "Regulatory Burdens: The Impact of Dodd-Frank on Community Banking: Testimony Before the House Committee on Oversight and Government Reform," July 18, 2013, http://mercatus.org/publication/ regulatory-burdens-impact-dodd-frank-community-banking.

6. Ibid.

7. "Update on Review of Asset Management Products and Activities," Financial Stability Oversight Council, link in "Financial Stability Oversight Council Releases Statement on Review of Asset Management Products and Activities," U.S. Treasury Press Release, April 18, 2016.

8. "Evidence-Based Policymaking: A Guide for Effective Government," Pew Charitable Trusts and MacArthur Foundation.

9. See Sheila Bair, *Bull by the Horns*, Simon & Schuster, 2012, p. 56, discussing how the federal government met congressionally mandated goals to support "affordable" housing.

10. Albert Durso, "US Regulator Targeting Lower Down Payment on Mortgages," *Yahoo News*, Oct. 14, 2014.

11. GAO, "Financial Market Regulation: Benefits and Risks of Merging SEC and CFTC," Statement of James L. Bothwell, May 3, 1995.

12. U.S. House Committee on Financial Services, "Frank and Capuano Introduce Legislation to Merge the SEC and CFTC," Press Release, Nov. 29, 2012. Sarah N. Lynch, "Retiring Lawmaker Barney Frank Seeks SEC-CFTC Merger," *Reuters*, Sept. 6, 2012.

13. The Volcker Alliance, "Reshaping the Financial Regulatory System," Apr. 20, 2015, p. 8.

14. "Statement of Commissioner Bart Chilton Regarding CFTC/SEC Merger," CFTC statement, Oct. 28 2008.

15. "Financial Market Regulation: Benefits and Risks of Merging SEC and CFTC."

16. "National Gambling Impact Study Commission, Final Report," June 18, 1999, pp. 2-1–2-5, http://govinfo.library.unt.edu/ngisc/reports/fullrpt.html. "The History of the Lottery in the United States," HistoryBuff.com.

17. "National Gambling Impact Study," pp. 2-1–2-5.

18. David Cay Johnston, "U.S. Lotteries and the State Taxman," Reuters.com, July 15, 2011, http://blogs.reuters.com/david-cay-johnston/2011/07/15/u-s -lotteries-and-the-state-taxman/.

19. Jeff Desjardins. "Why the Lottery Is a Regressive Tax on the Nation's Poorest," VisualCapitalist.com, http://www.visualcapitalist.com/lottery-regressive-tax-nations-poorest/. Max Galka, "The Lottery Is a Tax, an Inefficient, Regressive, and Exploitative Tax," Metrocosm, http://metrocosm.com.

20. Ibid.

21. Geoff Williams, "Poor People Spend 9% of Income on Lottery Tickets; Here's Why," AOL.com, http://www.aol.com/article/2010/05/31/poor-people-spend-9 -of-income-on-lottery-tickets-heres-why/19494428/?gen=1. Emily Hailsey, Romel Mostafa, and George Loewenstein, "Myopic Risk-Seeking: The Impact of Narrow Decision Bracketing on Lottery Play," *Journal of Risk and Uncertainty*, August 2008, vol. 37, no. 1, pp. 57–75.

22. Kim Bartel Sheehan, *Controversies in Contemporary Advertising*, second edition, Sage Publications, Thousands Oaks: California, 2014, p. 771. "Lottery Advertising," http://stoppredatorygambling .org/blog/category/research-center/ lottery-advertising/.

23. Paul Merrion, "Private Management Companies Line Up to Bid on Illinois Lottery's Outsourcing," *Crain's Chicago Business*, June 5, 2010.

24. 2014 Fact Sheet, Doorways to Dreams Fund, http://www.d2dfund.org/files/ publications/STW_MI_2014.pdf. "Closing the Gap: Innovations to Promote Americans' Financial Security," testimony before the U.S. Senate Special Committee on Aging, Tim Flacke, Executive Director, Doorways to Dreams, June 15, 2016. "Prize-Linked Savings FAQs" (PDF), Legislative Coordinating Commission, accessed July 28, 2016, commissions.leg.state.mn.us. "History of Save to Win," savetowin.org.

25. Peter Tufano, Nick Maynar, Jan-Emmanuel De Weve, "Consumer Demands for Prize-Linked Savings: A Preliminary Analysis," Harvard Business School Working Paper, hbs.edu.

26. Stuart Butler, "Prizes for Savings: A Bipartisan Success in Congress," Brookings Institution, Dec. 18, 2014, brookings.edu.

27. Laurie Hendrix, "Winning Ways to Use IRS Form 8888," University of Arkansas System, uaex.edu.

28. "History of Save to Win." See "Consumer Demand for Prize-Linked Savings." Commonwealth, Board of Directors, Peter Tufano, buildcommonwealth.org.

29. Thomas Jefferson to Charles Yancey, founders.archive.gov, Jan. 6, 1816.

INDEX

ABOUT THE AUTHOR

NORM CHAMP is the former Director of the Division of Investment Management at the U.S. Securities and Exchange Commission. Under his leadership, the SEC adopted a new rule in July 2014 to reform money market mutual funds. Norm is a partner in the Investment Funds Group at Kirkland & Ellis LLP. Norm is also a lecturer on investment management at Harvard Law School.

While at the SEC, Norm led the creation of the Division's Risk and Examination Office, which monitors the investment management industry to understand risks that regulations should address. He was the leader of the SEC's interactions with the Financial Stability Oversight Council as the Council turned its attention to designating asset management firms as "systemically important." He also worked on crisis management efforts at securities firms to protect customers of those firms. Additionally, Norm headed the creation of Guidance Updates and Senior Level Engagement, initiatives created to provide transparency to the industry and to engage with boards and senior managements of asset management firms, respectively. For his service in the Division of Investment Management at the SEC, Norm received the Chairman's Award for Law and Policy in 2014, the Chairman's Award for Labor-Management Relations in 2014, and the Chairman's Analytical Methods Award in 2013.

Prior to becoming the Director of the Division of Investment Management, he was the Deputy Director of the SEC's Office of Compliance Inspections and Examinations (OCIE) and the Associate Regional Director for Examinations in the SEC's New York Regional Office. In those capacities he supervised examinations of broker-dealers, investment advisers/investment companies, exchanges, clearing agencies and credit rating agencies. While at OCIE in 2011, Norm received the Chairman's Award for Law and Policy and the Chairman's Award for Labor-Management Relations.

Norm has an A.B., summa cum laude, in History from Princeton University and a J.D., cum laude, from Harvard Law School. He was a Fulbright Scholar at King's College London where he received his M.A. in War Studies.

He lives in Manhattan with his wife and four children.